GERMAN ROMANTIC STORIES

The German Library: Volume 35

Volkmar Sander, General Editor

GERMAN ROMANTIC STORIES

Edited by Frank G. Ryder

Introduction by Gordon Birrell

CONTINUUM · NEW YORK

1988

The Continuum Publishing Company
370 Lexington Avenue, New York, NY 10017

The German Library
is published in cooperation with Deutsches Haus,
New York University.
This volume has been supported by a grant
from Heidelberger Zement AG.

Printed in the United States of America

Library of Congress Cataloging-in-Publication Data

German romantic stories / edited by Frank G. Ryder; introduction by
Gordon Birrell

  p. cm.—(The German library; v. 35)
  ISBN 0-8264-0312-3.   ISBN 0-8264-0313-1 (pbk.)
  1. Short stories, German—Translations into English. 2. German
fiction—18th century—Translations into English. 3. German
fiction—19th century—Translations into English. 4. Short stories,
English—Translations from German. 5. English fiction—Translations
from German. I. Ryder, Frank Glessner, 1916– . II. Series.
PT1327.G394 1988
833'.01'08145—dc19   88-6991
                                                                 CIP

Acknowledgments will be found on page 269,
which constitutes an extension of the copyright page.

Contents

ADELBERT VON CHAMISSO

CLEMENS BRENTANO

ACHIM VON ARNIM

JOSEPH FREIHERR VON EICHENDORFF

Introduction

Romanticism by definition resists definition. With its celebration of diversity, its dedication to the principle of inclusiveness, its eagerness to embrace the most disparate phenomena, the Romantic movement was continually and necessarily at odds with itself. Still, if there was one thing Romantics can be said to have had in common, it was an emphatic sense of *background:* a sense that human beings are surrounded on all sides by mystery. In the Romantic view, human consciousness exists at the interface between two enigmatic worlds: on one side, the external realm of nature; on the other, the largely uncharted internal realm of the mind. The view, one may say, is blurred in either direction. Beyond our immediate perceptions, of ourselves and of the world, there stretches an immense backdrop of obscurity. For the adventuresome and enterprising spirit, however, it is an obscurity that beckons with promise and possibility. As in the great misty vistas of Romantic paintings, the landscapes within as well as outside of us are full of half-hidden shapes and patterns, barely recognizable forms that suggest an interconnectedness of meaning beyond the surmise of ordinary consciousness.

From the beginning, Romantic writers understood that it would be necessary to invent new literary forms, or extend the old ones, in order to accommodate this enlarged sense of background. They understood, too, that narrative fiction offered the richest possibilities for expressing their multidimensional vision of reality. Drama, for instance, can brilliantly depict human action and interaction but tends to emphasize the visible surface of things. Lyric poetry, on the other hand, is certainly capable of evoking a sonorous mood of mystery and wonder, and a number of Romantic poems must in fact be included among the finest ever written in the German language. But poetry is perhaps too localized, too intimate, to provide the panoramic sense of complexity that the Romantics were generally after. For this reason many Romantic poems, and for that matter some of the most frequently anthologized, appeared originally in novels or novellas, where they were subordinated to the larger aims of the narrative; the poems in Eichendorff's *Memoirs of a Good-for-Nothing* are a case in point.

While the Romantic preference for narrative fiction involved a number of factors, one can say without distorting matters too much that Romantics were drawn to narrative because it permitted both a temporal and a spatial extension of background. Like music, narrative unfolds sequentially in time. It records the unfolding of event and character, and it captures the linear or cyclical rhythms of temporal experience. But narrative also acknowledges the ways in which time can be nullified or reversed, through continuity, repetition, memory, and anticipation. Moreover, narrative may produce a kind of cumulative force of background, as individual images and motifs gather resonance through reiteration, variation, or association with other images. In spatial terms, narrative forms can—potentially at least—depict a whole world through a variety of perspectives, including dreams and inlaid stories or songs. The most important perspective of all is that of the narrator, the mediating consciousness through which the events of the story are filtered and refracted. In some forms of fiction, of course, the narrator can retreat practically to the point of invisibility. Romantic stories, however, tend to favor a narrator with a pronounced point of view, a distinctive voice that not only recounts the events of the story but simultaneously reacts to them. Through the device of the self-conscious narrator, Romantics were able to set up a complex, frequently ironic tension between observer and observed, subject and object, witness and world.

In Brentano's *Tale of Good Caspar and Fair Annie*, for instance, what we know of Caspar and Annie—and in fact we know astonishingly little about either of them—is communicated through the voice of their grandmother. We hear this voice in turn, however, through the ears of another figure, the first-person narrator of the story as a whole, an impressionable and insecure young writer. For the narrator (and for many readers) the grandmother represents a beacon of faith in a troubled world of false or questionable values. Yet the double perspective serves as a double blind: the grandmother's viewpoint, as convincing as it may seem at first, effectively obscures the complicated moral issues raised in the lives and the deaths of Caspar and Annie. The word *honor,* along with its multiple variants and combinations ("honor God alone," "pay him the final honors," "an honorable grave," and so on), rings out no fewer than sixty-five times in the course of the narrative; it occurs in the speech of every major character and gradually acquires so many associations and referents that its meaning becomes nearly opaque. The grandmother, with her flinty aphorisms and her clear sense of mission, has no difficulty cutting through the moral ambiguity around her. In the end, however, she functions as a commentator whose judgment is at best untrustworthy, at worst fatal to her grandchildren. In Brentano's story, as in many Romantic texts, the way events are perceived and assessed becomes a central issue of the narrative: the act of interpretation itself is presented to the reader *for* interpretation.

The Romantic sense of background understandably included a receptiveness to the "dark side of nature," the numinous world of parapsychological phenomena and the supernatural. While occult occurrences could be fascinating for their own sake, the more serious Romantic writers were equally intrigued with the ways in which the supernatural goes to work on the human mind. Like the other extraordinary events that typically form the heart of the Romantic novella, supernatural events serve as a kind of crucible, a stress test of character. In Kleist's "Beggarwoman of Locarno," for instance, the marquis responds to the spectral occurrences in his castle with the same cold-blooded determination and aggressiveness that had marked his previous dealings with the beggarwoman. In the end, the ghost represents such an extreme challenge to his existence that he annihilates both himself and his castle. By systematically setting fire to the four corners of the castle, he turns light and order, the emblems of a rational universe, into the agents of his destruction. In *Caspar and Annie,* too, supernatural events have a revelatory function. The curse of the flying teeth of Hunter Jürge not only adds a bit of grisly humor to the story, but significantly heightens the characterization of the grandmother: the old woman's fatalism, we see, is deep enough to embrace primitive superstition as well as the tenets of orthodox Christianity.

Fouqué's *Undine* contains by far the most fully realized supernatural world in this collection of stories, but even here the supernatural is less interesting, and certainly less complicated, than the reactions of the human beings who confront it. Despite a few superficial mysterious touches, the realm of the water sprites is literally crystal clear. Late in the story, Undine's mortal husband Huldbrand experiences a dream vision in which he hovers over the transparent waters of the Mediterranean, effortlessly gazing directly into the innermost heart of Undine's world. The laws that govern Undine's relations with mortals are likewise made abundantly clear, and even the mischievous tricks of the water sprites lack any real sense of supernatural eeriness. When Undine's uncle Kühleborn, a woodland river spirit, appears disguised as a coachman dressed in a white tunic, driving a coach covered with white linen and led by two white horses, the reader is less inclined to shudder with dread than to marvel at the water sprite's ingenious handling of mise-en-scène. In *Undine,* Fouqué appears to have deliberately limited the sense of background associated with the supernatural in order to set off a much more complex background: the depths of the human heart. Huldbrand and his erstwhile lover Bertalda move through the world in a peculiarly dreamy state of mind, only half aware of their own feelings and not much inclined toward self-examination. In their attempts to come to terms with Undine and her undeniably strange relatives, Huldbrand and Bertalda must contend with unpredictable, often violent emotional responses that well up from within them, responses born of commingled vanity, stubbornness, pride, and fear. The wild creature Undine, tamed and domesticated through marriage to a mortal, paradoxically finds herself confronting a wilderness of human passions that in the end nothing short of murder can subdue.

The literary symbol in its modern sense came into being as yet another aspect of the Romantic fascination with background. In the symbol, as Goethe put it, the universal shimmers through the particular. Romantic writers had no difficulty accepting this definition from their sometime adversary, but they preferred to place the primary stress on the word *shimmer*. Symbols invest the particular not only with universality but with mystery and allusiveness; they have a peculiarly opalescent quality that evokes a sense both of significance and obscurity. In *The Madman of Fort Ratonneau,* for instance, Arnim surrounds the central events of the story with a dense network of symbolic references to fire and water, illumination and darkness. These oppositions simultaneously support at least three different readings of the story. On one level, the origins and resolution of Francoeur's insanity may be accounted for in terms of diabolical possession and exorcism. On another level, but still illuminated by the same symbols, his madness appears to derive from a severe head wound and a resultant inflammation that is left unattended for nearly a year. Beyond the supernatural and the medical readings, however, lies a level at which religion, physical explanations, and psychology merge. From this vantage point, which requires yet another interpretation of the imagery, the novella records the kind of emotional derangement that can occur in the marriage of two unstable, impulsive young people. Francoeur's and Rosalie's love must be put to the most extreme and appalling test before they can acknowledge, intuitively at least, the mutual wholeness of their relationship and their sense of participation in the will of divine providence.

If Arnim's symbolism sustains a variety of interpretations, Chamisso's *Peter Schlemihl* offers a contrasting case: the symbol as void. This charming little story, so straightforward in every other respect, contains a central image of such astonishing ambiguity that a century and a half of critical studies have failed to pin down its meaning. The most that can be said with certainty about Peter Schlemihl's missing shadow is that it represents a radical form of alienation. Beyond that rather obvious statement the questions begin. The absence of a shadow does not cause the other characters in the story to react with supernatural horror—which after all would be the most sensible response under the circumstances—but with approximately the same mixture of pity, scorn, and indignation that they would feel if Peter Schlemihl were walking about naked. The inability to cast a shadow points to a fundamental lack of "solidity," socially as well as physically; but there is virtually nothing in the story that accounts for such a profound deficiency in its altogether likable young hero. It is as if one of Kafka's characters had fallen into Chamisso's nineteenth-century fairy tale: Peter Schlemihl suffers from a nameless disrepute, a shame that can be neither defined nor absolved. The enduring attraction of the tale may well reside in its appeal to the conscience of the individual reader, who is at liberty to project his or her most private insecurities into the great emptiness represented by Peter Schlemihl's missing shadow.

Background, as the Romantics experienced it, cannot be contained or demarcated. In literary and artistic works, formal roundedness and closure were regarded as a triumph of artifice over truth, a betrayal of the openness of existence, and an affront to the imagination as well. Romantics had a special affection for provisional forms of all kinds: fragments, sketches, musical improvisations and fantasias, unfinished poems and novels, or architectural ruins that the ravages of time have "restored" to an unfinished state. Even those literary works that conclude with a satisfying sense of resolution tend to leave important problems up in the air. In *Caspar and Annie,* the duke goes to remarkable lengths to promote the idea of a happy ending, erecting a statue that depicts himself and his bride as Justice and Grace, while figures representing True Honor and False Honor kneel at either side. Under closer examination, however, the statue freezes the central issues of the story into an allegorical statement that is almost laughably wrongheaded. In a tale full of misinterpretations, the final image represents a misinterpretation that is literally carved in stone. Peter Schlemihl, by the same token, may reach a point of reconciliation and resolution, yet he never escapes the stigma of his missing shadow. The best he can do—and it is perhaps good enough—is to convert his alienation into a kind of reborn innocence in the form of scientific objectivity. With the help of his seven-league boots, virtually all of the world becomes an immense botanical and zoological garden, a second Garden of Eden on a global scale.

The final story in this collection, Eichendorff's *Memoirs of a Good-for-Nothing,* may very well be the most beloved work in German literature. As of this writing, no fewer than twelve individual editions of the story are in print, quite apart from its inclusion in the several editions of Eichendorff's collected works. From beginning to end this story *sings,* with a strong, clear lyrical line reminiscent of Eichendorff's contemporary, Franz Schubert. Indeed, the musicality of the text is so great that some critics have been inclined to write the story off as a lighthearted frolic, as beautiful but as inconsequential as the song of a meadowlark. In fact, *Good-for-Nothing* is no less complex than the other stories in this collection. It too is saturated with background: its hero moves through a shimmering world of golden sunsets, moonlit gardens, enchanted castles, midnight carriage rides through lonely forests. In this case, however, the background proves to be marvelously intact. Like the heroes of folk fairy tales, the Good-for-Nothing is blessed with what could be called universal connectedness. No matter how far or how randomly he roams, the strangers he encounters turn out to be part of an intricate friendly network that eventually brings him home to his beloved "countess." But the Good-for-Nothing is also a child of nature. While the human network anchors and stabilizes his existence, his volatile young soul is forever open to the changing effects of landscape, weather, and time of day. With the pulsations of nature between sunlight and moonlight, high noon and twilight, rain and shine, field and forest, his emotions oscillate between elation and melancholy, wanderlust and homesickness. The hidden nexus of human associations may invest his life with continuous significance and unexpected coherence, but his emotional fluctuations call into question both that significance and that coherence. In the Good-for-Nothing's emotional economy, two mutually indispensable, mutually contradictory impulses play off against each other: the urge to belong and the urge to be long gone. For this reason the conclusion of the novella is as problematic as that of the other stories. On one level, everything points to a closing of the circle, to homecoming and consummation. On another level, one can scarcely overlook the fact that the romantic songbird has flown directly into a cage. Significantly, the Good-for-Nothing's immediate impulse is to reopen the circle by setting out once again, bride and all, for Italy. Whether he can succeed in remaining both footloose and snugly domesticated must remain an open question. The ability to live in a protected state of stability and simultaneously to enjoy the full intense range of one's emotions is a privilege that is perhaps reserved only for the young. In its depths, the *Memoirs of a Good-for-Nothing* sounds an elegiac tone, commemorating the time of life when such a wonderful balance was still—briefly—possible. In addition, the novella, which was completed in 1826, commemorates the passing of Romanticism itself. The concluding cry of the narrator expresses not only a farewell to youth but a farewell to the lost ingenuous exuberance of Romanticism as well: "And all of it, all of it was so good!"

GORDON BIRRELL

GERMAN ROMANTIC
STORIES

Anecdote from the Last Prussian War

Heinrich von Kleist

In a village near Jena an innkeeper told me, as I was on my way to Frankfurt, that several hours after the battle, when the village was already completely deserted by the troops of the Prince von Hohenlohe and surrounded by the French, who thought it still occupied, a lone Prussian cavalryman had appeared in it, and the innkeeper assured me that if all the soldiers who had fought that day had been as brave as he the French would assuredly have been beaten, even if they had been three times as strong as they actually were. This fellow, said the innkeeper, galloped up before my tavern all covered with dust and cried: "Landlord!" and when I asked what he wanted, replied, thrusting his sword into its scabbard: "A glass of brandy! I'm thirsty." My God, I say, won't you get out of here, friend? The French are practically in the village! "So what?" says he, laying the rein on his horse's neck, "I haven't had a drink all day." Damned if I don't think he's possessed of the devil! Hey, Liese! I cry, and bring him a bottle of Danzig Goldwater. There, I say, and try to press the whole bottle into his hand, just so he'll ride on. "What's this?" he says, shoving the bottle aside and taking off his hat: "What am I supposed to do with this stuff?" And: "Pour me a drink!" he says, wiping the sweat from his brow, "I don't have the time." You're a dead man, I say. There! I say, and pour him a glass, there! Drink and ride on! Good health to you! "Give me another!" the fellow says, while shots are already raining into the village from all sides. I say: Another one? Devil take you! "Another one!" he says and reaches me his glass—"and fill it up," he says, wiping his beard and blowing his nose on the ground with his fingers, "I pay cash!" Aye, dammit, I wish the devil—! There! I say, and pour him a glass like he said, a second one, and then a third, and ask: Are you satisfied now? "Hah!" the fellow says, shaking himself, "now that's good schnapps!—Well," he says and puts on his hat, "what do I owe you?" Nothing! nothing! I answer. In the devil's name, get out, the French will be here in a minute! "Well then," he says, feeling around in the top of his boot, "God reward you," and pulling a stumpy pipe out of his boot, he says, after blowing out the bowl: "Get me a light!" A light, I say, what's eating you—? "That's right, a light!" says he, "I want to smoke my pipe." Aye, the man's possessed for sure! Hey, Liese! I call to the girl, and while the fellow is filling his pipe, she brings him a light. "Now," says he, holding the pipe in his mouth after he's got it going, "now the French are going to catch it!" And pressing his hat over his eyes and seizing the rein, he turns his horse and draws his saber. You idiot! I say, you damned infernal gallows bird! Will you get the hell out of here? Three chasseurs— don't you see them?—are already at the gate! "So what?" says he, spitting on the ground and looking at the three fellows with a gleam in his eye. "I wouldn't be afraid if there were ten of them." And at that moment the three Frenchmen are already riding into the village. "*Bassa Manelka!*" the fellow yells, gives his horse the spur and gallops toward them, gallops right at them, as sure as God lives, and falls on them as though he had the entire Hohenlohe corps behind him, so that the chasseurs, not being sure whether there weren't more Germans in the village, halt for an instant, something they never do, and he, God bless me, before you could bat an eye, sabers them all from their saddles, rounds up the horses that are running around loose, gallops past me with the whole string and yells: "*Bassa Teremtetem!*" and: "You see how it's done, landlord?" and "So long!" and "I'll be seeing you!" and "ho! ho! ho!"—Such a fellow, said the innkeeper, I never saw in my life.

Translated by R. M. Browning

The Beggarwoman of Locarno

Heinrich von Kleist

At the foot of the Alps near Locarno in upper Italy there was once an old castle belonging to a marchese, which, on coming from the St. Gotthard, one now sees lying in ruins and rubble. It was a castle with high-ceilinged, spacious rooms, in one of which, on a litter of straw shaken out on the floor, the mistress, out of pity, had once bedded a sick old woman who had stopped to beg before the gate. The marchese, upon returning from the hunt, happened to enter the room, where he customarily stored his rifle, and brusquely ordered the woman to get up from the corner where she was lying and move over behind the stove. The old woman, as she tried to rise, slipped with her crutch on the polished floor, and seriously injured her back, so that, though she was able with infinite effort to get up and diagonally cross the room in the prescribed direction, she sank down groaning and whimpering behind the stove and expired.

A number of years later when the marchese, because of war and crop failures, found his fortunes in a dubious state, a Florentine knight came to visit him and offered to buy the castle because of its lovely site. The marchese, much interested in making a deal, instructed his wife to lodge the stranger in the aforementioned empty room, which was very handsomely and luxuriously furnished. But imagine how taken aback the couple was when at midnight the knight came down to them pale and troubled, swearing by all that is holy that there was a ghost in his room: something not visible to the human eye had gotten up in a corner of the room, making a noise as though it had been lying on straw, and had walked with clearly audible steps, slowly and feebly, diagonally across the room and sunk down behind the stove, groaning and whimpering.

The marchese, alarmed without knowing exactly why, laughed at the knight with forced jocularity and said he would go up at once and, to reassure him, spend the rest of the night with him in the room. But the knight begged the marchese to be kind enough to allow him to rest in an armchair in his own chamber, and when morning came had his team put to his carriage, made his adieus and departed.

To the marchese's intense displeasure this incident, which attracted inordinate attention, scared off a number of prospective buyers, and since, strangely and incomprehensibly, the rumor was also becoming current among his own servants that a ghost was haunting the upper room, the marchese determined, in order to lay this rumor by a decisive action, to investigate the matter himself the following night. Accordingly, with the coming of nightfall, he had a bed set up in the upper room and waited, without sleeping, for midnight. Imagine then how shaken he was when, just as the ghostly hour was striking, he heard that incomprehensible sound: as though someone were getting up out of rustling straw, walking diagonally across the room and then sinking down behind the stove with a deep sigh and a rattle in the throat.

When he came downstairs the next morning the marchesa asked him how his investigation had turned out, and when he glanced about with shy, furtive looks and, having locked the door, assured her that the room was indeed haunted, she started back in the greatest fright of her life and begged him, before he let the matter become known, to subject it once more, this time in her presence, to a cold-blooded examination. The next night however they and a faithful servant whom they had taken with them actually heard the same incomprehensible, ghostlike sounds, and only their ardent desire to get rid of the castle at any cost enabled them to suppress in the presence of the servant the terror that had seized them and attribute the incident to some innocent, fortuitous cause that was bound sooner or later to be discovered.

On the evening of the third day when both of them, hoping to get to the bottom of the matter, were again mounting the stairs to the guest room with pounding hearts, the house watchdog, which had been unchained, happened to appear before the door of the room, so that, without telling themselves exactly why, perhaps involuntarily wanting some third, living creature present besides themselves, they took the dog into the room with them. The couple, with two candles on the table, the marchesa fully clothed, the marchese with sword and pistols he had taken from the cupboard beside him, sat down toward eleven o'clock on separate beds, and, while they laboriously try to keep up a conversation, the dog curls up in the middle of the room and goes to sleep. Then, just at midnight, the terrifying sounds are heard again: someone whom no human eye can see rises, on crutches, in the corner of the room; there comes a rustling of straw, and with the first step: tap! tap! the dog awakens, suddenly gets up, pricking his ears, and growling and barking, just as though someone were walking toward him, backs off toward the stove. At this sight the marchesa, her hair on end, rushes out of the room and, while the marchese, who has seized his sword, cries: "Who's there?" and, when no one answers, begins slashing the air on every side with his sword, she has her carriage hitched up, determined to depart for town at once. But before she can pack a few belongings and rattle over the cobblestones out of the gate, she sees the castle going up in flames all around her. The marchese, crazy with terror, had taken a candle and, weary of life, set fire to the wood-wainscoted castle at every corner. In vain did she send in servants to rescue the unfortunate man; he had already perished in the most miserable manner, and his whitened bones, heaped together by his countrymen, still lie in the corner of the room from which he ordered the beggarwoman of Locarno to rise.

Translated by R. M. Browning

Story of a Remarkable Single Combat

Heinrich von Kleist

The knight Jean Carouge, a vassal of the Count d'Alençon, had to make an overseas journey to attend to domestic affairs. His young and beautiful wife he left behind in his castle. Another of the count's vassals, called Jacques le Gris, fell violently in love with this lady. Witnesses made deposition in court that at such and such an hour, on such and such a day, in such and such a month Jacques le Gris had mounted one of the count's horses and gone to see this lady in Argenteuil, where she was residing. She received him as a companion and friend of her husband and showed him the whole castle. He also wanted to see the keep, or watchtower, of the castle, and the lady took him there herself, without having a servant accompany her.

As soon as they were inside the tower, Jacques, who was a very strong man, shot the bolt on the door, took the lady in his arms and gave full rein to his passion. Jacques, Jacques, the lady said, weeping, you have disgraced me, but the disgrace will fall back on you as soon as my husband comes home from abroad. Jacques paid little heed to this threat, mounted his horse, and returned in full career. At four o'clock in the morning he had been seen in the count's castle and at nine o'clock of the same morning he also appeared at the count's levee.—We must take careful note of this circumstance. Jean Carouge finally returned from his journey and his wife received him with every mark of affection. But in the evening, when Carouge had gone to their chamber and to bed, she paced for a long while up and down in the room, crossing herself from time to time, at last fell on her knees before his bed and tearfully told her husband what had happened to her. He refused at first to believe it, but was finally forced to give credence to his wife's oaths and repeated assurances. Now, his only thought was revenge. He assembled his and his wife's relatives, and it was their unanimous opinion that the matter should be brought before the count and the decision left to him.

The count had the parties summoned to his presence, listened to their reasoning, and after much argument this way and that pronounced the decision that the lady had dreamed the whole story, since it was not possible for a man to cover 23 leagues and commit the deed of which he was accused, with all its accessory circumstances, in the short space of four hours and a half, which was all the time elapsed during which Jacques had not been seen in the castle. The Count d'Alençon therefore ordered that there be no further talk of the matter. But Sir Jean, who was a man of feeling and very touchy about his honor, did not submit to this decision but brought the case before the Parliament in Paris. This tribunal decreed single combat. The king, who was at that moment at Sluys in Flanders, dispatched a courier with orders to postpone the combat until his return, because he wished to be present himself. The Dukes of Berry, Burgundy, and Bourbon likewise journeyed to Paris to attend the spectacle. St. Catherine's Square was chosen as the place of combat and stands were erected for the onlookers. The combatants appeared, armed from head to foot. The lady was seated on a cart, dressed all in black. Her husband came up to her and said: Madame, in your cause and relying on your word I now risk my life to fight with Jacques le Gris; no one knows better than you whether my cause is good and just.—Sir knight, answered the lady, you can depend on the justness of your cause and go to fight with confidence. Carouge then grasped her hand, kissed it, crossed himself, and entered the lists. The lady prayed incessantly during the combat. Her situation was critical: if Jean Carouge was defeated, he would be hanged and she would be burned without mercy. When the field had been fairly divided between light and shade, the combatants sprang towards each other at a gallop, their lances leveled. But both were too skillful to come to harm in this fashion. They therefore dismounted and drew their swords. Carouge received a wound in the thigh; his friends trembled for him, and his wife was more dead than alive. But he pressed his opponent with so much rage and skill that he threw him to the ground and thrust his sword into his breast. Thereupon he turned to the spectators and asked in ringing tones whether he had fulfilled his obligation? With one voice they answered, Yes! Immediately the hangmen took charge of Jacques's corpse and hung it on the gallows. Sir Jean threw himself at the king's feet; the king praised his bravery, had one thousand livres paid out to him at once, decreed for him a lifelong salary of two hundred livres, and made his son a chamberlain. Carouge then hastened to his wife, embraced her publicly, and went with her to church to give God thanks and to sacrifice at the altar. Froissart tells this story, and it actually happened.

Translated by R. M. Browning

An Unexpected Reunion

Johann Peter Hebel

In Falun in Sweden a good fifty years ago and more, a young miner kissed his pretty fiancée and said to her: "On St. Lucia's Day our love will be blessed by the priest's hand. Then we shall be man and wife and will build ourselves a little nest of our own." "And peace and love shall dwell in it," said the lovely woman with a sweet smile, "for you are my One and my All, and without you I would rather be in the grave than in another place." But when the clergyman had read the banns in church for the second time before St. Lucia's Day: "If any of you can show just cause why these two may not lawfully be joined together in holy matrimony," Death spoke up. For when the youth walked past her house next day in his black miner's garb (the miner always wears his shroud), he knocked on her window once more and said good morning to her but never again good evening. He never returned from the mine, and on that same morning she hemmed a black kerchief for him with a red border for their wedding—in vain. But when he did not come, she laid it aside and wept for him and never forgot him. Meanwhile the city of Lisbon in Portugal was destroyed by an earthquake, and the Seven Years' War passed by, and the emperor Francis I died, and the Jesuit order was abolished, and Poland was partitioned, and the empress Maria Theresa died, and Struensee was executed, America became free, and the combined French and Spanish power could not capture Gibraltar. The Turks locked up General Stein in the Veterani Cave in Hungary, and the emperor Joseph died too. King Gustav of Sweden conquered Russian Finland, and the French Revolution and the long war began, and emperor Leopold II went to his grave too. Napoleon conquered Prussia and the English bombarded Copenhagen, and the farmers sowed and harvested. The miller milled and the blacksmiths hammered, and the miners dug for metal veins in their underground workshops. But when in the year 1809, shortly before or after Midsummer Day, the miners of Falun wanted to dig through an opening between two shafts, a good three hundred ells deep under the earth, they dug out of the rubble and vitriol water the corpse of a youth completely saturated with iron sulphate but otherwise showing no sign of decomposition and completely unaltered, so that one could still fully recognize his facial features and his age, as if he had died only an hour ago and had fallen into a light sleep at his work. But when he was brought up into the light of day, no one claimed to recognize the sleeping youth or to know anything about his accident (his father and mother, friends, and acquaintances had long been dead) until the appearance of the former fiancée of the miner who had one day gone down into the shaft and never returned. Gray and shriveled she came on a crutch to the public square and recognized her betrothed; and more in joyful rapture than in pain she sank down upon the beloved corpse; and only after she had recovered from a long, severe emotional crisis, she finally said: "He is my betrothed, for whom I have mourned for fifty long years and whom God is letting me see once more before my end. A week before our wedding he went down into the pit and never came up again." Then the spirits of all the bystanders were moved to sadness and tears at the sight of the former bride in the form of withered, feeble age and the bridegroom still in his youthful beauty and when they saw how after fifty years the flame of youthful love awakened again in her breast; but he did not open his mouth to smile or his eyes in recognition; and how she finally had him carried by the miners to her small room, as the only person who belonged to him and who had a claim on him, till his grave was prepared at the cemetery. The following day when his grave in the cemetery was prepared and the miners fetched him, she unlocked a little box, tied the black silken kerchief with the red border around his neck, and accompanied him in her Sunday dress as if it were her wedding day and not the day of his burial. For when he was laid in his grave in the cemetery, she said: "Now sleep well for another day or so in your cool wedding bed and don't let time weigh heavy on you. I have only a little more left to do and will come soon, and soon it will be day again."—"What the earth has given back once, it will not keep for a second time," she said, as she went away and looked back once more.

Translated by Harry Steinhauer

Kannitverstan

Johann Peter Hebel

In Emmendingen and Gundelfingen, as well as in Amsterdam, a man has the opportunity every day, I daresay, to reflect on the inconstancy of all earthly things—if he wants to—and to learn how to be satisfied with his lot even though life is no bed of roses. But it was by the oddest roundabout route that a German journeyman in Amsterdam came, through error, to the perception of this truth.

After he had come to that great and prosperous city of commerce, full of splendid houses, heaving ships, and busy people, his eye fell upon a house larger and more beautiful than any he had ever seen on all his travels from Tuttlingen to Amsterdam. For a long time he gazed in wonder at this costly building, at the six chimneys on its roof, at its beautiful cornices, and at the high windows, each larger than the front door to his father's house.

Finally, yielding to an impulse, he addressed a passerby. "My good friend," he asked, "can you tell me the name of the gentleman who owns this marvelous house with the windows full of tulips, asters, and gillyflowers?" But the man, who probably had something more important to attend to and, unfortunately, understood just as much German as his questioner did Dutch—to wit, nothing—growled: *"Kannitverstan,"* and whisked by. This is a Dutch word—or three of them, if one looks at it properly—and means no more than "I cannot understand you."

But the good stranger thought it to be the name of the gentleman he'd asked about. "That must be a mighty rich man, that Mr. Kannitverstan," he said to himself, and walked on.

Making his way through the narrow streets, he came at length to the estuary that is called Het Ey, meaning "the Y." There stood ship after ship and mast after mast, and he was beginning to wonder how he could ever manage to take in all of these marvels with his own two eyes, when his glance fell upon a large merchantman that recently had put in from the East Indies and was being unloaded. Whole rows of piled crates and bales stood side by side on the wharf, and more were being rolled out: casks full of sugar and coffee, full of rice and pepper, and with them—pardon—mouse droppings too.

After he had watched for a long time, he asked a fellow who was carrying a crate on his shoulders the name of the fortunate man to whom the sea had brought all these wares. "*Kannitverstan,*" was the answer.

Then he thought: "Aha, so that's how it is! If the sea floats him such riches, no wonder he can put up houses with gilt-potted tulips in the windows." So he went away, sorrowfully reflecting how poor a man he was among so many rich people in this world. But just as he was thinking: "I wish I, too, would be as well off some day as this Mr. Kannitverstan," he turned a corner and saw a great funeral procession. Four black-draped horses were pulling a black-covered hearse slowly and lugubriously, as though they were aware they were carrying a dead man to his peace. A long cortege of friends and acquaintances of the departed followed behind, pair after pair, muffled in black cloaks, and mute. A solitary bell sounded in the distance. Our stranger was seized by the melancholy feeling that no good man can suppress at the sight of a funeral, and he remained standing reverently, with his hat in his hands, until all was over. Then he attached himself to the last mourner (who was just figuring how much he would make on his cotton if the bale price should rise ten florins), tugged at his coat, guilelessly begged his pardon, and said: "He must indeed have been a good friend of yours, the gentleman for whom the bell is tolling, that you follow his coffin so grieved and pensive."

"*Kannitverstan,*" was the answer.

A few large tears descended from the eyes of our good journeyman from Tuttlingen, and he felt sad and relieved at once. "Poor Kannitverstan," he exclaimed, "what have you now of all your riches? Exactly what I shall get one day from my poverty: a linen shroud! And of all your beautiful flowers, you have, perhaps, a rosemary on your cold breast, or some rue." With these thoughts he accompanied the funeral procession to the grave as though he belonged with it, and saw the supposed Mr. Kannitverstan sink down to his final resting place, and was more moved by the Dutch funeral oration, of which he understood not a word, than by many a German one to which he had paid no attention.

He left with the others and went away with a light heart, and at an inn where German was understood, he ate, with relish, a piece of Limburg cheese. And whenever afterward his heart became heavy because so many people in this world were so rich and he was so poor, he only thought of Mr. Kannitverstan of Amsterdam—of his big house, his opulent ship, and his narrow grave.

Translated by Paul Pratt

Undine

Friedrich de la Motte Fouqué

Undine dear, since first you stole
 Out of the darkness of the past,
 And your strange radiance round me cast,
How often have you charmed my soul!

How many times have you and I
 Sat close, while many a hope and fear
 Was softly whispered in my ear,
You darling child, half-spoilt, half-shy!

And with my lyre I have tried
 To sound abroad on golden strings
 All these your gentle whisperings,
Till they were famous far and wide.

Thus other hearts have ceased to doubt you,
 And learnt to love your naughty ways;
 And many people nowadays
Are asking for a book about you.

Well, here it is, so they can see
 What you are like. No, don't be shy,
 My little one, or start to cry:
Come in, and face the company.

Curtsy politely to the men
   And confidently take your stand
   Before the ladies of the land;
They like you now—will love you then.

If you are asked, by any chance,
   Who I am, say: "A gallant knight
   That serves the ladies day and night
At banquet, tournament and dance."

CHAPTER 1

How the Knight Came to the Fisherman

Once upon a time, many hundreds of years ago, there was a good old fisherman, and one beautiful evening he was sitting in front of his door, mending his nets. He lived in most delightful surroundings. His cottage was built on a green tongue of land that ran out into a big lake, so that it looked as if the land had fallen in love with the wonderfully clear blue water and plunged headlong into it, and as if the water had stretched out loving arms to embrace that glorious meadow, with its tall, waving grasses and flowers, and the refreshing shade of its trees. Each was enjoying the other's hospitality, and that is why they were both so beautiful.

Admittedly there was little or nothing in the way of human society to be found on this lovely spot, for behind it lay a very wild forest, which most people kept well clear of, partly because it was so dark and so easy to get lost in, and partly because of the weird and wonderful creatures that one was said to meet there. But the good old fisherman never had the slightest difficulty in getting through it, when he took the delicious fish that he caught in his lake to a big town the other side of the forest. Perhaps the chief reason why he found it so easy was that there were no evil thoughts in his mind, and every time he entered the sinister shadows he started singing hymns at the top of his voice.

This evening, however, as he sat quite unsuspecting beside his nets, he felt a sudden thrill of terror as he heard what sounded like a man on horseback coming through the darkness of the forest towards him. All the things that he had dreamed on stormy nights about the mysteries of the forest came crowding into his mind, and in particular the vision of a gigantically tall, snow white man, who kept nodding his head in a very curious manner. Sure enough, as he raised his eyes towards the forest he seemed to see, through the tracery of the leaves, that very same nodding man; but he soon took heart again, reflecting that as no harm had ever come to him even in the middle of the forest, here out in the open the power of the Evil One would be still less able to touch him. At the same time, firmly and with deep conviction, he recited aloud a text from the Bible, which completely restored his courage, so that he almost burst out laughing as he realized his mistake. For the white, nodding figure turned all of a sudden into a familiar stream that ran foaming out of the forest into the lake; and the source of the noise was a splendidly dressed knight, who now came into sight among the shadows of the trees, riding towards the cottage.

A scarlet cloak hung down over his gold-embroidered violet doublet; from his golden cap fluttered red and violet plumes, and on his golden baldric flashed an exceptionally fine and richly decorated sword. The white stallion that he rode was built on unusually slender lines for a war-horse, and stepped so lightly over the turf that its carpet of variegated green remained completely undamaged.

The old fisherman was still not quite easy in his mind, but he told himself that there could not be anything really bad beneath such a delightful exterior. So he politely took off his hat to the strange gentleman, and remained quite calmly beside his nets.

The knight came to a halt, and asked if he and his horse could be found accommodation for the night.

"So far as your horse is concerned, sir," replied the fisherman, "I can't suggest a better stable than this shady meadow, or any better fodder than the grass that grows in it. But as for yourself, I'll be happy to give you supper and lodging for the night in my little cottage here, such as it is."

The offer was gladly accepted. The knight jumped down from his horse, helped the fisherman to remove the saddle and bridle, and then let the animal trot away into the flowery pasture.

"Even if I'd found you less kind and hospitable, my dear old fisherman," he remarked to his host, "you still wouldn't have got rid of me tonight. For I see there's a broad lake in front of us, and Heaven forbid that I should ride back into that eerie forest with twilight coming on!"

"We won't talk too much about that, if you don't mind," said the fisherman, and led his guest into the cottage.

It was quite dark indoors, but the clean and tidy living room was dimly lit by a small fire that was burning on the hearth, and beside it the fisherman's aged wife was sitting in a big armchair. She rose politely to welcome her distinguished guest, but immediately sat down again in the place of honor, without offering it to the visitor, at which the fisherman smiled and said:

"You mustn't be offended, young sir, at her refusing to give up the best chair in the house. That's how it is with us poor people—the best chair's always reserved for the old ones."

"Why, husband, what can you be thinking of?" said his wife with a placid smile. "Our guest's a Christian like anyone else, I imagine. Why should a nice young man like that want to turn an old woman out of her chair? Sit down, young sir," she went on, turning to the knight. "That's not a bad little chair over there, only you mustn't be too rough with it, for one of the legs isn't quite as firm as it used to be."

Very cautiously the knight pulled up the chair in question and sat down on it. He immediately felt as though he was one of the family, and had just that moment come home from somewhere a long way off. The three good people soon struck up a friendly conversation, though the old man was rather uncommunicative about the forest, which was the subject of several inquiries from the knight.

"Don't let's talk about that," he said. "Especially not just now, when it's getting dark."

However, the old couple were only too glad to discuss their own affairs, and much enjoyed hearing the knight's account of his travels. He told them that he had a castle near the source of the Danube, and was called Sir Huldbrand von Ringstetten.

Several times in the course of the conversation the stranger heard a splash at the low window, as if someone was squirting water against it. Every time it happened, the old man frowned irritably; but when at last a great shower of water dashed against the pane and started bubbling in round the badly fitting frame, he got up in a rage and shouted threateningly through the window:

"Undine! Will you ever stop being childish? Besides, we've got a strange gentleman with us today."

There was silence outside, only broken by a faintly audible giggle, and the fisherman returned to his place, saying:

"You must forgive her for this piece of naughtiness, my honored guest, and probably for many more. But she doesn't mean any harm by it. You see, it's our foster child, Undine, and she simply won't grow up, though she's already getting on for eighteen. But as I say, at bottom she's got a thoroughly good heart."

"It's all very well for you to talk," rejoined the old woman, shaking her head. "When you come home from fishing or from a journey, there may be something quite nice about her fun. But when you have her hanging round your neck all day long, and never hear her speak a word of sense, and instead of finding her a help about the house as she grows older, always have to make sure she doesn't get into serious trouble with her silliness—that's quite another matter, and it's enough to try the patience of a saint."

"There, there," smiled her husband. "You have the same trouble with Undine as I do with the lake. It's always breaking my dams and bursting my nets, but I love it just the same, and with all your trials and tribulations you feel much the same about that pretty child. Now don't you?"

"One can't really be cross with her," admitted the old woman, smiling.

The door flew open, and a beautiful fair-haired girl slipped laughing into the room.

"You've been pulling my leg, Father," she said. "Where's this strange gentleman of yours?"

But at that moment she caught sight of the knight, and stood staring at the handsome youth in astonishment. Huldbrand was drinking in her charming appearance, and trying hard to impress her lovely features on his memory, for he assumed it was only her surprise that was giving him time to do so, and thought she would soon turn away with all the more embarrassment to escape his scrutiny. But nothing of the sort happened. After looking at him for quite a long time, she stepped right up to him without a trace of shyness, knelt down in front of him, and fingering a gold medallion that hung on a fine chain round her neck, exclaimed:

"Why, you nice, handsome stranger, how did you finally get to our poor little cottage? Did you have to go wandering for years all over the world before you found us? Have you come from the wild wood, my lovely new friend?"

The old woman's rebuke left him no time to answer. She told the girl to behave herself, and get up and go on with her work. Undine made no reply, but placing a small footstool beside Huldbrand's chair, sat down on it with her sewing, and said sweetly:

"I'll do it here."

The old man did what parents of spoiled children usually do on these occasions. He pretended not to have noticed Undine's naughtiness, and tried to change the subject. But the girl would not let him.

"I asked our guest where he came from," she said, "and he hasn't told me yet."

"You're quite right, I come from the forest, you pretty little creature," replied Huldbrand.

"Then you must tell me how you came to be there in the first place," she continued, "And what adventures you had in it, for something strange always happens there."

At this reminder Huldbrand gave a slight shiver, and glanced involuntarily towards the window, for he felt as though one of the weird figures that had met him in the forest was grinning in at him. He saw nothing but the deep, black night which by now lay outside the pane. So he pulled himself together, and was just about to begin his story, when the old man interrupted him.

"Don't do anything of the sort, sir," he said. "This isn't at all a good time for anything like that."

Undine jumped up angrily from her stool, put her pretty hands on her hips, and planting herself squarely in front of the fisherman, burst out:

"So he's not to tell me, Father? He's not to? But I want him to! He shall tell me! He shall!"

And the pretty little foot stamped violently on the floor; but the whole thing was so charmingly done that Huldbrand found it even harder to take his eyes off her now she was in a rage, than he had found it when she was being friendly. At this point, however, the old man's suppressed fury suddenly flared out. He rated Undine severely for her disobedience and rudeness towards the visitor, and the good old woman chimed in with similar reproaches.

"Very well," said Undine. "If you're determined to quarrel, and won't do what I want, you can spend the night by yourselves in your smoky old cottage!"

Swift as an arrow she was out of the door, and flying off into the darkness.

CHAPTER 2

How Undine Had Come to the Fisherman

Huldbrand and the fisherman leapt up from their seats to go after her, but before they could get to the door Undine had already disappeared in the misty darkness outside, her light feet making no sound to indicate which way she was running. Huldbrand looked inquiringly at his host. He almost felt as if the whole lovely vision, which had plunged so quickly back into the night, had merely been a continuation of the strange delusions that had haunted him in the forest.

"It's not the first time she's done this to us," grumbled the old man. "Now we'll be awake all night worrying; for who knows what may happen to her if she stays out there in the dark all alone until morning?"

"Then for God's sake let's go after her!" cried Huldbrand anxiously.

"What's the use?" said the old man. "It wouldn't be right to let you go chasing after the silly girl by yourself after dark in a lonely place like this—and she's such a tomboy that my old legs would never catch her up, even if we knew which way she was running."

"Well, we must at least try calling her, and asking her to come back," said Huldbrand, and began to call in the most persuasive tones: "Undine! Undine! Do come back!"

"Shouting won't help," said the old man, shaking his head. "You've no idea how stubborn the little one can be."

Even so, he could not resist following the knight's example, and shouting again and again into the darkness of the night: "Undine! Oh, dear Undine! Please do come back, just this once!"

But it was exactly as he had said. There was no sign of Undine to be seen or heard, and as the old man absolutely refused to let Huldbrand go in pursuit of the runaway, in the end they both had to return to the cottage. By this time the fire was nearly out, and the mistress of the house, who took Undine's disappearance and dangerous situation far less to heart than her husband, had already gone to bed. The old man blew on the coals, put some dry wood on top of them, and by the light of the resulting flames brought out a jug of wine, which he placed between his guest and himself.

"You're worried about that stupid girl too, sir," he said, "and we'll do better to spend part of the night talking and drinking, than tossing about on the rushes trying to get to sleep. Don't you agree?"

Huldbrand was quite in favor of the arrangement, so the fisherman invited him to take the place of honor vacated by his wife, and they sat talking and drinking together like a couple of very old friends. Needless to say, every time there was the slightest noise at the windows, and once or twice when there was none at all, one of them would glance up and say: "There she is!" Then they would both keep quiet for a few moments, and when no one appeared, carry on with their conversation, shaking their heads and sighing.

However, as neither of them could think of anything but Undine, the only subject of conversation that occurred to either of them was how Undine came to be there in the first place. So the fisherman began the story as follows:

"One day, it must be about fifteen years ago, I was on my way through the forest, taking my fish to market. My wife as usual had stayed at home. At that time she had a very pleasant reason for doing so, for though even then we were getting on in years, God had sent us a child. It was a little girl, and we'd already been discussing whether we shouldn't leave our pretty cottage beside the lake, so as to give our dear little gift from heaven the benefit of a better education in a less lonely neighborhood. Of course, what poor people mean by education probably isn't quite what you, sir, would mean by it—but goodness knows, we must all do the best we can.

"Well, on the way there this problem kept going round and round in my head. I was so fond of this place of ours, and I couldn't help shuddering when, in the midst of all the noise and wrangling in the town, I had to tell myself: before very long you'll be living in a place like this, or somewhere not much quieter! Still, I hadn't ever murmured against the Lord, but silently given Him thanks for the newborn child. And I can't say I came across anything out of the ordinary on the journey, for I've never seen anything at all uncanny in the forest—the Lord has always been with me among those eerie shadows."

He pulled his cap off his bald head, and remained for a moment in prayer. Then he put it on again, and continued:

"No, it was on this side of the wood, alas, that sorrow met me. My wife came out streaming with tears. She was wearing mourning.

" 'Good God!' I cried. 'Where's our darling child? Tell me!'

" 'She is with Him, dear husband,' she replied, and we went indoors together, weeping quietly. I looked round for the little body—and then I heard how it had happened. My wife had been sitting with the child beside the lake, and while she was happily playing with it, without a care in the world, the little creature suddenly bent forwards as if it had seen something absolutely beautiful in the water. My wife saw it laugh, the little angel, and stretch out its tiny hands—and the next moment it had shot out of her arms and disappeared beneath the surface of the water. I've often tried to find the little body, but it was no use. There wasn't a trace of it to be found.

"That evening, we were sitting quietly together in the cottage, feeling utterly bereft. Neither of us felt like talking, even if our tears had allowed us to do so. We just sat staring at the fire. Suddenly there was a rustling at the door. It flew open, and there on the threshold stood a lovely little girl, smiling in at us. She was beautifully dressed, and looked about three or four years old. We remained quite dumb with astonishment, and at first I didn't know if it was a real little human being, or merely some sort of delusion. Then I saw that water was trickling down from its golden hair and its fine clothes, and realized that the poor little thing must have fallen in the lake, and was badly in need of help.

" 'Wife,' said I, 'nobody could save our own dear child for us. But at least let's do something for someone else that would have made us happy for life, if anyone could have done it for us.'

"We undressed the little girl and put her to bed, and brought her hot drinks. While we were doing so, she never spoke a word, but just stared at us out of those heavenly blue eyes of hers, and smiled. Next morning it was fairly clear that she had taken no serious injury, and I asked her about her parents, and how she came to be there. But all we got out of her was a very confused and curious story. She must have been born somewhere a long way off, for not only have I failed in fifteen years to discover anything about her origin, but also from time to time she used to say such extraordinary things—in fact, she still does—that one really can't be absolutely sure she didn't drop down from the moon! For she talks about golden castles, and roofs of crystal, and goodness knows what else. The clearest account that she's ever given us is that she went sailing with her mother on the big lake, fell out of the boat into the water, and first came to her senses under the trees here, where she felt quite comfortable again on the pleasant grassy bank.

"Now we had a very difficult problem. We soon made up our minds to keep the little girl that we'd found, and bring her up in the place of the darling that we'd lost—but who could say if the child had been baptized or not? She herself couldn't give us any information on the subject. Her usual answer was that she knew she was a creature made for the glory of God, and she was quite prepared to have anything done for her that would increase His glory. My wife and I looked at it like this: if she hasn't been baptized, then there's no time to be lost in getting it done. And if she has, well, you can't have too much of a good thing. So we started trying to think of a good Christian name, for in the meantime we really didn't know what to call her. Finally we decided that the most suitable name would be Dorothea, because I'd once heard that it meant 'gift of God,' and she'd certainly been given us by God, to comfort us in our sorrow. But she wouldn't hear of it. She said her parents had called her Undine, and Undine was what she meant to go on being called. Now that seemed to me rather a heathenish kind of name, the sort you wouldn't find in any calendar, so I consulted a priest in the town about it. He wouldn't hear of Undine either, and at my earnest request he came back with me through the forest, to perform the baptism here in the cottage.

"Well, the little one stood there, looking so sweet in her pretty clothes, that the priest's heart fairly leapt up at the sight of her, and she coaxed him so cleverly, and sulked so charmingly, that by the time she'd finished he'd completely forgotten all his objections to the name Undine. So Undine she was christened, and her behavior during the ceremony was very sweet and proper, wild and restless as she always was otherwise. For my wife's quite right, we've had a lot to put up with from her. If I were to tell you—"

At this point the knight interrupted him, to draw his attention to a sound of rushing water which he had noticed before, while the old man was speaking, and which could now be heard roaring with increasing fury right outside the cottage windows. Both men dashed to the door. And there they saw, by the light of the rising moon, that the stream which ran out of the forest had burst its banks and was sweeping along great stones and tree trunks in its wildly swirling waves. As though awakened by the uproar, the storm now broke out of the mighty clouds that were racing across the moon, the lake began to shriek beneath the beating wings of the wind, and the trees on the tongue of land started groaning in every branch, and reeling down giddily over the tempestuous waters.

"Undine! For God's sake, Undine!" shouted the two men in alarm.

No answer came back to them, and forgetting every other consideration, they went dashing off in different directions, searching and calling.

Chapter 3

How They Found Undine

The longer he went on searching for Undine among the shadows of the night, without finding her, the more worried and perplexed Huldbrand became. The thought that she had been merely a vision of the forest came over him again with new conviction; and what with the shrieking of the waves and the wind, the creaking of the trees, and the complete transformation of what a few moments ago had been a quiet and pleasant scene, he was almost prepared to regard the whole tongue of land, including the cottage and its inhabitants, as some sort of mocking illusion. But in the distance he could still hear the fisherman anxiously shouting "Undine!," and the loud prayers and hymns of the old woman rising above the roaring of the storm.

At last he came to the brink of the swollen stream, and saw by the moonlight that its raging waters now flowed right in front of the haunted forest, thus turning the tongue of land into an island.

"O God!" he thought to himself. "What if she's actually gone into the forest, to satisfy her pretty anger at not hearing about it from me? What if she's been cut off by this stream, and is over there at this moment sobbing with terror, all by herself among the ghosts?"

A cry of horror escaped him, and he started clambering down over stones and uprooted pine trunks towards the rushing stream, determined to wade or swim across it and get to the poor girl somehow. He thought of all the strange, grisly things that had met him during the daytime under the boughs that were now grinding and shrieking overhead; and he actually had the impression that a tall white man, whom he recognized all too well, was grinning and nodding at him from the further bank. But these horrible visions only served to strengthen his resolution, when he pictured Undine all by herself among them, being frightened to death.

He had already seized a stout pine branch, and using it to steady him, was boldly advancing through the swirling waters, though it was all he could do to keep himself upright—when from somewhere quite close at hand a sweet voice cried:

"Careful! Careful! He's not to be trusted, that old stream!"

He recognized those lovely tones, and stood bewildered among the shadows, which had now blotted out the moon, made dizzy by the surging waves that he could see racing past his legs. But he still would not give up.

"Even if you're not really there," he exclaimed, "even if you're just an illusion, I want to die, too, and become a wraith like you, dear, dear Undine!"

And with these words he stepped even deeper into the stream.

"Turn round, turn round, you beautiful, silly boy!" came the voice again from just beside him. He spun round, and there in the light of the moon, which had now come out again, beneath the tangled boughs of the trees, on a little island created by the flood, he saw Undine, all smiles and loveliness, nestling in the deep grass.

In how different a spirit the young man now wielded his staff of pine! A few strides, and he had crossed the raging flood that separated them, and was standing beside her on the little patch of turf, in a secret sanctuary beneath the rustling shelter of the ancient trees. Undine had raised herself slightly, and the moment he entered the leafy tent, she flung her arms round his neck, and pulled him down on to the soft grass beside her.

"You shall tell me your story here, my handsome friend," she whispered. "The grumpy old people can't overhear us now. And it's quite as comfortable here, beneath our roof of leaves, as it is in that wretched cottage!"

"It's Heaven!" cried Huldbrand, embracing her and kissing her passionately.

Meanwhile the old fisherman had arrived at the brink of the stream, and now called across:

"Why, sir, I thought you were an honest man, or I shouldn't have taken you in—but here you are making love to my daughter on the sly—and what's more, letting me go on worrying about her, and running round in the dark looking for her!"

"I've only just this moment found her myself, old fellow," the knight called back.

"So much the better," said the fisherman. "Well, bring her over to dry land as quickly as you can."

But Undine would not hear of it. She said she would rather stay in the forest with the handsome stranger forever, than go back to a place where no one would let her have her own way, a place which the knight would soon be leaving, anyway. And with her arms still round Huldbrand, she sang very sweetly:

> A wave set out from a misty lea
> About the world to roam.
> It plunged among the waves of the sea,
> And never more came home.

The old man wept bitterly at this song, but she seemed quite unmoved. She went on kissing and caressing her loved one, until at last he said to her:

"Undine, if the old man's grief doesn't touch your heart, it certainly touches mine. We must go back to him."

At this she opened her big blue eyes in astonishment. Finally she answered, slowly and hesitantly:

"If you say so, all right then. I'll do anything you say. But first of all the old man must promise not to raise the slightest objection to your telling me what you saw in the forest, and secondly—but that doesn't matter."

"Only come back! Come back!" cried the fisherman. They were the only words he could get out. At the same time he stretched out his arms towards her over the water, and nodded his head to signify that he agreed to her terms—which made his white hair fall oddly over his face, so that Huldbrand could not help thinking of the nodding white man in the forest. But without letting this upset him, he picked up the lovely girl in his arms and carried her across the narrow gulf of raging water that separated them from dry land.

The old man fell upon Undine's neck, and could not kiss her enough, he was so overjoyed. The old woman came up, too, and affectionately welcomed her back. There were no more reproaches, especially as Undine had quite forgotten her ill humor, and almost overwhelmed her foster parents with caresses and endearments.

When they had finally got over the joy of having her back, the rising sun was already shining across the lake, the storm had dropped, and the birds were singing merrily on the wet branches. As Undine still insisted on hearing the knight's story, the two old people smilingly assented. So they took their breakfast out under the trees beside the lake, and sat down there very contentedly on the grass— Undine, needless to say, at the knight's feet, since she absolutely refused to sit anywhere else. And Huldbrand began to tell the following story.

CHAPTER 4

What Had Happened to the Knight in the Forest

"About a week ago I arrived in the town on the other side of the forest. Soon after I got there, they put on a big tournament, so naturally I tried my luck with my lance and my old hack. Well, as I stopped for a moment beside the lists to rest from my pleasant labors—I'd just handed my helmet to one of my squires—I suddenly caught sight of a strikingly beautiful woman in a gorgeous dress, standing on one of the platforms among the spectators. I asked the knight next to me who the ravishing creature was, and learned that she was called Bertalda, and was the foster daughter of a powerful Duke who lived in the neighborhood. I noticed that she had her eyes on me, too, and as you might expect, my riding, which had been pretty good before, was now positively inspired. That evening at the dance I was Bertalda's partner, and remained so every night of the tournament."

At this point Huldbrand was interrupted by a sharp pain in his left hand, and looked down to see what had caused it. Undine had sunk her pearly teeth deep into his finger, and her face was dark with rage. But suddenly she looked up into his eyes with a gently wistful expression, and whispered very softly: "You did ask for it, you know." Then she turned her face away, and the knight went on with his story, feeling strangely confused and thoughtful:

"She's a proud and difficult girl, Bertalda. I didn't like her nearly so much on the second day as I had on the first, and on the third I liked her even less. But I went on hanging round her, because she was nicer to me than to any of the other knights, and so it came about that, quite as a joke, I asked her for one of her gloves.

" 'Certainly,' she said, 'if you'll go off by yourself into that forest that I've heard such unpleasant stories about, and tell me what it looks like.'

"Well, I wasn't particularly interested in the glove, but I couldn't very well go back on what I'd said, and a man of honor doesn't need asking twice to accept a challenge like that."

"I think she must have been fond of you," broke in Undine.

"It did look rather like it," admitted Huldbrand.

"Then she must be very stupid," said the girl, laughing. "Fancy driving away something one's fond of! And into a dangerous forest, too! If I'd been her, the mysteries of the forest would have had to wait!"

"Well, I started off yesterday morning," continued the knight, smiling affectionately at Undine. "The tree trunks looked so rosy and slender in the early sunlight that was flooding across the green grass, and the leaves were whispering so merrily to one another, that I couldn't help laughing to myself at the idea that there could be anything sinister about such a delightful spot. It won't take me long to trot to the other side of the wood and back, I thought, and I felt so easy and cheerful in my mind about it, that before I'd realized, I'd plunged deep into the green shadows and left the plain far behind me. Then it suddenly occurred to me that I might easily lose my way in that huge forest, and that this was perhaps the only really dangerous thing about the place. So I stopped to check the position of the sun, which had meanwhile got rather higher. As I glanced up, I noticed a black object among the branches of a tall oak. At first I thought it was a bear, and grasped my sword—until it shouted down at me, in a very hoarse and unpleasant human voice:

" 'What are we to roast you on at midnight, if I don't nibble off some of these twigs up here for firewood, Mr. Nosy Parker?'

"As it said this, it grinned and rattled the branches up and down until my poor horse took fright and bolted, before I'd had a chance to make out what sort of devilish creature it actually was."

"You mustn't use that word," said the old fisherman, and crossed himself. His wife silently did the same, but Undine raised her bright eyes to gaze at her sweetheart, saying:

"The best part of the story is that they haven't really roasted you after all. Go on, you sweet boy."

The knight continued his tale:

"In its panic my horse narrowly missed dashing me against the tree trunks and branches. It was dripping with sweat from terror and overheating, and simply wouldn't stop whatever I did. Finally it went plunging down a rocky slope, when all of a sudden I thought I saw a tall white man fling himself across the path of the maddened stallion. The shock brought it to a standstill. I got it under control again, and only then discovered that my rescuer was not a white man after all, but a silvery stream that came dashing down from a nearby hill, thus violently interrupting my horse's mad career."

"Oh, you darling stream, thank you!" cried Undine, clapping her hands. But the old man shook his head, and remained deep in thought with his eyes fixed on the ground.

"I'd scarcely recovered my seat in the saddle," continued Huldbrand, "and got hold of the reins again, when a funny little man appeared at my elbow. He was absolutely tiny and quite repulsive to look at, for he was a yellowish brown all over, and his nose was nearly as big as the rest of him put together. His wide slit of a mouth was contorted into a grin of imbecile politeness, and he kept bowing and scraping at me until I got quite sick of it. So with a brief word of thanks I turned my still trembling horse, and decided to go in search of further adventure, or failing that, to try and find my way home, for by this time the sun had passed its zenith and was already sinking towards the West. But quick as a flash the little fellow whipped round and stood in front of the horse again.

" 'Out of my way there!' I shouted angrily. 'The animal's had a bad fright, and is liable to run you down.'

" 'You don't say!' whined the little creature, with a horrible, idiotic laugh. 'Well, first of all give me a tip for catching your horse. If it weren't for me he'd be lying on the rocks down there, and, my word, so would you!'

" 'Oh, stop pulling faces and take your money, then,' I said. 'But it's a lie all the same, for you can see for yourself it was that blessed stream over there that saved my life, not you, you wretched little object!'

"And I dropped a gold coin into the queer little cap that he'd pulled off his head and was holding out to me like a beggar. Then I started trotting away, but he set up a yell behind me, and all of a sudden, with an incredible turn of speed, he'd caught me up again. I put my horse into a gallop—he galloped along beside me, though it seemed to cost him a fearful effort, and he went through the most extraordinary contortions, half-comic and half-horrible, as he kept waving the gold coin about in the air, and at every bound shrieked out: 'False coin! False money! False coin! False money!' The words came wheezing out so breathlessly that I thought he'd drop dead on the ground if he went another step, and all the time his ugly red tongue kept lolling farther and farther out of his mouth. I stopped, appalled, and asked:

" 'What on earth are you yelling about? Have another piece of gold, have two more if you like, only leave me alone!'

"At that he started up his hideous bowing and scraping again, and whined, 'It's not gold—it's not exactly gold that I want, my dear young gentleman. I have plenty of that to play with already. Look, I'll show you.'

"All of a sudden the solid ground at my feet became transparent, like green glass, the flat earth seemed to curve into a sphere, and inside it I could see hundreds of little goblins playing with silver and gold. They were turning somersaults, pelting each other in fun with the precious metals, and puffing gold dust into each other's faces. My ugly little companion was standing half-in, half-out of the ground, getting the others to hand him up vast quantities of gold, and showing it to me and laughing, then chucking it down again, clinking and clattering, into the abyss. After that he showed the goblins down there the gold coin that I'd given him, and they laughed themselves almost sick, and started booing and hissing at me. Finally they all pointed their sharp, metal-stained fingers at me, and getting wilder and madder every moment, began swarming up thick and fast towards me. I got into a panic, just as my horse had done before. I clapped my spurs into him, and how far I went on this second mad dash through the forest, goodness only knows.

"When at last I came to a standstill, it was the cool of the evening. Through the branches I caught sight of a white footpath, which I thought must lead back to the town. I tried to reach it, but was stopped by a dim white face, with continually shifting features, which seemed to be staring at me through the leaves. I tried to get away from it, but whichever way I turned, it was there in front of me. In the end I lost my temper and galloped straight at it—but it blinded me and my horse with a shower of white spray, so that we had to turn back. Thus it forced us, step by step, away from the footpath, and made it absolutely impossible for us to move in any direction except one. But as soon as we started going that way, it appeared close behind us. However, it didn't do us the slightest harm. When I looked round from time to time, I noticed that the white, spray-dashed face was attached to an equally white body of gigantic proportions. Once or twice I got the impression that it was a sort of walking fountain, but I couldn't ever make absolutely sure. By this time my horse and I were both so exhausted that we simply gave in, and let the white man drive us wherever he wanted. He kept on nodding his head, as if to say: 'That's it! That's it!' So finally we reached the edge of the forest here, and saw grass, and a lake, and your little cottage ahead of us—and the tall white man disappeared."

"Good riddance to him!" said the old fisherman, and went on to discuss his guest's best method of getting back to his friends in the town. At this Undine started chuckling to herself. Huldbrand noticed it, and said to her:

"I thought you liked having me here. Why are you so amused at the idea of my going away?"

"Because you *can't* go away," replied Undine. "Just you try getting across that swollen stream, either in a boat or on horseback or on foot, whichever takes your fancy! Or rather, don't try anything of the sort, for you'd only be smashed to pieces by the stones and tree trunks that are hurtling down it. As for crossing the lake, I know my father would never get as far as that in a tiny little boat like his."

Huldbrand got up with a smile, to see if she was right; the old man accompanied him, and the girl went dancing merrily along beside them. They found that the situation was just as she had described it, and the knight had to resign himself to staying on the tongue of land, which had now become an island, until the floods subsided. As the three reentered the cottage after their tour of inspection, he whispered in Undine's ear:

"Well, how do you feel about it, Undine darling? Are you annoyed that I'm going to stay!"

"Oh, stop it!" she snapped peevishly. "Who knows what wouldn't have come out in your story about Bertalda, if I hadn't bitten you?"

CHAPTER 5

How the Knight Lived on the Island

Dear reader, have you ever had the experience, after rushing up and down all over the world, of coming to a place that really suited you—a place where the love of one's own fireside, of peace and quiet, that is born in each one of us, welled up in you once more—where you felt that you were at home, a home bright with all the flowers of childhood, and with the purest and truest love, resurrected from the costly tomb in which it had been buried—felt that here it would be good to live and build a humble dwelling? Whether the feeling was mistaken, and whether you had to pay a painful penalty afterwards for your mistake, is quite beside the point; and you probably have no wish to torment yourself with the memory of that bitter after-taste. But just try to recall that inexpressibly sweet sensation, that angelic salutation, "Peace be with you" and you will have some vague idea how Huldbrand felt during his life on the island.

With deep satisfaction he watched the forest stream growing more turbulent every day, cutting a wider and wider channel for itself, and thus prolonging his period of seclusion on the island. Part of his time he spent wandering about with an old crossbow that he had found in a corner of the cottage and got into working order, on the lookout for any birds that might fly past; and when he managed to hit one, it made a splendid contribution to the household food supply. On such occasions, when he came in with his bag, Undine nearly always scolded him for his cruelty in robbing the dear little creatures of their happy lives up there in the blue sea of air; in fact, she often burst into tears at the sight of the dead birds. But on other occasions, when he came home without shooting anything, she scolded him just as much for being lazy and inefficient.

"Now, thanks to you, we've got nothing to eat but fish!" she would grumble. She was so charming, however, in her anger, that he enjoyed every minute of it, especially as she usually tried to make up for her bad temper by being all the more affectionate afterwards.

The old people had come to accept the intimacy between the two young ones, and regarded them as an engaged, or rather as a married couple who had been sent to support them in their old age, cut off as they were on the island. Indeed this very isolation gave Huldbrand the firm impression that he was already betrothed to Undine. For him the world beyond the surrounding water had practically ceased to exist—or even if it still existed, he saw no prospect of any further contact with the rest of humanity. And when, from time to time, his grazing horse whinnied, as if to remind him of knightly deeds, or his coat of arms seemed to glance sternly at him from the embroidery on his saddlecloth and trappings, or his beautiful sword suddenly fell off its nail on the cottage wall, and as it fell, slipped half out of its sheath, he would set his mind at rest by telling himself:

"Undine's no ordinary fisherman's daughter. She's something far better than that! She probably comes from a royal house in some foreign country."

The one thing he really hated was when the old woman scolded Undine in his presence. Admittedly the girl herself generally took the whole thing as a joke, but to Huldbrand it seemed like a reflection on his own honor—and yet he could not really blame the fisherman's wife, for Undine always deserved at least ten times as much scolding as she ever got. So he remained on good terms with his hostess, and life went on in the same quiet, pleasant way as before.

Eventually, however, they ran up against a problem. The fisherman and the knight had got into the habit of enjoying a jug of wine over their midday meal, and another in the evening, when the wind was howling outside, as it nearly always did towards nightfall. But now they had exhausted the whole stock of wine that the fisherman had collected little by little from the town, and both men were quite upset about it. Undine spent the day valiantly poking fun at them, without getting the usual cheerful reaction from either. Towards evening she left the cottage, saying that she could not stand the sight of their long, dull faces any longer. When twilight brought the threat of another storm, and the waters of the lake were already roaring and shrieking, the knight and the fisherman got worried and dashed out to bring her home, remembering that night of terror when Huldbrand had first arrived at the cottage. But Undine came running to meet them, clapping her hands.

"What will you give me, if I get you some wine?" she asked. "Or rather, you needn't give me anything, for I'll be quite content if you'll only look a bit more cheerful, and have a few bright ideas for a change, instead of being as boring as you have been all today. Come with me—there's a cask washed up on the bank of the stream, and you can send me to bed for a week, if it isn't full of wine!"

The men followed her and sure enough, among the bushes at a bend in the stream, they found a cask which gave every indication of containing the precious liquid for which they craved. Without further delay, they started rolling it as fast as they could towards the cottage, for a heavy storm was coming up in the evening sky, and through the twilight the waves of the lake could be seen lifting up their white, foaming heads, as if to look for the rain that would soon be dashing down on them. Undine did her best to help the two men, and when all too soon the storm wind suddenly started screaming overhead, she shouted merrily towards the gathering clouds:

"Hoy! You up there! Mind you don't soak us to the skin! We're not nearly home yet!"

The old man rebuked her for her sinful presumption, but she went on chuckling quietly to herself, and certainly no harm seemed to come of her remark. On the contrary, surprisingly enough all three of them were still perfectly dry when they reached their cozy fireside with their prize; and it was only when they had actually opened the cask and found some remarkably good wine in it, that the rain finally burst out of the dark clouds, and the storm went roaring through the tops of the trees and over the surging waves of the lake.

Some bottles had soon been filled from the big cask, which promised to keep them supplied for many days, and they were sitting together round a blazing fire, drinking and joking and feeling comfortably protected against the raging storm, when suddenly the old fisherman became very solemn.

"Good God!" he exclaimed. "Here we are enjoying this precious gift, when its original owner may quite possibly have lost his life in the floods!"

"Oh, he won't have done that!" said Undine with a smile, and poured out some more for the knight, who replied:

"Upon my honor, if I could only find him and come to his rescue, I shouldn't mind how far I had to go, or how many risks I ran. But this much I can tell you—if I ever get back to civilization, I'll certainly make a search for him or his heirs, and give them two or three casks of wine in return."

The old man was delighted. He nodded approvingly at the knight, and drained his mug with a much easier conscience, and with far greater enjoyment. But Undine said to Huldbrand:

"As for giving it back, you're entitled to do what you like with your own money. But it's stupid to talk of running off to look for him. If you went and got lost as a result, I'd cry my eyes out—and I'm sure you'd far rather stay here with me and this excellent wine, now wouldn't you?"

"I certainly would," replied Huldbrand with a smile.

"Well then," said Undine, "it was a very stupid thing to say. One's got to look out for oneself—what does anyone else matter?"

At this the old woman turned away with a sigh, shaking her head, and the fisherman, forgetting his usual affection for the pretty little creature, started scolding her angrily:

"To hear you talk," he concluded, "anyone would think you'd been brought up by Turks and heathens! God forgive me and you, you wicked child!"

"Well, whomever I've been brought up by, that's what I think, so there!" retorted Undine. "And nothing you can say will make the slightest difference!"

"Hold your tongue!" shouted the fisherman, and Undine, who in spite of her impudence was extremely nervous, started back and clung trembling to Huldbrand.

"Are you cross with me, too?" she whispered.

The knight squeezed her soft hand and stroked her hair. He could not say a word, for the old man's harsh treatment of Undine had made him too angry to speak. So for a while the two couples sat facing one another in embarrassed and hostile silence.

Chapter 6

A Wedding

The silence was broken by a gentle knock on the door, which made everyone in the cottage start; for even a tiny thing can give one a terrible shock, if it happens quite unexpectedly. And in this case there were the additional factors that the dreadful forest was not far away, and that the tongue of land was apparently inaccessible to any human visitor.

They stared at one another in bewilderment. The knock came again, accompanied by a deep groan. The knight started reaching for his sword, but the old man whispered:

"If it's what I fear, no weapon is going to help us!"

Undine meanwhile had gone to the door, and now called out in quite angry and confident tones:

"If you start playing any of your tricks here, you earth-spirits, Kühleborn will soon teach you better manners!"

This extraordinary speech made the others even more alarmed. They gazed at her in dismay, and Huldbrand was just plucking up courage to ask her a question, when a voice outside said:

"I'm no earth-spirit, but I'm certainly a spirit, and I'm certainly dwelling in an earthly body. If you're God-fearing people, you there inside the cottage, please open the door and help me."

At these words Undine promptly opened the door and shone a light into the stormy darkness outside, revealing the figure of an aged priest, who started back in alarm at the unexpected sight of the girl. To see such a lovely apparition emerge from a humble cottage door convinced him, as well it might, that some sort of magic was at work, and he began to pray:

"O all ye spirits of righteousness, praise ye the Lord!"

"I'm not a ghost," said Undine, smiling. "Do I look as bad as all that? Besides, you can see for yourself I'm not frightened by your holy words. I know about God, too, and I know we all ought to praise Him—everyone after his own fashion, of course—and that's why He created us. Come in, reverend Father—we're all good people here."

The priest came in, bowing to everyone in the room, and presenting a most pleasant and venerable appearance, except that water was dripping from every fold of his black clothing, and from his long white beard, and from the white hair on his head. The fisherman and the knight led him into a bedroom and provided him with a change of clothes, handing his cassock to the women in the living room, to dry by the fire. The white-haired stranger thanked them most humbly and politely, but absolutely refused to put on the gorgeous cloak that the knight held out to him, choosing instead an old gray overcoat of the fisherman's.

The moment they returned to the living room, the old woman vacated her big armchair, and was not satisfied until she had made the priest sit down in it.

"For you're old and tired," she explained, "and besides, you're a priest."

Undine pushed her little stool underneath the stranger's feet, and generally looked after the old man in the most courteous and charming fashion. Huldbrand whispered a teasing remark about it into her ear, but she replied quite seriously:

"Why, he's a servant of God, who made us all! It's not a thing to laugh about."

The knight and the fisherman encouraged the priest to refresh himself with food and wine, and when he had somewhat recovered, he began to tell his story. It appeared that he came from a monastery on the far side of the lake, and had set out from there the day before on a visit to the bishop, whom he wished to inform of the great distress that the recent heavy floods were causing in his monastery and its dependent villages. After a long detour, necessitated by the floods in question, he had this evening found himself compelled to ask two worthy boatmen to ferry him across a place where the lake had overflowed its banks.

"But our little vessel had scarcely got out among the waves," he continued, "when the frightful storm broke out that's still raging over our heads. It seemed as if the water had just been waiting for us to arrive, before it went into a sort of wild, whirling dance. The oars were soon torn out of the boatmen's hands, smashed to pieces, and swept farther and farther away from us by the waves. We ourselves, left completely at the mercy of blind natural forces, were driven out across the open lake towards these distant shores of yours, which we could already see looming up through the mist and spray. Faster and faster the boat spun round, until we were absolutely giddy—and whether in the end it capsized, or I was thrown out, I have no idea. All I know is that I floated on through the darkness, in imminent danger of a horrible death, until a wave threw me ashore here, under the trees on your island."

"You may well call it an island!" said the fisherman. "A few days ago it was a peninsula—but now that the stream and the lake have gone completely crazy, things look rather different."

"I guessed that something like that must have happened," said the priest, "for while I was groping my way in the dark along the edge of the water, and finding nothing but tumult in every direction, I finally noticed a footpath that led straight into the roaring waves. Then I saw the light in your cottage, and ventured to come to you for help— and I cannot thank my heavenly Father enough, not only for saving me from the water, but also for guiding me to such good people as you—especially as I have no reason to expect that I'll ever see another human being in my lifetime, apart from you four."

"Why, what do you mean?" asked the fisherman.

"Well," rejoined the priest, "have *you* any idea how long this strife of the elements will last? And I'm an old man. The stream of my life may easily run dry and sink into the earth, long before that stream out there returns to its usual channel. Altogether, it's quite within the bounds of possibility that more and more water will rush foaming between you and the forest, until you're so cut off from the rest of the world that you'll never be able to reach it in your little fishing boat, and the people over there will be far too much taken up with their own amusements to remember two old folk like you."

At this the old woman started, and crossed herself, saying: "God forbid!" But the fisherman smiled at her, and exclaimed:

"There's human nature for you! Why, what difference would it make to you, my dear? You've never gone farther than the edge of the forest for years. And what other human beings have you seen, besides Undine and me? It's only just lately that the knight and the priest have come to join us. And they'd have to stay here, if this became a forgotten island—so you'd really be far better off!"

"I don't know about that," said his wife, "but it makes one feel queer to think of being cut off from other people for ever, even if one never sees them or knows them anyway."

"Then you'll have to stay with us, you'll have to stay with us!" whispered Undine very softly—but it was almost a song of triumph, and she nestled even closer to Huldbrand. The young man, however, was lost in strange thoughts of his own. The priest's last words had seemed to push the world across the water farther and farther away into the darkness, while the green and flowery island on which he lived took on a brighter and brighter aspect in his mind. His bride-to-be shone forth as the loveliest rose in this little spot of earth, and indeed in the whole world—and there was the priest ready at hand. Moreover, at this moment the old woman shot an angry glance at Undine, for sitting so close to her sweetheart in the presence of the priest, and it looked as if a stream of unpleasant remarks was about to follow. The result was that the knight turned to the priest, and out came these words:

"You see, reverend sir, we're engaged to be married, and if this young lady and her foster parents have no objection, I'd like you to perform the ceremony this very evening."

The old man and his wife were extremely surprised. Admittedly they had often thought that something of the sort would happen, but they had never actually put it into words, and when the knight did just that, the whole idea struck them as quite novel and unexpected. Undine became very solemn all of a sudden, and sat looking thoughtfully in front of her, while the priest asked for further details of the situation, and inquired if the old people gave their consent. After a great deal of discussion, they finally agreed. The old woman went off to prepare the bridal chamber, and also to find, for the purposes of the wedding, two consecrated candles which she had long kept by her.

Meanwhile the knight seized his golden chain, and started trying to work off two of the links, so that he could use them as rings to exchange with his bride. But as soon as she saw what he was doing, she came out of her reverie with a start.

"No!" she cried. "My parents didn't send me into the world completely destitute. In fact, they must have somehow guessed, even then, what was going to happen tonight."

With these words she dashed out of the door, and returned a moment later with two valuable rings, one of which she gave the bridegroom, keeping the other for herself. The fisherman was absolutely amazed, and his wife, who had just come back, was even more so, for neither of them had ever seen these pieces of jewelry in the girl's possession before.

"My parents had them sewn into the pretty dress that I was wearing when I came to you," explained Undine. "They told me on no account to breathe a word about them to anybody before my wedding night. So I quietly cut them out, and kept them hidden until now."

They had no time for further questions, for the priest now lit the consecrated candles, placed them on the table, and instructed the young couple to stand in front of him. Then, with a few short words, they were solemnly united, the old people gave them their blessing, and the bride, looking very thoughtful and trembling a little, pressed close against the knight.

"What strange people you are!" exclaimed the priest all of a sudden. "Why did you tell me you were the only human beings on the island? Throughout the whole ceremony I could see a tall handsome man in a white cloak watching us through the window. He must be still standing outside the door, if you'd care to invite him in."

"God forbid," said the old woman, shuddering. The fisherman shook his head in silence, and Huldbrand dashed to the window. For an instant he, too, imagined he saw a streak of white, but it quickly disappeared into the darkness. He managed to convince the priest that he had been totally mistaken, and they all sat down in a friendly circle round the fire.

CHAPTER 7

Further Events on the
Wedding Night

Before and during the ceremony Undine had been very quiet and well behaved, but now all the odd fancies that she had been keeping down seemed to come bubbling irrepressibly to the surface. She played all kinds of childish tricks on the bridegroom, on her foster parents, and even on the priest, for whom she showed far less respect than before, and the old woman was just about to protest when the knight forestalled her with a few serious remarks, in the course of which he tried to silence Undine by calling her, with great emphasis, his wife. By that time even he was quite as annoyed as the others at her childish behavior; but nothing he could do in the way of nudging her, or clearing his throat, or making disapproving comments, had the slightest effect. Admittedly, whenever she noticed his annoyance, which did happen from time to time, she would quiet down a little, and sit beside him and caress him, or whisper something in his ear to smooth away the frown that was gathering on his brow. But the next moment she would be off on some new flight of folly, and things would get worse than ever.

"My sweet child," said the priest, in serious but very kindly tones, "you're certainly a delight to behold, but it's time you started trying to tune your soul in harmony with your husband's."

"My soul!" said Undine, laughing. "That sounds very nice, and it may be a very edifying and useful rule for the majority of people. But if one hasn't got a soul, what, may I ask, is one to tune? Because that's how it is with me."

The priest was too deeply offended and annoyed to make any reply: he merely turned sadly away. But she went over to him and said coaxingly:

"No, do listen to the whole story before you look so cross—

because when you look cross like that, it hurts me, and you shouldn't hurt a person that's never done you any harm. Just be patient with me, and I'll tell you properly what I mean."

She was evidently about to give a long and detailed explanation, when suddenly she stopped short, as if gripped by some inner fear, and burst into a flood of bitter tears. No one knew what to make of her any more, and they just stared at her in silence, with all sorts of different anxieties going through their minds. At last she dried her eyes and looked earnestly at the priest.

"There must be something very precious, but also very dreadful about a soul," she said. "For God's sake, tell me, wouldn't it be better not to have one at all?"

She was silent again, as if waiting for an answer, trying hard not to cry. Everyone in the cottage had got up, and was shrinking away from her, but she seemed to have no eyes for anyone but the priest, and an expression of fearful curiosity appeared on her face, which communicated her terror to the others.

"A soul must be a heavy burden," she went on, since no one replied. "A very heavy one! For even the vague idea of it fills me with grief and terror. And oh, how happy and lighthearted I used to be!"

And she burst into another flood of tears, and buried her face in her hands. At this the priest looked very grave. He stepped over to her, and adjured her, in the name of all that was holy, to throw aside the bright veil that covered her, and reveal whatever evil was within. But she fell on her knees before him, repeating every word he uttered, praising God, and swearing that she was in love and charity with all mankind.

Finally the priest said to the knight:

"Well, sir, I will leave you alone with your wife. So far as I can make out, there is no evil in her, though there is much that is very strange. I advise you to be cautious, loving, and faithful."

So saying he went out, and the fisherman and his wife followed, crossing themselves.

Undine remained on her knees, but now uncovered her face and looked timidly up at Huldbrand.

"Oh, now you'll never keep me!" she wailed. "And yet I've done nothing wrong, poor, poor child that I am!"

As she said this, she looked so infinitely sweet and touching, that forgetting all the mystery and terror of his position, the bridegroom rushed towards her and raised her in his arms. She smiled at him through her tears: it was like the morning sun sparkling on the waters of a little stream.

"You can't give me up!" she whispered with deep conviction, and stroked the knight's cheek with her soft hand. It was enough to banish all the dreadful thoughts that had been lurking in the back of his mind, trying to persuade him that he had married a fairy, or some evil, mocking creature from the spirit-world. The only question that he could not help asking was this:

"Darling Undine, do tell me just one thing. What did you mean by what you said about earth-spirits, when the priest knocked on the door, and about Kühleborn?"

"It was only a joke, that's all," said Undine, laughing and quite restored to her usual high spirits. "First I frightened you by it, and then you frightened me. And that's the end of the story, and of our whole wedding night."

"It's not the end of that yet," whispered the knight, intoxicated with passion. He blew out the candles, and by the pleasant light of the moon, which shone brightly in through the window, he smothered his beautiful darling with kisses, and carried her into the bridal chamber.

Chapter 8

The Day After the Wedding

The young couple were woken by the bright morning sunlight. Undine hid shyly under the bedclothes, and Huldbrand lay still, thinking. Every time he had fallen asleep during the night he had been disturbed by horrible dreams of furtively leering ghosts that tried to disguise themselves as beautiful women, and of beautiful women who all of a sudden turned into dragons. Again and again he started up in terror, but there was nothing to be seen except the moonlight, pale and cold outside the window. Fearfully he would turn his eyes towards Undine, in whose arms he had gone to sleep, and there she would be, as sweet and lovely as ever, resting quietly beside him. Then he would lightly touch her rosy lips with his own and go to sleep again, only to be woken by new horrors.

Now that he was thoroughly awake and had thought it all over, he reproached himself for having had the slightest doubts about his beautiful wife. He even apologized for doing her such an injustice; but she only stretched out her lovely hand towards him, sighed very deeply, and lay still. In her eyes, however, was a look of such infinite tenderness as he had never seen before, which convinced him that she bore him no ill will.

He leapt cheerfully out of bed, and prepared to join the others in the living room. They were sitting round the fire, looking very anxious, though nobody had yet dared put his fears into words. The priest seemed to be praying silently for all possible evil to be averted. But when the young husband appeared in such excellent spirits, their furrowed brows became smooth again, and the old fisherman actually started cracking jokes—of the most polite and respectable kind—at the knight's expense, so that even the old woman began to smile quite cheerfully.

By this time Undine had finally got dressed, and now appeared in the doorway. They all started towards her, then stopped and gazed in astonishment: there was something so strange and yet so familiar about her. The priest was the first to approach her, his eyes bright with fatherly affection, and as he raised his hand to bless her, the lovely creature sank reverently to her knees. In a few humble words she begged his forgiveness for any foolish things that she might have said the night before, and entreated him to pray for the salvation of her soul. Then she got up, kissed her foster parents, and thanked them for all their kindness.

"Oh, now I feel in my inmost heart," she said, "how much, how infinitely much you have done for me, you dear, dear people!"

She flung her arms round them, and was quite unable to tear herself away, until she noticed that the old woman's eye was on the breakfast table, whereupon she promptly stationed herself by the fire, and did all the cooking and serving herself, refusing to allow her good old foster mother to be given the slightest trouble on her account.

She was like that all day—quiet, kind and attentive, a little house-wife and a shy, sensitive young girl, both at the same time. The three

people who had known her longest expected at any moment to see
one of the sudden changes of mood that were characteristic of her.
But they waited in vain. Undine remained as sweet and gentle as an
angel. The priest simply could not take his eyes off her, and more
than once he told the bridegroom:

"Sir, by the grace of God, and by my unworthy agency, you had a
real treasure committed to your care last night. Look after it, as it
deserves, and it will prove your salvation in this world and the next."

Towards evening, with a humbly affectionate gesture Undine took
the knight's arm, and drew him gently out of doors, where the
setting sun shone pleasantly across the green grass, and bathed the
tall, slim trunks of the trees with light. Her eyes were swimming
with tears of wistful tenderness, and about her lips there seemed to
hover some secret anxiety, which only betrayed itself by a few
scarcely audible sighs. In silence she led her husband farther and
farther away. When he spoke, she responded only with her eyes,
which while giving no direct answer to his questions, revealed a
whole world of love and tremulous devotion.

At last they reached the bank of the swollen stream, and the
knight was astonished to see that it was not nearly so deep and rapid
as it had been, and its waves had subsided into the gentlest of
ripples.

"By the morning it will have all dried up," said his beautiful wife
sadly, "and then you'll be able to go wherever you want to."

"Not without you, Undine darling," he replied with a smile.
"Besides, even if I wanted to leave you, church and state would
immediately interfere, and bring your runaway husband back
again!"

"It all depends on you. It all depends on you," whispered the little
creature, half-crying and half-laughing. "But I think you'll want to
keep me. I do love you so much. Now carry me across to that little
island over there. Then we can settle it, one way or the other. I could
easily slip across by myself, but it feels so good to rest in your arms,
and if you're going to give me up, I'd like to feel them round me just
once more, if it's only for the last time."

Feeling strangely moved and alarmed, Huldbrand was unable to
reply. He just picked her up in his arms and started to carry her over;
and only then did he realize that it was the very same island from
which he had brought her back to the fisherman on the night of his

arrival. Once across, he lowered his lovely burden on to the soft grass, and was just about to sit down close beside her, when she said:

"No. Over there, facing me. I want to read the answer in your eyes, before your lips have time to move. Now listen carefully to what I'm going to tell you.

"You must know, my sweet darling," she began, "that the elements are full of creatures that look exactly like you, but very seldom let you see them. Fire is the playground of strange, glittering creatures called Salamanders. Deep down in the earth live mischievous, wizened little things called Gnomes. Through the woods wander the wood-spirits, who belong to the element of air, and the lakes and streams and brooks are inhabited by innumerable water-spirits. It's wonderful to live down there beneath echoing vaults of crystal, through which the sky looks in with the sun and all the stars. And one can wander about over the pure sea-sand, and over lovely shells of every color in the rainbow. And there are all the relics of the ancient world, beautiful things that people nowadays have lost the right to enjoy, covered over by the waves with their mysterious veil of silver. There one can see tall and stately monuments glistening with drops of living water, and all overgrown with splendid flowers of moss and clusters of reeds. The men and women who live there are very beautiful to look at—far more beautiful than most human beings. From time to time a fisherman is lucky enough to be within earshot, when a delicate sea-maiden rises above the waves to sing. When this happens, the man is never tired of telling how beautiful she was, and so there are many stories about these strange women, who are commonly called Undines. But you, at this moment, my dearest friend, are actually looking at an Undine."

The knight tried to persuade himself that his lovely wife was in the grip of one of her queer fancies, and had made up this ingenious story just to tease him. But try as he would, he could not believe it for a moment. A shudder went through him. Unable to bring out a word, he just stared fixedly at her. Sadly she shook her head, and with a deep sigh proceeded as follows:

"We'd be far better off than you other human beings—for we call ourselves human, too, and so far as our physical appearance goes, that's what we are—if it weren't for one thing. When we and other elemental spirits die, we disappear without leaving any trace of our existence. You others will awake one day to a purer life, but we just remain where we were, with sand and sparks and wind and waves. For we have no souls. Our element sets us in motion, and obeys us, so long as we're alive. But as soon as we're dead, it disperses us for ever. So we live merrily, without a care in the world, like a nightingale, or a goldfish, or any other pretty child of nature. But everything aspires to be higher than it is, and my father, who's a powerful Water-King in the Mediterranean, wanted his only daughter to have a soul, even if it meant suffering the pains that creatures with souls endure. And people like us can only acquire a soul by being united in true love with someone of your race. So now I have a soul, and from my soul I thank you for it, you inexpressibly dear one—and I'll thank you even more, if you don't make me unhappy for life. For what's to become of me, if you shrink from me and cast me off? But I couldn't bear to keep you by a lie. So if you want to cast me off, do it now, and go back to the other bank alone—and I'll dive into this stream, which is my uncle, who leads a strange, solitary life here in the forest, far away from all his friends. But he's extremely powerful, and owns many great rivers, and just as he brought me here to the fisherman, a merry laughing child, so he will take me back again to my parents, a loving, suffering woman with a soul."

Huldbrand was deeply moved, and before she could say any more, he put his arms gently round her and carried her over to the other bank. Only then did he swear, with many tears and kisses, that he would never desert his sweet wife, and thought himself even luckier than the Greek sculptor, Pygmalion, whose beautiful stone statue was brought to life by Venus and became his bride.

Happily reassured, Undine walked slowly back to the cottage, leaning on his arm; and now for the first time she felt in her heart how little she need regret having said good-bye to her strange father's palace of crystal.

CHAPTER 9

How the Knight Took His Young Wife Away with Him

When Huldbrand woke up next morning, his lovely bedfellow had disappeared, and once more he began to be overcome by the curious feeling that his marriage, and the ravishing Undine herself were merely an illusion. At that moment, however, she came in through the door, kissed him, and sat down beside him on the bed.

"I went out early," she explained, "to see if my uncle had kept his word. And he has. He's brought all the floodwater back into his own quiet stream, and now he's flowing along through the forest in his old thoughtful, solitary way. His friends in water and air have also gone to sleep, and the whole neighborhood's going to be calm and peaceful from now on—so you can start home as soon as you like without getting your feet wet."

Wide awake as he was, Huldbrand felt as though he was still dreaming, for he found it very hard to get used to the idea of his wife's extraordinary relations. But he kept his doubts to himself, and soon her infinite sweetness and charm had rocked all uneasy thoughts to sleep. And when, a few minutes later, he was standing with her outside the door and contemplating the green tongue of land with its bright margin of water, he felt so happy in this cradle of his love that he said:

"Why should we be in such a hurry to start off? We may never find such happiness in the world outside as we've known in this little sanctuary of ours. Let's watch the sun set here two or three times more."

"Just as you wish," replied Undine submissively. "The only thing is that the old people will hate saying good-bye to me in any case, and if they realize at the last moment that I've got a faithful heart, and a real capacity for love and reverence, it may be almost more than they can bear. At the moment they think my present quietness and good behavior is merely a passing mood—like the calmness of the lake when the wind has dropped for a while—and they'll soon be able to forget me, and transfer their affection to a flower or a tree. I mustn't let them suspect the change that's come over me, just when they're going to part from me forever—but how can I possibly conceal it, if we stay here any longer?"

Huldbrand agreed that she was right. So he went and talked to the old people about leaving, and said he wanted to start within the hour. The priest offered to go with them, and after a brief farewell he and the knight lifted the girl on to the horse, and went striding off at a good pace beside her, across the dry bed of the stream towards the forest. Undine wept bitterly, but in silence, and her foster parents loudly bewailed her departure. Some dim suspicion of what they were losing at that moment seemed somehow to have penetrated their minds.

The three travelers silently made their way into the shadowy depths of the forest. Beneath the green vault of leaves they made a delightful picture: the lovely girl riding that noble stallion with its magnificent trappings, and the two men striding along to right and left of her—on one side the venerable priest in the white robe of his order, on the other the fresh young knight with his bright, colorful clothes and his flashing sword. Huldbrand had no eyes for anything but his wife, and Undine, who had dried her sweet tears, had no eyes for anything but him; and soon they struck up a wordless interchange of looks and gestures, in which they remained absorbed until they suddenly realized that the priest was having a quiet conversation with a fourth traveler, who had unobtrusively joined them.

He wore a white robe, very like the priest's habit, except that the cowl hung down over his face, and the rest of his clothing billowed round him in such ample folds that he kept having to pick them up and throw them over his arm, or otherwise rearrange them—not that this seemed to hamper his progress in the slightest. When the young couple first became aware of him, he was saying:

"And so, reverend sir, I've lived here in the forest for many years, although I'm not exactly a hermit in your sense of the word. For as I said, I don't know anything about penances, and I don't feel any particular need for them. My only reason for being so fond of the forest is that it has a certain beauty all of its own, and it amuses me to go rushing along in my billowing white clothes through the dark shadows of the leaves, and sometimes to see a pleasant ray of sunlight flash down on me unexpectedly."

"You're a very remarkable person," replied the priest, "and I'd like to hear more about you."

"And who are you, come to that?" asked the stranger.

"They call me Father Heilmann," said the priest, "and I belong to the Mariagruss monastery on the other side of the lake."

"Do you indeed?" said the stranger. "My name is Kühleborn, or if you want to know my exact title, I suppose you might reasonably call me Herr von Kühleborn, and say that I'm the freeholder of this forest—for I'm as free as the bird on the wing, if not slightly more so. Just now, for example, I've got something to say to that young lady over there."

In a twinkling of an eye he was on the other side of the priest, close beside Undine, and stretching up high in the air, so as to whisper something in her ear. But she turned away in horror, saying:

"I don't want anything more to do with you."

"Oho!" laughed the stranger. "What a frightfully grand marriage we must have made, if we've given up knowing our own relations! Don't you recognize your Uncle Kühleborn, who brought you all the way here on his back?"

"Yes, but please don't let me see any more of you," answered Undine. "I'm frightened of you now, and my husband might get to dislike me, if he often saw me in such peculiar company."

"Don't forget, little niece," said Kühleborn, "I'm here to act as your guide. Otherwise the naughty earth-spirits might start playing their silly tricks on you. So just let me go quietly along beside you. That old priest there seems to remember me better than you do, by the way. He told me just now that there was something strangely familiar about me, and that I must have been with him in the boat, when he fell into the water. I certainly was—for I was the waterspout that swept him out of it, and carried him all the way to land to officiate at your wedding!"

Undine and the knight glanced towards Father Heilmann, but he seemed to be wandering along in a dream, quite unaware of what was being said.

"That's the edge of the forest now ahead of us," said Undine. "We don't need your help any more, and there's nothing to frighten us now except you. So please, for goodness' sake, go away and leave us in peace."

This seemed to annoy him. He pulled an ugly face and grinned at Undine, who gave a little shriek and called for help. Quick as a flash the knight darted round the horse and lunged with his sharp sword at Kühleborn's head. But all he hit was a waterfall that came foaming down from a high cliff beside them, and with a splash that sounded exactly like laughter, suddenly gushed out over them and soaked them to the skin.

"I've been expecting something like that to happen," said the priest, suddenly waking up. "That stream's been running along the top of the hill quite close to us for some time. In fact, just for a moment I thought it was a person talking to us."

But Huldbrand could still hear a voice speaking in the roar of the waterfall:

> Hasty knight
> Of valor tried,
> Fear no spite
> From thy guide,
> Always fight
> For your bride,
> Hasty knight
> Of valor tried.

A few more steps and they were out in the open. The great town lay glittering before them, and the evening sun that was gilding its towers was also kind enough to dry the travelers' dripping clothes.

CHAPTER 10

How They Lived in the Town

The sudden disappearance of the young knight, Huldbrand von Ringstetten, had made a great sensation and caused great sorrow in the town, for the people there had grown very fond of him, not only because of his skill at tournaments and dances, but also because of his gentle and friendly behavior. His servants refused to leave the place without their master, but none of them had the courage to follow him into the dreadful shadows of the forest. So they just stayed at their inn, vaguely hoping for the best, as people usually do on such occasions, and keeping his memory alive by constantly bewailing his loss.

Soon the great storms and floods removed all doubt from everyone's mind that the handsome stranger was dead, and Bertalda wept for him quite openly, cursing herself for having sent him off on that disastrous ride into the forest. The Duke and Duchess, her foster parents, had come to fetch her away, but she persuaded them to remain with her in the town, until she could get definite information whether Huldbrand was alive or dead. She even tried to persuade various young suitors of hers to search for her noble knight-errant in the forest; but she could not bring herself to offer her hand as a reward for the perilous enterprise, perhaps because she still had hopes that Huldbrand might come back and marry her himself. And no one was prepared, for the sake of a glove or a ribbon, or even for a kiss, to risk his own life in an attempt to bring back a dangerous rival.

When Huldbrand now returned, quite suddenly and unexpectedly, his servants were naturally delighted, and so was everyone else in the town—except Bertalda. The others were only too glad to see him turn up with such a beautiful wife, and with Father Heilmann to vouch for the marriage, but Bertalda could not help feeling upset by it. For one thing, she had developed a genuine affection for the young man, and for another, her distress during his absence had made her feelings embarrassingly obvious. However, like the intelligent woman that she was, she accepted the situation, and got on very friendly terms with Undine, who was generally thought to be a princess that Huldbrand had released from some evil spell in the forest. But when they questioned her or her husband about it, they got no answer, or only an evasive one; and as for Father Heilmann, his lips were sealed for all such idle gossip, and in any case he returned to his monastery soon after his arrival. So people had to be satisfied with their own curious conjectures, and even Bertalda knew no more of the truth than anyone else.

Meanwhile Undine was growing more and more fond of that charming young lady every day.

"We must have known each other somewhere before," she often used to say, "or there must be some strange affinity between us. For one doesn't get so fond of another person, as I did the moment I saw you, unless there's some reason for it, some deep, mysterious reason."

And even Bertalda could not conceal from herself the strange sense of familiarity that attracted her to Undine, in spite of her bitter resentment against her fortunate rival. The result of this mutual attraction was that Bertalda persuaded her foster parents to keep postponing their departure, and Undine persuaded her husband to do the same. In fact, there was already talk of Bertalda's going to stay with Undine for a while at the castle of Ringstetten, near the source of the Danube.

They were discussing the idea one fine evening as they wandered by starlight round the tree-fringed marketplace. Late as it was, the young couple had dragged Bertalda out for a walk, and the three of them were strolling up and down beneath the deep blue sky, often interrupting their familiar talk to admire the splendid fountain in the middle of the square, with its wonderful jet of rushing, bubbling water. They had a delightful sense of intimacy. Gleams of light from nearby houses stole through the shadows of the trees, and all around them they could hear a quiet murmuring from children at play and from people walking about like themselves. They felt very much alone, and yet very much a part of the cheerful, lively world around them. In this pleasant mood, what had looked like difficulties during the day seemed to straighten themselves out of their own accord, and the three friends could not think of any possible reason why they should not all travel together.

Just as they were trying to fix a day for their departure, a tall man came towards them from the middle of the marketplace, bowed politely to the company, and said something in Undine's ear. Annoyed at being disturbed, and at the person who had disturbed her, she allowed the stranger to lead her a few paces away, and the two started whispering to one another, apparently in a foreign language. Huldbrand thought he recognized this curious individual, and stared at him so fixedly that he neither heard nor answered Bertalda's astonished questions.

All at once Undine clapped her hands delightedly, and with a smile turned her back on the stranger, who strode hastily away, angrily shaking his head, and climbed into the fountain. Huldbrand now felt quite certain of his identity, but Bertalda asked:

"My dear Undine, what on earth did the man from the fountain have to say to you?"

The girl laughed quietly to herself and replied:

"The day after tomorrow, on your birthday, you shall hear all about it, my sweet creature."

And that was all they could get out of her. She invited Bertalda and her foster parents to come to lunch on the day in question, and soon afterwards they parted.

"Kühleborn?" asked Huldbrand with a shudder when they had taken their leave of Bertalda and were walking home alone through the darkening streets.

"Yes, that's who it was," replied Undine. "And he was trying to say all kinds of silly things, but in the middle of it, quite by mistake, he gave me a piece of extremely good news. If you want to hear it right away, my darling, you've only got to say so, and I'll come right out with it. But if you'd like to give your Undine a very, very great pleasure, you'll leave it until the day after tomorrow, and then you can enjoy the surprise too."

The knight readily assented; and just as she was dropping off to sleep, Undine smiled and murmured to herself: "How pleased she'll be, and how surprised, when she hears the news that the man from the fountain brought me—dear, dear Bertalda!"

Chapter 11

Bertalda's Birthday

The luncheon-party was in progress. At the head of the table sat Bertalda, decked like a goddess of spring with all kinds of flowers and jewels presented by her friends and foster parents, and on her right and left sat Huldbrand and Undine. When the sumptuous meal came to an end, and dessert was being served, the doors were left open, in accordance with a good old German custom, so that the people of the neighborhood could watch and join in the celebrations. Servants went round supplying the spectators with wine and cakes.

Huldbrand and Bertalda waited with secret impatience for the promised revelation, and hardly took their eyes off Undine. But she still remained silent, and only smiled to herself with inward satisfaction. It was obvious to those who knew about her promise that she was going to let out her delightful secret at any moment, but was making a great effort to hold it back, just as children keep their favorite tidbits to the last. Bertalda and Huldbrand shared this blissful sense of anticipation, and waited, half in hope and half in fear, for the new happiness that was soon to fall like dew from her lips.

Then various members of the company asked Undine for a song. It seemed to suit her purpose exactly, for she at once sent for her lute, and began to sing as follows:

> Morning so bright,
> Flowers so gay,
> Grass so sweet-scented and tall
> On the shore of the rippling lake!
> What is that gleaming on the grass?
> Is it a flower of heavenly birth
> Dropped on the lap of mother earth?
> Why, it is a little child,
> Playing heedlessly with flowers,
> Clutching at the golden sunlight!
> Where have you come from, little darling?
> Have the waters of the lake
> Brought you here from a distant shore?
>
> Stretch not out those tiny hands,
>   Begging for a warm caress;
> No fond parent by you stands,
>   Flowers feel not your distress.
>
> With their beauty and their smell

They can cheer you all the day,
    But not kiss and make you well:
    Mother's breast is far away!

Life's dim threshold scarcely crossed,
    Heaven's joys not yet forgot,
Have you then so early lost
    Life's best gift, and know it not?

See, a Duke comes riding by,
    Stops and gazes in surprise;
Rears you in his castle high,
    Teaches to be pure and wise.

Happy now beyond expressing,
    You are fairest in the land;
But you lost your greatest blessing
    When you left that unknown strand!

With a sad smile Undine put down her instrument. The eyes of
Bertalda's foster parents were full of tears.

"That's exactly what it was like, that morning when I found you,
my poor, sweet little orphan," said the Duke, deeply moved. "Our
pretty songstress is quite right—we've still not been able to give you
the best gift of all."

"Now let's hear what happened to the poor parents," said Undine, and striking up again on her lute, she sang:

Mother goes from room to room,
    Searching, searching in distress:
All the house is wrapt in gloom,
    All she finds is emptiness.

Emptiness! where once a child
    Sweetly played the livelong day;
Where at night its mother smiled
    O'er the cradle where it lay.

On the trees new leaves will grow,

In the sky new suns will burn,
But no spring will end her woe:
What she seeks will not return.

Evening comes, and at the door
    Soon her husband's step she hears;
But she smiles not as of yore,
    For her smile is drowned in tears.

So the white-haired father finds
    Deathly silence there to meet him;
Finds a wife whom sorrow blinds,
    And no childish laugh to greet him.

"Oh, for God's sake, Undine, where are my parents?" cried Bertalda through her tears. "You know exactly where they are, you've found it out somehow, you extraordinary creature, or you wouldn't have pierced me to the heart like this. Are they actually here perhaps? Could that be it?"

Her eyes swept the distinguished company, lingering for a moment on a member of the royal family who was sitting next to her foster father. Undine, her eyes overflowing with joy, nodded towards the door.

"Well, where *are* those poor parents, who've waited so long?" asked Bertalda—and from the crowd of spectators the old fisherman and his wife stepped nervously forward. Their eyes went questioningly from Undine to the beautiful girl who was said to be their daughter.

"Yes, it's her!" faltered Undine, overwhelmed by the joy that she was giving, and the two old people flung themselves, weeping and praising God, on the neck of their newly found daughter.

Horrified and enraged, Bertalda tore herself free. Such a revelation was more than her proud spirit could bear, at a moment when she had been confidently expecting to rise to new heights of splendor, and had pictured a crown at least descending on her head. It seemed to her as if the whole thing had been deliberately contrived by her rival as an exquisite method of humiliating her before Huldbrand and all the world. She flew out at Undine and the old couple, and ugly words like "Treachery!" and "Bribery!" burst from her lips.

The old woman made no reply, except to murmur quietly to herself: "Oh, God, she's turned into a wicked woman—but all the same I can't help feeling she's my own child!"

The old fisherman, however, had clasped his hands, and was silently praying that she was not his daughter.

Undine staggered, deadly pale, from the parents to Bertalda, from Bertalda to the parents, dashed down all at once from the heaven that she had dreamed of into a hell of fear and horror, such as she had never experienced even in her worst nightmares.

"Have you no heart, Bertalda? Have you really no heart at all?" she cried again and again, as if trying to shock her angry friend out of a momentary delusion, or to startle her out of some fantastic dream. But when this only increased Bertalda's violence; when the rejected parents burst into tears, and the company started taking sides and broke into noisy argument, Undine suddenly made such an earnest and dignified appeal to be heard in her own husband's house, that in a twinkling of an eye there was complete silence. With a strange blend of pride and humility, she stepped to the head of the table, where Bertalda had been sitting, and with every eye upon her, spoke as follows:

"Ladies and gentlemen, how angry and upset you look! You've completely spoiled my party! Good heavens, I'd no idea how stupid you were, how stupid and hard-hearted, and I'll never get used to it as long as I live. It's not my fault that everything's been turned upside down, not my fault, I assure you, but yours, however little you may think so. That's why I've very little to say to you, but one thing must be said: I have not been lying. I neither can nor will give you any proof, apart from my own assurance, but I'll swear to the truth of what I say. I have it on the authority of the very person who lured Bertalda away from her parents into the water, and then laid her in a green meadow for the duke to find."

"She's a witch!" cried Bertalda. "She has dealings with evil spirits! She admits it herself!"

"I do no such thing," said Undine, a world of faith and innocence in her eyes. "I'm no witch—you've only to look at me to see that."

"She's lying!" screamed Bertalda. "She's trying to bluster it out. But she'll never get anyone to believe I'm the child of vulgar people like them. My noble parents, please take me out of this low company, and out of this town, where no one does anything but insult me."

But the honest old duke stood his ground, and said to his wife:

"We must find out for certain what the situation is. God forbid that we should stir a foot from this room until we've done so."

At this the fisherman's wife went up to them, bowed low to the duchess and said:

"I know I can open my heart to a God-fearing person like you, my lady. There's something I want to tell you. If this wicked girl is my daughter, she has a birthmark, the shape of a violet, between her shoulders, and another on her left instep. If she'd only come outside with me for a moment—"

"I'm not going to undress in front of a peasant-woman!" snapped Bertalda, haughtily turning her back.

"But in front of me you will," replied the duchess with great emphasis. "You will follow me into the next room, young lady, and the good old woman will come too."

The three disappeared, and the others stayed behind in silent expectation. After a while the women came back. Bertalda was deadly pale, and the duchess said:

"It's no good tampering with the truth. Our hostess is perfectly right. Bertalda is the fisherman's daughter, and that's all that anyone here needs to know."

Then she and her husband left the room with their foster daughter, followed, at a gesture from the duke, by the fisherman and his wife. The other guests withdrew in silence, or with scarcely audible comments, and Undine collapsed in Huldbrand's arms, weeping bitterly.

CHAPTER 12

How They Left the Town

Huldbrand, needless to say, would have preferred things to have turned out differently; but as it was, he could not help being delighted by the gentle, good-natured and affectionate way in which his wife had behaved. "If I've given her a soul," he told himself, "I seem to have given her a far better one than my own!" So now his only thought was to comfort her in her distress, and take her away as soon as possible from a place which today's events were bound to have made disagreeable to her. Not that anyone criticized her part in the affair. As people had always looked on her as something out of the ordinary, her strange revelation of Bertalda's parentage took nobody by surprise, and the only person criticized by those who heard the story was Bertalda herself, for having lost her temper. Of this, however, the knight and his wife were as yet unaware; and even if she had known it, Undine would have been equally distressed, so it was obviously best to leave the walls of the ancient city behind them as soon as they possibly could.

So at crack of dawn next day a handsome carriage for Undine drew up outside their inn, and Huldbrand's and his squire's horses were soon pawing the pavement beside it. The knight and his wife were just emerging from the inn, when a fisher-girl came up to them.

"It's no use trying to sell us anything now," said Huldbrand. "We're just leaving."

At this the fisher-girl burst into tears, and it was only then that they recognized her as Bertalda. They took her back at once into their room, and learned that the duke and duchess had been so annoyed by her violent and unfeeling behavior the day before, that they had completely withdrawn their support, though not before they had given her a substantial dowry. The fisherman had also been presented with a large sum of money, and he and his wife had started back the same night to their home by the lake.

"I wanted to go with them," she continued, "only the old fisherman who's supposed to be my father——"

"But he really is, Bertalda," interrupted Undine. "You see, that man from the fountain, as you called him, told me the whole story. He was trying to persuade me not to take you with us to Ringstetten, and in the process he let out this secret."

"Well, my father, then, if that's how it's got to be," said Bertalda. "My father said, 'I'm not going to take you with me until you've had a change of heart. Let's see if you're prepared to make your own way to us through the forest, all by yourself. That'll show if you have any real feeling for us. But don't come to me as a young lady—come as a fisher-girl.' Well, I want to do as he says, because everyone else has deserted me, and I might as well go and live with my humble parents, like any other poor fisherman's daughter. But I'm simply terrified of the forest. They say it's full of all sorts of horrible ghosts, and I'm such a coward. But what else can I do? The only reason I've come here now is to ask Lady von Ringstetten's pardon for my rudeness to her yesterday. I know you meant it kindly, sweet lady, but you didn't realize how much it would hurt me, and in my horror and surprise I said all sorts of stupid insulting things. Oh, forgive me, forgive me! I'm so very unhappy. Just think what I was yesterday morning, what I was even at the beginning of your party, and what I am now!"

She ended in a flood of tears, and Undine fell on her neck, weeping just as bitterly. She was deeply moved, and it was some time before she could speak, but at last she said:

"You shall come with us to Ringstetten. Everything's going to be just as it was before. Only please stop being so distant with me, and calling me Lady von Ringstetten! Don't you see, we got mixed up with one another when we were children. Our lives were bound up with each other even then, and from now on we're going to bind them together so tightly that no power on earth shall ever separate us. But first of all come with us to Ringstetten. Then we can discuss how to go shares in everything, just as though we were sisters."

Bertalda looked up shyly at Huldbrand. Feeling sorry for the girl, he took her by the hand and urged her in most affectionate tones to entrust herself to their care.

"We'll send a message to your parents," he said, "explaining why you've not come——" and he would have spoken further in the good old couple's defense, had he not noticed her start of embarrassment at the mere mention of them; so he thought it best to drop the subject. He simply took her arm and helped her into the carriage, then did the same for Undine, mounted his horse, and started trotting cheerfully along beside them. He encouraged the driver to go at such a rattling pace that they had soon left the outskirts of the town, and all painful memories, behind them; and now the two women were better able to enjoy spinning along through the beautiful country that lay on either side of the road.

After a few days' traveling they arrived, one fine evening, at the castle of Ringstetten. The knight had a great deal to discuss with his steward and other members of his staff, so Undine and Bertalda were left to themselves. They went for a walk on the high castle wall, enjoying the delightful view of the Swabian countryside that stretched away from them in all directions. While they were doing so, a tall man approached them, who greeted them politely, and looked to Bertalda very much like the man they had met in the marketplace. The resemblance became even more unmistakable when Undine, with an angry if not positively threatening gesture, motioned him away, and he hurriedly strode off, shaking his head as he had done before, and disappeared among the trees. But Undine merely said:

"Don't be frightened, Bertalda darling. This time the horrid fellow isn't going to do you any harm."

And she proceeded to tell Bertalda the whole story, explaining who she was, and how she had come to take Bertalda's place in the fisherman's family. At first the girl was horrified: she thought her friend must have suddenly gone mad. But Undine's story was so coherent in itself, and so consistent with previous events, that Bertalda soon became convinced of its truth, especially as it aroused that instinctive feeling which always helps us to distinguish true from false. It was strange to feel that she was actually taking part in one of those curious adventures of which she had previously only heard at second hand. She stared at Undine with awe, and an uncontrollable thrill of terror came between her and her friend. At supper that evening, she could not help feeling surprised at the knight's familiar and affectionate behavior towards one who, in the light of what she had heard, seemed to her more like a ghost than a human being.

CHAPTER 13

How They Lived at the Castle

Dear reader, as this story is being told by one who finds it extremely moving, and wishes you to do so too, will you do him a favor? Allow him at this stage to pass rapidly over a fairly long period, describing what took place only in very general terms. Doubtless it would be possible to explain, step by step, the exact process by which Huldbrand's heart began to turn from Undine to Bertalda; how his affection was more and more ardently returned by Bertalda, and they both came to regard the poor young wife as an alien being, more to be feared than pitied; how Undine wept, and her tears aroused pangs of conscience in the knight's heart, but failed to reawaken his old love, so that from time to time he treated her quite kindly, but a cold thrill of terror would soon drive him away again, back to the ordinary humanity of Bertalda. All this, the writer is well aware, might be set out systematically, and possibly ought to be; but he would suffer too much in the process, for he has experienced something of the sort himself, and is afraid even to remember what it was like. You, dear reader, will probably recognize the feeling, for these things are liable to happen to all of us. You may count yourself lucky if you have been the victim rather than the cause of such unhappiness; for in these matters it is more blessed to receive than to give. If so, the mention of such things will merely produce a yearning pain in your heart, and perhaps make a gentle tear steal down your cheek, at the thought of those withered flowers in which you once took such delight. But let that be enough: we have no wish to inflict on the heart a thousand separate stabs of pain, but only to state briefly that the situation was now as I have described.

Poor Undine was deeply distressed, and the other two did not feel exactly happy about it. Bertalda especially was apt to interpret the slightest opposition to her wishes as evidence of jealousy on the part of her ill-used hostess. For that reason she tended to adopt a rather dictatorial attitude, to which Undine sadly submitted, and the infatuated Huldbrand generally took Bertalda's side.

What upset everyone even more was the series of extraordinary apparitions, without precedent in living memory, that met Huldbrand and Bertalda in the vaulted passages of the castle. The tall white man, whom Huldbrand knew only too well as Uncle Kühleborn, and Bertalda as the ghostly man from the fountain, often appeared threateningly before them, especially before Bertalda, who was sometimes so sick with terror as a result that she had to take to her bed, and frequently thought of leaving the castle altogether. But for one thing, she was too fond of Huldbrand, and too convinced of her own innocence, since there had never been any actual declaration between them; and for another, she had no idea where else to go. On receipt of Huldbrand's message that Bertalda was with them, the old fisherman had sent a short, almost illegible scrawl, such as you might expect from a man of his age who had never done much writing, to this effect: "I am now an unhappy old widower, for my dear faithful wife has died. But lonely as I am, sitting here in the cottage, I'd rather Bertalda was with you than me. Only mind she doesn't do any harm to my dear Undine, or she'll have my curse on her."

As often happens in such cases, Bertalda paid no attention whatever to the last sentence of the letter, but the part about keeping away from her father stuck fast in her memory.

One day, when Huldbrand was out riding, Undine collected all the servants, and told them to fetch a big stone and place it carefully over the mouth of the spring that rose in the middle of the courtyard. They protested that they would then have to fetch up water from the valley far below.

"My dear children," replied Undine with a sad smile. "I'm sorry to increase your work. I'd far rather carry up the bucket myself, but this spring simply must be closed. Take my word for it, it's the only way to avoid something even worse."

They were only too glad to oblige their sweet mistress, and without any further questions they got hold of a huge stone. They had already picked it up and were poising it over the spring, when Bertalda came running out and shouted for them to stop. She told them she always used this water to wash in, because it was so good for her skin, and she would never agree to having the spring sealed off. Undine, however, though sweet and gentle as usual, was more than usually determined. She replied that, as mistress of the house, she must do as she thought best so far as household arrangements were concerned, and was accountable to nobody but her husband.

"Oh, but look, look!" cried Bertalda in anger and alarm. "The poor lovely water is writhing about in agony at the prospect of being shut off from the light of the sun, and never again reflecting sweet human faces, as God meant it to do!"

Sure enough, the water in the spring was hissing and bubbling in a most remarkable manner, as though something was trying to fight its way out; but Undine was all the more insistent that her orders should be obeyed. However, her insistence was scarcely needed, for the castle servants were hardly more eager to obey their gentle mistress than they were to override Bertalda's insolence; so, storm and threaten as she would, the stone was soon firmly fixed over the mouth of the spring.

Undine leaned against it, deep in thought, and with her pretty fingers scribbled something on its surface; but she must have had something very sharp in her hand at the time, for when she turned away and the others came nearer, they noticed all kinds of curious signs engraved on the stone, which no one had ever seen there before.

When the knight came home that evening, he was greeted by Bertalda with tearful complaints about Undine's behavior. He shot a stern glance at his unfortunate wife, who sadly dropped her eyes, but responded with great composure:

"My husband would never think of scolding even a serf, without hearing what he had to say for himself, still less his own wedded wife."

"Well, then, what made you do such an extraordinary thing?" asked the knight, frowning.

"I'd rather wait until we're alone," said Undine with a sigh.

"You can tell me just as well with Bertalda here," he retorted.

"Very well, if you insist," said Undine, "but please don't. Please, please don't!"

She looked so sweet and humble and obedient, that a ray of sunshine from earlier, happier days found its way into the knight's heart. He took her affectionately by the arm, and led her into his own room, where she began to speak as follows:

"My dear husband, you know my wicked Uncle Kühleborn. You've often had the annoyance of meeting him in the passages of your castle, and he's sometimes made Bertalda quite ill with fright. Well, the reason is that he's got no soul. He's just a sort of mirror of the external world, and is quite incapable of reflecting the world within. From time to time he sees that you're cross with me, and that I, in my childish way, am unhappy about it—and perhaps at that very moment Bertalda may happen to laugh. So he gets all sorts of wrong ideas into his head, and keeps thrusting himself into our affairs. What's the use of scolding him? What's the use of saying I want him to go away? He doesn't believe a word of it. A poor creature like that simply can't understand that the joys and pains of love look very much the same from outside, and are so closely connected that no power on earth can separate them. Tears can so easily turn into smiles, and a smile can so easily make us cry."

Smiling through her tears, she looked up at Huldbrand, whose heart was suddenly filled with all the magic of his old love. Sensing the change, she pressed him closer to her, and weeping now for joy, continued:

"Well, as the disturber of our peace wouldn't listen to reason, the only thing I could do was to bar the door against him. And the only door through which he can come to us is that spring. He's quarreled with all the other water-spirits in the neighborhood, the ones who live in the valleys round about, and his own kingdom doesn't start until much farther down the Danube, where the river is joined by some very good friends of his. That's why I had the stone put over the spring, and wrote some signs on it which will cripple all his efforts to interfere with either you, or me, or Bertalda. Of course, the signs won't make the slightest difference to human beings—they'll be able to move the stone just as easily as before. So if you like, do as Bertalda asks—but believe me, she doesn't know what she's asking. That naughty Kühleborn has got his eye on her particularly, and if things were to turn out as he says they will—and they very well might, without your meaning any harm—oh darling, even you wouldn't be safe!"

Deep in his heart Huldbrand felt his sweet wife's magnanimity, in so busily barring out her formidable protector—and then being scolded by Bertalda for doing so. He threw his arms around her, much affected, and said:

"The stone stays where it is, and everything shall be just as you want it, now and always, my darling Undine!"

Humbly, overjoyed to hear the words of love for which she had waited so long in vain, she caressed him, and finally said:

"My dearest one, as you're being so particularly gentle and kind today, dare I ask you a favor? You see, you're like a day in summer. Just when it's at its loveliest, it puts on a flaming crown of thunder and lightning, to show its divine and kingly nature. In much the same way, you sometimes thunder at me, and lightning flashes from your eyes and tongue, and it suits you very well, even though I'm sometimes stupid enough to cry about it. But never do it when we're on the water, or even anywhere near any water. For then I'd be in the

power of my relations. In their merciless rage they'd snatch me away
from you, thinking that one of their race was being insulted, and I'd
have to spend the rest of my life down there in those palaces of
crystal—or else they might send me up again to visit you, and, O
God, that would be infinitely worse! No, no, my darling, don't let it
ever come to that, if your poor Undine is at all dear to you."

He solemnly promised to do as she said, and they left the room
with hearts full of love and happiness. Up came Bertalda with some
workmen that she had meanwhile sent for, and in the peevish tone
that was now habitual with her, said:

"So the private conversation is over at last, and the stone can be
removed. You men there, go and see to it."

Disgusted by her insolence, the knight curtly replied:

"The stone stays where it is."

He then proceeded to rebuke Bertalda for her rudeness to his
wife, whereupon the workmen went away, smiling broadly, and
Bertalda turned pale and hurried off to her room.

Suppertime came, and they waited in vain for Bertalda to reap-
pear. A servant was sent to fetch her, but he found her room empty,
and all he brought back was a sealed sheet of paper, addressed to the
knight. In dismay Huldbrand opened it and read:

> I realize to my shame that I am nothing but a poor fisher-girl.
> For my mistake in forgetting it for a moment, I shall do penance
> in the wretched hovel where my father lives. I hope you and your
> lovely wife will be very happy together.

Undine was cut to the heart. She passionately entreated
Huldbrand to hurry after her friend and bring her back. But, alas, he
needed no urging: his passion for Bertalda had returned with increased violence. He went rushing round the castle, asking if anyone
had seen which way she had gone. Nobody knew, and he had
already mounted his horse in the courtyard, intending, for lack of a
better plan, to search the road by which he had originally brought
her to the castle, when a page turned up with the news that he had
met the lady on the path leading to the Black Valley. Swift as an
arrow, the knight was through the gate and galloping in the direction indicated, without hearing Undine's agonized cry from the
window:

"The Black Valley? Oh, not there! Huldbrand, not there! Or, for God's sake, take me with you!"

Finding that all her shouting had no effect, she hurriedly ordered her white palfrey to be saddled, and started trotting after him, refusing to let any of the servants accompany her.

CHAPTER 14

How Bertalda Came Home with the Knight

The Black Valley lies deep among the mountains. What it is called now, I have no idea, but in those days it derived its name from the profound darkness into which it was plunged by the tall trees that grew in it, most of which were firs. Even the stream that went swirling along between the rocks looked completely black for the same reason, and not nearly as cheerful as water normally does when it has the blue sky immediately above it. Now, with twilight falling, this cleft in the mountains had become particularly wild and gloomy. The knight rode anxiously along the bank of the stream, afraid at one moment of letting the runaway get too far ahead of him, and at another of missing her in his haste, if she was deliberately hiding from him.

By this time he had penetrated fairly deep into the valley, and expected to overtake Bertalda before very long, assuming that he was on the right track; but the suspicion that he might not be, made his heart beat faster and faster with terror. For where was a delicate creature like her to spend the night, if he failed to find her, with a storm gathering over the valley and threatening to burst at any moment?

At last he saw something white on the hillside glimmering through the trees. He thought he recognized Bertalda's dress, and started making his way towards it. But his horse refused to climb the slope. It reared so violently, and he was so anxious not to lose any time—especially as it might be difficult anyway to get through the undergrowth on horseback—that he dismounted, tied his snorting steed to an elm, and started cautiously, working his way through the bushes on foot. Branches, cold and clammy with dew, dashed against his forehead and cheeks, distant thunder muttered on the other side of the hill, and everything looked so strange that he began to feel quite afraid of the white figure that now lay on the ground not far ahead of him. Still, it was obviously a woman, either asleep or in a dead faint, wearing a long white dress such as Bertalda had worn that day. He stepped close up to her, rustled a branch up and down, rattled his sword—she did not move.

"Bertalda!" he said, quietly at first and then louder and louder. She did not seem to hear. When finally he shouted the beloved name at the very top of his voice, a series of dull echoes came stammering back from the mountain caves: "Bertalda! Bertalda! Bertalda!" But the sleeper did not stir.

He bent down towards her. The darkness of the valley, intensified by the approach of night, prevented him from distinguishing her features. With a dreadful question in his mind, he lay down close beside her, and at that moment a flash of lightning suddenly lit up the valley. A few inches from his own he saw a hideously contorted face, and heard a hollow voice say:

"Give me a kiss, you lovesick fool!"

With a shriek of terror, Huldbrand jumped up, and the ugly figure came after him.

"Go home!" it muttered. "The fiends are awake. Go home—or I've got you!"

And it made a grab at him with its long white arms.

"Kühleborn!" cried the knight, plucking up courage. "So it's you, you devil? All right, there's your kiss for you!"

And he slashed furiously at the figure with his sword. But it promptly disappeared, and a drenching shower of water removed any doubts he may have had about his opponent's identity.

"He's trying to scare me away from Bertalda," he said aloud to himself. "He thinks I'll be so frightened by his silly jokes that I'll leave that poor girl completely at his mercy. But I'm not afraid of a wretched little spirit like him! He's no idea, with all his childish conjuring tricks, what a human being can do when he really puts his heart and soul in it!"

As the truth of his words came home to him, he found he had

given himself new courage. It also began to seem as if luck was on his side, for no sooner had he got back to his tethered horse than he heard, above the mounting uproar of the thunder and the gale, Bertalda's voice crying piteously not far off. He went flying in the direction of the sound, and found the trembling girl desperately trying to climb up the hill in an effort to escape from that dreadful darkness. He stepped up and put his arm round her, and for all her proud determination earlier, she was now only too thankful to be rescued from her solitude by her beloved friend, and to see such kind arms outstretched to welcome her back to the cheerful, friendly life of the castle. After only a moment's hesitation, she followed him back to where his horse was tethered, but she was so exhausted that he was extremely relieved to get her there. Hastily he untied the horse and prepared to lift her on to its back, intending then to lead it by the bridle until they were clear of the valley.

But the strange apparition of Kühleborn had sent the animal quite mad. Huldbrand himself would have found it hard enough to mount the rearing, wildly snorting beast: as for lifting the trembling Bertalda on to its back, it was completely impossible. He therefore decided to take her home on foot, dragging the horse behind him by the bridle, and using the other arm to support the girl. Bertalda summoned up all her remaining energy, so as to get through the dreadful valley as quickly as possible, but her weariness weighed her down like lead, and all her limbs were shaking, partly from the aftereffects of the terror with which Kühleborn had inspired her, and partly from her continuing fear of the storm that was roaring and thundering through the mountain forest.

Finally she slipped from his supporting arm and collapsed on the moss, gasping:

"It's no use—I'm going to be punished for my foolishness by dying here of terror and exhaustion!"

"Sweet creature, I'll never leave you!" cried Huldbrand, vainly struggling to get the plunging stallion under control, and only making it rage and foam more than ever. In the end it was all he could do to drag it away from the girl, so as not to increase her terror; but no sooner had he put a few paces between her and the maddened animal, than she started uttering the most piteous cries, thinking that he was going to abandon her in that horrible wilderness. He simply did not know what to do. He would gladly have given the raging beast its freedom, and let it work off its frenzy by itself, but the pass was so narrow that its brazen hooves were almost bound to go thundering over the very spot where Bertalda lay.

In this desperate dilemma, he was infinitely relieved to hear a cart being slowly driven down the stony track behind him. He shouted for help, and was answered by a man's voice, which told him to keep his spirits up, for help was on its way. Soon afterwards two white horses became visible through the undergrowth, then the white smock of a carter beside them, and finally the great white sheet of canvas that covered his wares. With a loud "Whoa!" from their master, the horses came obediently to a standstill. The carter ran up to the knight and started helping him to control his foaming steed.

"I know what's the matter with him," he said. "When I first came into this neighborhood, my horses were just as bad. The thing is, there's an evil water-spirit living in these parts, who's very fond of playing tricks like this. But I've learned a text to deal with it. If you'll allow me to whisper it in the horse's ear, it'll make him as tame as my two over there."

"Try anything you like, only be quick about it!" cried the knight impatiently. So the carter dragged down the head of the rearing horse towards him, and said a few words in its ear. At once it became completely tame and quiet, with nothing to show how violent it had been a moment before, except a certain amount of panting and steaming. There was no time for Huldbrand to inquire at any length into how it had been done. He and the carter agreed that the latter should take Bertalda into his cart, which, as he explained, was full of soft bales of cotton, and so convey her to the castle of Ringstetten, while the knight accompanied them on horseback. The stallion, however, appeared to be far too exhausted by its fit of madness to carry him anything like that distance, so the carter persuaded Huldbrand to climb inside with Bertalda. The horse could then be tied on behind.

"It's downhill, after all," he said, "so it'll be easy work for my two animals."

The knight accepted the offer, and climbed in beside Bertalda. The stallion followed patiently behind, and the sturdy carter strode along beside them.

In the silence of the darkening night, broken only by the thunder that was dying away in the distance, in the delicious consciousness of safety and escape from danger, Huldbrand and Bertalda found it easy to talk to one another. He scolded her affectionately for her headstrong behavior, and she made a humble and sincere apology; but every word she said was like a lamp shining in the darkness, to show her lover that her heart was his. Huldbrand was far too much aware of what she meant to pay any attention to the actual words that she used, and it was only to her meaning that he replied.

All at once the carter yelled out:

"Gee-up, you two! Pick those feet up! Get a move on! Don't forget whose horses you are!"

The knight poked his head out of the cart, and saw that the horses were walking, if not actually swimming, through a great expanse of foaming water, the wheels of the cart were gleaming and splashing like mill wheels, and the carter himself had climbed aboard the vehicle to escape from the rising flood.

"What sort of road is this supposed to be?" shouted Huldbrand to the carter. "It's going right into the middle of a stream!"

"Oh no, sir!" laughed the carter. "It's exactly the other way round. The stream's going right into the middle of the road! Just take a look round, and you'll see that everything's under water!"

Sure enough, the whole valley had turned into a surging, roaring sea of visibly mounting waves.

"It's that evil spirit, Kühleborn, trying to drown us!" yelled Huldbrand. "Don't you know any text to deal with him, old fellow?"

"I certainly used to," said the carter, "but I simply can't use it, until you tell me who I am."

"Is this a moment for asking riddles?" shouted Huldbrand. "The flood's getting higher and higher all the time, and what difference does it make to me who you are?"

"It makes quite a lot of difference to you," said the carter, "for I am Kühleborn."

And a hideously contorted face grinned back into the cart. But the cart was no longer a cart, and the white horses were no longer white horses. Everything dissolved into foam and ran away in a hissing surge of water, while the carter himself reared up into a gigantic wave, which swept the struggling stallion beneath the surface, and then started growing again, growing high over the heads of the swimming couple, like a great tower of water, and was just about to bury them forever—when Undine's sweet voice was heard above the uproar, the moon came out of the clouds, and Undine herself became visible on the hillside above the valley. She hurled down reproaches and threats at the floods below, until the menacing tower-like wave subsided with an angry hiss, the surface of the water became smooth and glittering in the moonlight, and like a white dove Undine came flying down from the hill, seized the knight and Bertalda, and lifted them on to a fresh green patch of grass, where with exquisite cordials she dispelled their faintness and terror. Then she helped Bertalda on to her own white palfrey, and thus all three returned to the castle of Ringstetten.

Chapter 15

The Journey to Vienna

After this incident life at the castle was very quiet and peaceful. The knight came more and more to appreciate the angelic goodness that his wife had shown in hurrying after him and saving his life in the Black Valley, where Kühleborn's power began again. Undine herself enjoyed that peace of mind which goes with the knowledge that one is doing the right thing; and besides, her husband's newly awakened love and respect were bringing her some faint glimmerings of hope and happiness. Bertalda, on her part, was grateful, humble and modest in her behavior, without claiming any credit for such conduct, as she had always done in the past. If either of her friends attempted to explain the sealing of the spring or the adventure in the Black Valley, she earnestly begged them to spare her, saying that she felt ashamed enough already about the one, and was still too frightened even to think of the other. So neither of them pursued the subject further, for after all, what was the point of doing so? Peace and happiness had evidently come to stay at the castle of Ringstetten: they felt quite sure of it, and imagined that the fruits and flowers of life were all they need expect from now on.

In these pleasant circumstances the winter came and went, and spring with its bright green shoots and clear blue skies returned to visit the three happy people. Their hearts were in tune with the season, and the season was in tune with their hearts; so no wonder the arrival of the storks and swallows made them want to travel, too.

One day, when they were going for a walk to the source of the Danube, Huldbrand was singing the praises of that noble river, and telling them how it flowed, ever broadening, through many fertile countries; how its banks were bright with delicious, sparkling wines, and how altogether, at each stage of its journey, it increased in power and beauty.

"How glorious it would be, if we could travel down it to Vienna one day!" exclaimed Bertalda. Then, relapsing into the mood of self-effacing modesty that was now habitual with her, she blushed and was silent. For this very reason Undine felt deeply touched, and in her eagerness to give her dear friend a treat, she answered:

"Why shouldn't we start right away?"

Bertalda almost jumped for joy, and the two women immediately began to paint the prospect of a journey down the Danube in the brightest colors of the imagination. Huldbrand joined in with equal enthusiasm, though once he whispered anxiously in Undine's ear:

"But doesn't Kühleborn's power begin again farther down the river?"

"He's welcome to see what he can do," she replied with a laugh. "I shall be there, and he won't risk starting any nonsense with me!"

Thus the last obstacle was removed. Preparations were made for the journey, and they set off in the gayest spirits and the highest hopes. But do not be surprised, my good people, if everything turns out differently from what they expected. The malicious power that is always lurking to destroy us likes to sing its chosen victims to sleep with sweet songs and golden stories. On the other hand, the heavenly messenger that comes to save us often frightens us by the violence with which he knocks at our door.

The first few days of their journey down the Danube were extremely enjoyable. The further they sailed down the proudly flowing stream the more beautiful everything became. But when they reached an otherwise-delightful district, which with its splendid scenery seemed to promise the greatest enjoyment, the unruly Kühleborn began to show quite unmistakably that they had entered his sphere of influence. Admittedly he confined himself to practical jokes, for Undine merely had to rebuke the winds or waves that were trying to delay them, and instantly the enemy's power was reduced to humble submission. But then the attacks would start again, and again Undine would have to use her authority, so that the little party of travelers had their pleasure completely spoiled. Besides, the boatmen were always whispering nervously in one another's ears and glancing suspiciously at the three passengers, whose own servants became more and more inclined to believe that there was something sinister at work, and gave their employers some very odd looks.

"It all comes of not marrying someone of my own sort," Huldbrand often told himself. "What else can you expect, when a human being goes and gets himself tied up with a mermaid!"— though, of course, to excuse himself, as we all like to do, he usually added, "But as for that, I'd no idea she *was* a mermaid. It may be my misfortune to be perpetually badgered by her relations with these idiotic tricks, but it's certainly not my fault." He derived a certain amount of comfort from this reflection, but even so he grew more and more irritable, and more and more hostile to Undine. There was a sulky expression on his face whenever he looked at her, and the poor creature knew perfectly well why it was. The strain of this situation, and of her constant efforts to counteract Kühleborn's maneuvers, exhausted her so much that towards evening, lulled by the pleasant motion of the boat, she fell fast asleep.

Scarcely had she closed her eyes, when everyone else in the boat, no matter in which direction he was looking, thought he saw a ghastly human head rising above the water, not like that of a swimmer, but sticking up quite vertically as though it was impaled on the surface of the river, and was floating down it like the boat. Everyone started trying to show his neighbor the grisly object he had seen, with its half-laughing, half-menacing expression, only to find his neighbor looking equally terrified, but staring and pointing in a totally different direction. While they were still trying to make one another understand, and everybody was shouting, "Look there! No, *there*," all the heads became suddenly visible to everyone, and the whole stretch of water round the boat seemed to be swarming with gruesome apparitions. The resulting shrieks of terror were enough to wake Undine, but the moment she opened her eyes the whole nightmarish vision disappeared.

Huldbrand, however, had been so disgusted by the hideous spectacle that he would have burst into a stream of wild curses, had not Undine looked at him appealingly and whispered:

"For God's sake, my dear husband! We're on the water! Please don't be cross with me now!"

The knight sat down in silence, and relapsed into thought.

"Wouldn't it be better, darling," Undine whispered in his ear, "if we gave up this silly expedition altogether, and returned in peace to the castle?"

But Huldbrand only muttered angrily:

"So I'm to be a prisoner in my own castle, am I? And never draw a breath in peace unless the spring's covered up? I wish to goodness all your crazy relations——"

Here Undine laid her pretty hand caressingly on his lips. He said no more, and kept his thoughts to himself, remembering what she had told him.

Bertalda, meanwhile, was lost in bewilderment. She knew a good deal, but not all, about Undine's origin; and Kühleborn in particular still remained for her a terrifying but completely inexplicable mystery. She had never even heard his name. While puzzling over all the curious things that had happened, she absent-mindedly unfastened the golden necklace that Huldbrand had recently bought from a traveling salesman for her, and dangled it over the surface of the river, dreamily contemplating its bright reflection in the darkening water.

Suddenly a great clutching hand came out of the Danube, seized the necklace, and drew it down out of sight. Bertalda gave a loud shriek, and a mocking laugh answered her from the depths of the river.

At this the knight lost his temper completely. He jumped up and started hurling abuse into the water, cursing all those responsible for this constant interference in his private life, and challenging them, water-spirits, sirens, or whatever they might be, to come out into the open and face his naked sword. Meanwhile Bertalda bewailed the loss of her precious ornament, and thus added fuel to the flames of Huldbrand's anger, while all the time Undine, with one hand in the water, was muttering away to herself under her breath, only occasionally interrupting her strange, secret whispering to say imploringly to her husband:

"My dearest one, don't scold me here! Scold me as much as you like when we're somewhere else, only don't do it here! You know why!" And though he was positively stammering with rage, he managed to avoid saying anything directly against her. Then she raised her wet hand from the water. In it was a beautiful necklace of coral, which glittered with such splendor that they were all nearly dazzled.

"Take it," she said, holding it out to Bertalda. "I've had it brought to make up for the other one, so don't be unhappy any more, you poor child."

But the knight leapt between them. He tore the pretty ornament out of Undine's hand and hurled it back into the river, shouting furiously:

"So you still have dealings with them? Then by all the witches in hell, go and stay with them, and take all your presents with you, only leave us human beings in peace, you juggling hag!"

With tears streaming down her cheeks, poor Undine stared at him. The hand was still outstretched, with which she had so kindly offered the pretty gift to Bertalda. Then she began to cry as if her heart would break, like a child that is scolded when it has done nothing wrong, and feels bitterly hurt. At last she said faintly:

"Oh, my sweet friend, good-bye! They shan't do anything to you. Only be faithful, and I'll be able to keep them away from you. But now I can stay no longer, stay no longer in this world that is still so new to me. Alas, alas, what have you done? Alas! Alas!"

And then she disappeared over the side of the boat. Whether she stepped of her own accord into the water, or was swept away by it, no one knew. It might have been both, or neither. But the next moment she had completely vanished into the Danube. Nothing was left of her but a few ripples sobbing and whispering round the boat, which seemed to say: "Alas! Alas! Oh, be faithful! Alas! Alas!"

But Huldbrand lay dissolved in hot tears, and soon unconsciousness drew a merciful veil over his sufferings.

CHAPTER 16

How Things Went with Huldbrand

Unfortunately—or should I say, fortunately?—sorrow does not last very long. I mean really deep sorrow, the kind that springs from the very sources of life, and becomes so identified with the loved one who has been lost, that he ceases to be lost at all, and our whole life is dedicated to the contemplation of his image, until we too cross the barrier that divides him from us. Of course, there are many worthy people who really do live such dedicated lives, but even then it is not the same true sorrow that it was at first. Sooner or later, extraneous images thrust themselves into our consciousness, and we finally have to admit that the transience of all earthly things applies even to our grief. That is why I am compelled to say: unfortunately, sorrow does not last very long.

Such, at any rate, was Huldbrand's experience: whether it was to his advantage or not, will appear in the sequel. At first, he could only weep bitterly, just as his poor, kind Undine had wept when he tore the shining necklace out of her hand, the hand that was trying so generously to make amends. And then he would stretch out his hand, as she had done, and burst into tears again, like her. He even cherished a secret hope that he would finally dissolve in tears altogether—have not many of us had the same idea at a time of great sorrow? Bertalda wept with him, and for a long time they lived quietly together at the castle of Ringstetten, honoring Undine's memory, and almost forgetting their former passion for one another. Perhaps that was why, during this period, Undine often appeared in Huldbrand's dreams, softly and kindly caressing him, and then going away again, weeping silently, so that he sometimes wondered, when he woke up, why his cheeks were so wet: was it only with his own tears, or with Undine's too?

As time went on, however, such dreams became less frequent, and the knight's grief less intense. Even so, he might well have been content to spend the rest of his life quietly thinking and talking about Undine, had not the old fisherman suddenly turned up at the castle and earnestly begged to have Bertalda back as his child. He had heard of Undine's disappearance, and did not want his daughter to go on staying at the castle in the company of an unmarried man.

"Whether she's fond of me or not," he explained, "doesn't interest me now. For her honor is at stake, and where honor's concerned, nothing else matters."

The old fisherman's attitude, combined with the horrible loneliness that lay in wait for the knight in every room and passage of the castle threatening to seize on him after Bertalda's departure, reawakened what had been lulled to sleep and completely forgotten in his grief—his passion for the beautiful Bertalda. The fisherman raised several objections to the marriage which was now proposed. Undine had been very dear to him, and he took the view that there was no knowing as yet whether she was really dead or not. And even if her corpse was indeed lying, stiff and cold, at the bottom of the Danube, or being swept out to sea by the current, still Bertalda was partly responsible for her death, and it ill became her to take the place of the poor woman that she had driven away. On the other hand, the fisherman was also very fond of Huldbrand, and he was further influenced by the entreaties of his daughter, who was far more gentle and submissive these days, and also by her tears for Undine. So it became clear that he would finally have to give his consent, for there was no question of his leaving the castle, and a courier was sent to ask Father Heilmann, who in happier days had given his blessing to the marriage of Huldbrand and Undine, to come and officiate at the knight's second wedding.

No sooner had the good man read Huldbrand's letter than he set out for the castle, traveling at even greater speed than the courier himself. Whenever he got out of breath, or his old limbs ached with weariness, he said to himself:

"There may still be time to prevent this wrong being done. Bear up, my feeble frame, until I reach my destination!"

Then with renewed energy he would wrench himself up again, and walk and walk, without ever stopping for rest, until late one evening he entered the leafy courtyard of the castle.

The bride and bridegroom were sitting arm in arm beneath the trees, with the old fisherman beside them, plunged in thought. As soon as they recognized Father Heilmann, they jumped up and started clustering round to welcome him. After only a few words of greeting, he beckoned the bridegroom into the castle, but when Huldbrand showed surprise and reluctance to follow him, the worthy priest said:

"Very well. Why should I insist on speaking to you in private, Sir Huldbrand? What I have to say concerns Bertalda and the fisherman just as much as you, and what one has got to hear one day, one might as well hear as soon as possible. Well, then, Sir Huldbrand, are you quite sure that your first wife is really dead? That is not my impression. I say nothing about the strange circumstances of her disappearance, for indeed I have no certain knowledge of them. But this much is beyond all doubt: she was a good and faithful wife. And for the last fortnight she has kept on appearing in dreams beside my bed, anxiously wringing her hands, and groaning again and again: "Oh, stop him, dear Father! I'm still alive! Oh, save his body! Oh, save his soul!" I didn't understand at first what the dreams meant, but then your letter arrived, and I hastened to come here, not to marry you, but to separate for ever two people who don't belong together. You must part from her, Huldbrand! You must part from him, Bertalda! He still belongs to another. Can't you see, on those pale cheeks of his, the sorrow that he still feels for his vanished wife? No real bridegroom looks like that, and my heart tells me that even if you refuse to leave him, you'll never be happy with him."

The three people felt in their souls that Father Heilmann was right, but they simply refused to believe it. Even the old fisherman was by now so attached to the plan which had been so often discussed during the last few days, that he could not conceive of any departure from it. So they all started arguing with an uneasy, fanatical obstinacy against the priest's warnings, until he finally left the castle, sadly shaking his head. He could not even be persuaded to stay the night, or to taste any of the refreshments that were offered him.

Huldbrand, however, managed to convince himself that the priest's objections were merely fanciful, so first thing next morning he sent for a member of a nearby monastery, who professed himself perfectly willing to perform the ceremony in a few days' time.

CHAPTER 17

The Knight's Dream

The following day, just before dawn, Huldbrand was lying in bed, half-asleep and half-awake. Every time he started to go right off to sleep, something seemed to warn him of the terrible dreams that might come, and scared him back into wakefulness. But every time he tried to wake up properly, he seemed to hear swans beating their wings all round him, and the sound was so delightfully soothing that he soon went drifting back into a state of semiconsciousness.

In the end, however, he must have really gone to sleep, for the swans that he had heard actually lifted him up on their wings, and carried him far over land and sea, singing sweetly all the while.

"Swans singing—swansong—doesn't that mean death?" he kept saying to himself. But no doubt it could have some other significance.

All at once he seemed to be floating above the Mediterranean, and one of the swans sang loudly in his ear: "This is the Mediterranean Sea!" As he looked down at the waves, they turned into pure crystal, so that he could see right through them to the bottom, and there, to his delight, he saw Undine, sitting beneath the bright crystal vaults. But she was weeping bitterly, and looking far more distressed than he had ever known her in those happy days that they had spent together at the castle, especially at the beginning, and then again later, just before their ill-fated voyage down the Danube. The knight could not help thinking back over every detail of their life together; but Undine seemed to be unaware of his presence.

Meanwhile Kühleborn had come up to her, and started scolding her for crying so much. At this she drew herself up, and gazed at him with such an air of dignity and authority that he was almost afraid of her.

"I may have to live down here beneath the waves," she said, "but

I've brought my soul with me—so I have good reason to weep, even if you're incapable of understanding what such tears mean. For they're tears of joy—to a faithful heart, everything is joyful."

He shook his head incredulously, and after a moment's reflection continued:

"All the same, niece, you're still subject to our laws, and you must sentence him to death if he's unfaithful to you and marries again."

"Up to this moment he's still a widower," replied Undine, "and he still mourns for me and loves me in his heart."

"Perhaps so, but he's also a bridegroom," said Kühleborn with a scornful laugh. "In a few days the priest will have given them his blessing, and then you'll have to go up and arrange for the bigamist's death."

"I can't do that," said Undine, smiling. "I've closed up the spring too securely for anyone like me to get through."

"But suppose he leaves the castle?" asked Kühleborn. "Or suppose one day he has the spring opened again? For he doesn't pay much attention to these things."

"For that very reason," said Undine, still smiling through her tears, "for that very reason he's now floating in spirit over the Mediterranean, and dreaming of this conversation of ours. I've arranged it specially as a warning for him."

At this Kühleborn glared up at the knight with a threatening scowl, and stamped his feet with rage; then he shot off like an arrow beneath the waves. In his fury he seemed to have swollen to the size of a whale. The swans started singing again, and beating their wings, and flying: the knight seemed to be floating along over mountain ranges and rivers, until he finally floated down into the castle at Ringstetten, and woke up in his own bed.

He really did wake up in his own bed, and at that moment his squire came in to tell him that Father Heilmann was still in the neighborhood. He had seen him in the forest the night before, living in a hut that he had built for himself, with plaited branches for walls and a roof of moss and brushwood. When asked what he was there for, if not to perform the marriage ceremony, he had replied:

"There are other ceremonies, you know, besides the marriage ceremony. Even if I've not come for that, I may be needed for some other purpose. We can only wait and see. After all, there's not so very much difference between wedding and weeping, as anyone can see who doesn't willfully shut his eyes to the facts."

These words, and the memory of his dream, aroused all kinds of strange thoughts in Huldbrand's mind; but once a person has got an idea firmly fixed in his head, it is very hard to shift it—so everything remained as it was.

CHAPTER 18

How Huldbrand Got Married

If I were able to convey to you what the wedding celebrations at the castle of Ringstetten were like, you would feel as if you were looking at a vast accumulation of bright and beautiful objects, with a piece of black crepe spread over them, which so darkened all their splendor, that the total effect was less suggestive of enjoyment than of a satire on the nothingness of earthly things. Not that the festive company were disturbed by any ghostly manifestations, for, as we know, the castle had been made impregnable to the attacks of water-spirits. But the knight, and the fisherman, and almost everyone present had the feeling that the guest of honor had not yet arrived, and that this guest of honor was the lovable, kindhearted Undine. Every time the door opened, all eyes were turned involuntarily towards it, and when they saw it was only the butler bringing in another course, or the wine steward bringing a fresh supply of fine old wine, they turned back in disappointment, and the sparks of wit and merriment that had started flashing to and fro were quenched in melancholy recollections.

The bride was by far the most thoughtless person present, and therefore the most cheerful; but from time to time even she felt it strange to be sitting there in her green bridal wreath and her gold-embroidered clothes at the head of the table, while Undine's body was lying stiff and cold at the bottom of the Danube, or being swept out to sea by the current—for ever since her father had spoken these words, they had gone on ringing in her ears, and today she found it impossible to forget them for a moment.

The company dispersed immediately after it got dark, not hurried off by the bridegroom's eager impatience, as is normally the case, but simply forced apart by their own joyless melancholy and premonitions of disaster. Bertalda and the knight went off to undress, she with her maids and he with his servingmen: there was no question, in the circumstances, of having a jolly procession of laughing girls and boys to escort the bride and bridegroom to bed.

Bertalda tried to cheer herself up by examining a splendid piece of jewelry that Huldbrand had given her, and having all her fine clothes and veils laid out beside it, so that she could choose the gayest costume for the morning. Her maids took the opportunity to make all sorts of cheerful remarks to the young bride, not omitting to praise her beauty in the liveliest possible terms. The subject became more and more absorbing, until finally Bertalda glanced in a mirror.

"Oh dear!" she sighed. "Just look at those freckles on the side of my face!"

They looked, and sure enough there the freckles were; but they told her there was nothing to be seen but a dear little mole, a tiny speck that only served to enhance the whiteness of her soft skin. Bertalda shook her head, saying that it was a blemish all the same.

"And I could have so easily got rid of it," she complained. "But now the spring's closed up, that I always used to get such splendid water from to cleanse my skin. Oh, if only I had a bottle of it now!"

"Is that all you want?" laughed one of her maids, and slipped out of the room.

"She's surely not crazy enough to have the stone taken off at this time of night?" asked Bertalda, pleasantly surprised. But even as she spoke, they heard men walking across the courtyard, and saw from the window that the obliging maid was leading them straight to the spring, and that they were carrying crowbars and other tools on their shoulders.

"I must admit, it's just what I want," smiled Bertalda. "That is, if it doesn't take too long."

And enjoying the feeling that a hint from her was now enough to achieve what had been so painfully refused before, she stood watching the progress of the work in the moonlit courtyard below.

The men started heaving away with a will at the big stone, though from time to time one of them would sigh at the thought of undoing the work of their beloved former mistress. As it turned out, it was a far easier job than they expected, for some power in the spring itself seemed to be helping to raise the stone.

"Why, anyone would think it was a waterspout or something!" said the men to one another in surprise.

The stone lifted higher and higher, and with hardly any assistance from the workmen rolled over with a dull thud on to the flagstones. From the mouth of the spring, what looked like a white column of water rose solemnly into the air: at first they thought it really was a waterspout, until the ascending form revealed itself as that of a pale-faced woman veiled in white. Weeping bitterly, and wringing its hands in anguish, it started moving at a grave, deliberate pace towards the castle buildings. The servants scattered in all directions, while at the window, surrounded by her maids, the bride stool pale and rigid with terror. As the figure reached a point directly below her room, it raised its weeping face towards her, and beneath the veil Bertalda thought she recognized the pale features of Undine. But the mournful shape passed on, with heavy, reluctant, lingering steps, like those of a man going to the scaffold. Bertalda shrieked for someone to call the knight; but all her maids were rooted to the spot, and even she relapsed into silence, as if terrified by the sound of her own voice.

While they stood in terror at the window, motionless as statues, the strange visitant reached the castle entrance, climbed the well-known steps and walked through the well-known hall, weeping silently all the while. Oh, how different it had been the last time she had walked here!

The knight had already dismissed his attendants. He was standing, half-undressed and lost in gloomy thought, before a tall mirror. A candle burned dimly beside him. Very, very softly a finger tapped on his door. It was exactly how Undine had once tapped, when she wanted to play a joke on him.

"I must have imagined it," he said to himself. "It's time I went to bed with my wife."

"Yes, to bed, but a very cold one!" came the tearful voice from outside the room, and then in the mirror he saw the door slowly, slowly opening, saw the white figure come in, and shut the door carefully behind her.

"They have opened the spring," she said quietly. "And I have come for you, and you must die."

His heart seemed to stand still, and he knew that there was no escape; but he put his hands in front of his eyes and said:

"Then at least don't let me die mad with fear. If there's a face of terror behind that veil, please don't lift it. Kill me quickly, before I've had time to see you."

"Oh, won't you take one last look at me?" she said. "I'm just as beautiful as I was when you wooed me beside the lake."

"If only that were true!" sighed Huldbrand. "If only you would kill me with a kiss!"

"Most willingly, my beloved," she replied. She threw back her veil, and there was her sweet face smiling at him, in all its glorious beauty. Trembling with passion and the thought of approaching death, he bent down towards her. She gave him a heavenly kiss, but then, instead of letting him go, she pressed him still closer to her, and wept as though she was weeping her soul away. Tears gushed into his eyes, and a sea of blissful anguish went surging through his breast, until at last breath failed him and his lifeless body slipped from her lovely arms and sank softly to the cushions of his couch.

"I have wept his life away!" she told the servants who encountered her in the antechamber. Then she walked slowly through the panic-stricken crowd, and out towards the spring.

CHAPTER 19

How the Knight Was Buried

As soon as the news of Huldbrand's death was known in the neighborhood, Father Heilmann set off for the castle; and his arrival almost coincided with the departure of the terrified monk who had married the unfortunate couple.

"It's just as well," said Heilmann, when they told him about it. "Now it's all my responsibility, and I need no one to share it with me."

His first step was to try and comfort the bride, who was now a widow, though his words bore little fruit in her worldly mind. The old fisherman, on the other hand, while deeply grieved, resigned himself far more easily to the fate which had overtaken his daughter and son-in-law; and to Bertalda's incessant abuse of Undine as a witch and a murderess, his only answer was:

"It couldn't have been otherwise. I can only see it as God's judgment—and I dare say no one feels more deeply about Huldbrand's death than the one who had to carry out the sentence, poor, forsaken Undine!"

In this spirit he helped to arrange a funeral on a scale befitting the dead man's rank.

Soon Huldbrand's shield and helmet were lying on his coffin, ready to be lowered into the grave with it, for he was the last of his line. The sad procession of mourners moved off, while from their lips funereal music rose into the bright, quiet blue of the sky. Heilmann led the way with a tall crucifix, followed by the inconsolable Bertalda, supported on her aged father's arm.

Suddenly, among the black-robed mourners following the widow, they were aware of a snow-white figure, heavily veiled and wringing its hands in passionate lamentation. The women next to her felt a secret thrill of horror, and shrank back or sideways to avoid her, thus communicating their panic to others, and increasing their alarm when the white stranger approached them in their turn, until the whole procession began to be thrown into confusion. Some soldiers had the courage to address the mysterious figure, and tried to hustle it out of the procession, but it slipped somehow through their hands and the next moment was seen still moving, with slow and solemn steps, through the cortege. The women kept shrinking away from it, until it finally reached a position immediately behind Bertalda. It then began to move more slowly still, so that the widow was unaware of its presence, and thus the quiet, humble figure was allowed to follow her undisturbed.

This went on until they reached the churchyard, and the procession formed a circle round the open grave. Bertalda now caught sight of the uninvited mourner, and starting forward half in anger and half in fear, commanded her to stand aside from the knight's last resting-place. But the veiled figure shook its head in gentle refusal, and raised its hands in humble entreaty towards Bertalda, who was so moved that she burst into tears, remembering that day on the Danube when Undine had so kindly offered her the coral necklace. Moreover, at this point Father Heilmann made a sign enjoining silence, so that all could pray devoutly over the corpse, above which a mound of earth was already beginning to rise. Bertalda said no more, but knelt down, and everyone followed her example, including the gravediggers themselves, as soon as their work was finished.

When they stood up again, the strange white figure had vanished. On the spot where she had been kneeling a silvery spring was gushing out of the grass. It went trickling on and on, until it had almost encircled the mound of earth over the knight's grave; then it ran off into a quiet pool that lay beside the churchyard. Until quite recent times, the local villagers are said to have pointed out this spring to their children, and cherished the firm belief that it was the poor, rejected Undine, still clasping her sweetheart in her loving arms.

Translated by Paul Turner

The Strange Story of
Peter Schlemihl

Adelbert von Chamisso

1

After a successful, but for me very difficult sea voyage, we finally reached port. As soon as I got off the tender, I loaded all my possessions on my back and, pushing my way through the teeming crowd, entered the first humble house that had a sign in front of it. I asked for a room. The clerk sized me up with a single glance and took me to the attic. I asked for fresh water and for precise instructions as to where I could find Mr. Thomas John. "At the north gate, the first country house on the right, a large, new house built of red and white marble, with many columns." Good. It was still early, I undid my bundle at once, took out my black coat, which I had newly turned, dressed in my best clean clothes, put the letter of recommendation in my pocket, and immediately set out on the road to the man who was to help me realize my modest plans.

After I had walked up the long North Street and reached the gate, I soon saw the columns gleaming through the green foliage. "So this is it," I thought. I wiped the dust from my feet with my handkerchief, arranged my cravat and pulled the bell rope for good or ill. The door sprang open. In the entrance hall I had to undergo an examination; but the porter had me announced, and I had the honor of being summoned to the park, in which Mr. John was strolling with a small company. I recognized the man at once by his aura of corpulent self-satisfaction. He received me very well, as a rich man receives a poor devil; he even looked at me, but without turning away from the rest of the company, and took the letter from my outstretched hand. "So, so, from my brother; I have heard nothing from him for a long time. He's in good health, I hope?" "There," he continued to the company without waiting for an answer, and pointing with the letter to a hill, "that's where I'm going to have the new building erected." He broke open the seal without breaking off the conversation, which was turning to the subject of wealth. "A man who isn't master of at least a million," he interjected, "is, if you'll pardon the word, a rogue." "Oh, how true!" I exclaimed, with full, overflowing emotion. This must have pleased him, because he smiled at me and said, "Stay here, dear friend, I may perhaps have time later on to tell you what I think about this"—he pointed to the letter, which he then put in his pocket, and turned to the company again. He offered his arm to a young lady; other gentlemen addressed their attention to other fair ones; all who belonged together found each other; and they made a pilgrimage to the hill blooming with roses.

I stole along behind them without burdening anyone; for not a soul paid any more attention to me. The company was in good spirits, there was sporting and jesting. At times they spoke with importance of frivolous matters, more often, frivolously of important ones; and gradually their wit was directed especially to absent friends and their affairs. I was too much a stranger to understand a great deal about all this, too concerned and introverted to have a mind for such puzzles.

We had reached the copse of roses. The beautiful Fanny, who seemed to be the mistress of the day, wanted to break a branch herself, out of sheer stubbornness; she pricked herself on a thorn and a deep red flowed down her delicate hand as if it had come from the dark roses. This event threw the whole company into confusion. A search was made for English plaster. An elderly man, tall and thin, who was walking beside me and whom I had not noticed before, immediately put his hand into the tightly fit back pocket of his old-fashioned gray taffeta coat, took out a little portfolio, opened it and, with a humble bow, handed the lady what she wished. She received it without thanks and without glancing at the donor. The wound was bandaged and the company went on up the hill, from whose ridge they wished to enjoy the spacious view extending from the green labyrinth of the park toward the boundless ocean.

The sight was truly grand and glorious. A bright point appeared on the horizon between the dark water and the blue of the sky. "A telescope here!" cried John, and even before the servants who had answered the call had started out, the gray man, bowing modestly, had already put his hand in his coat pocket. He drew a handsome Dollond telescope from it and handed it to Mr. John. The latter at once put it to his eye, and informed the company that it was the ship that had set out yesterday being held back within sight of the harbor by adverse winds. The telescope went from hand to hand but not back into those of its owner. I looked at the man in astonishment, failing to understand how such a big instrument had come out of that small pocket. But it seemed not to have surprised anyone else, and they paid no more attention to the gray man than to me.

Refreshments were served, the rarest fruits from every part of the world in the most costly dishes. Mr. John did the honors with a light grace, and at that point addressed a second sentence to me: "Do eat. You didn't have this at sea." I bowed but he did not notice, for he was already talking to someone else.

Had it not been for the damp ground, they would have liked to lie down on the lawn, on the slope of the hill facing the panoramic landscape. It would be heavenly, one of the guests said, if they had Turkish carpets to spread out there. The wish had hardly been uttered when the man in the gray coat already had his hand in his pocket and, with a modest, indeed humble, gesture, busied himself with drawing out an expensive Turkish carpet embroidered with gold thread. Servants took hold of it as if this was the most inevitable and natural thing to do, and spread it out at the desired place. The company took their places on it without ceremony. Once more I looked in astonishment at the man, his pocket and the carpet: it was more than twenty feet long and ten feet wide. I rubbed my eyes, at a loss about what to think, especially since no one else found anything remarkable about it.

I wanted very much to learn something about the man and to ask who he was, but I did not know to whom I might turn, for I was almost more afraid of the lordly servants than of the lords they served. I finally mustered my courage and approached a young man who seemed to be less important than the others and who had frequently stood alone. I asked him softly to tell me who the obliging gentleman in the gray suit was. "That one, who looks like an end of thread that has escaped a tailor's needle?" "Yes, the man standing by himself." "I don't know him," he replied and, apparently in order to avoid a lengthy conversation with me, turned away and spoke to another man about some trivial matter.

The sun now began to shine more intensely and became a nuisance to the ladies. The beautiful Fanny addressed the gray man, who had not yet been acknowledged by anyone, and asked him casually if he had a tent with him too. He replied with a very deep bow, as though an undeserved honor had been bestowed on him. He already had his hand in his pocket, from which there soon emerged tools, poles, ropes, hardware, in short, everything necessary for the most splendid pleasure-tent. The young gentleman helped open the tent, which extended over the whole area of the carpet. Still no one found anything extraordinary in this.

By that time I had long felt queer, in fact faint at heart. How much more so when, at the next wish that was expressed, I saw him pull three black horses—I tell you, three beautiful, large horses with saddles and harness—imagine, in Heaven's name! three saddled horses out of the same pocket out of which had come a portfolio, a telescope, a twenty-by-ten-foot Turkish carpet, a pleasure-tent of the same dimensions, with all the hardware pertaining to it!—If I didn't swear that I saw it with my own eyes, you would certainly not believe it.

However embarrassed and humble the man himself seemed to be, however little attention the others paid him, his pale figure, from which I could not tear my eyes, became so gruesome to me that I could no longer bear it.

I decided to steal away from the company, which, in view of the insignificant role I was playing there, seemed to me an easy thing to do. I wanted to return to town, try my luck with Mr. John again the next morning, if I found the courage to do so, and question him about the strange gray man. If only I had been lucky enough to get away!

I had actually succeeded in stealing through the rose copse, down the hill, and was on an open lawn when, afraid that I might be seen walking through the grass beside the path, I cast a searching glance behind me. Imagine my terror when I saw the man in the gray coat coming behind me and toward me. He lifted his hat to me at once and bowed lower than anyone had ever done to me. There was no doubt about it, he wanted to talk to me, and I could not avoid him without being rude. I took my hat off, too, returned his bow, and stood there bareheaded in the sun, as though rooted to the spot. I looked at him, rigid with fear, and felt like a bird charmed by a snake. He himself seemed to be deeply embarrassed; he did not raise his eyes, kept bowing repeatedly, came closer to me and addressed me in a soft, uncertain voice, somewhat like that of a beggar:

"I hope you will excuse my importunity, sir, for daring to seek you out in this way without knowing you; but I have a request to make of you. Will you most graciously grant . . ." "But in the name of Heaven, sir," I exclaimed in my anxiety, "what can I do for a man who . . ." We both stopped and it seems to me that we turned red.

After a moment of silence he resumed: "During the short time in which I enjoyed the pleasure of being near you, I was able, sir, to study—allow me to say so, several times—really in inexpressible admiration, the beautiful, beautiful shadow you cast in the sun, with a certain aristocratic disdain, so to speak, without any effort, this splendid shadow here at your feet. Pardon my bold presumption; but would you possibly feel not disinclined to let me have your shadow?"

He was silent and my head began to spin like a mill wheel. What was I to make of this strange proposal of his to buy my shadow from me? He must be insane, I thought, and in an altered tone of voice, which better fitted the humility of his, I therefore replied:

"Oh, oh, my good friend, isn't your own shadow enough for you? I call this a most unusual bargain." He continued at once: "I have in my pocket many things that might not appear unworthy to you, sir. For this invaluable shadow I consider the highest price too small."

Now a cold shudder seized me again as I was reminded of his pocket, and I could not understand how I could have called him a good friend. I spoke again, trying, if possible, to rectify my error with the utmost politeness:

"But, my dear sir, pardon your most humble servant. I don't really understand your attitude. How could I possibly sell my shadow?" He interrupted me: "I ask Your Honor's permission to pick up this noble shadow, here on the spot and pocket it; how I do it is my business. But in evidence of my gratitude to you, sir, I permit you to choose from among all the treasures which I carry with me in my pocket: spring root, mandrake, change pennies, robber dollar, the napkin of Roland's page, a mandragora at your own price: but I don't suppose these are things for you. The wishing cap of Fortunatus, new and durably restored, would be better. Also a moneybag like his." "Fortunatus' moneybag," I interrupted him, and great though my anxiety was, he had with this one word captured my whole mind. I became dizzy, and objects like double ducats danced before my eyes. "Will you be kind enough, sir, to examine and test this bag." He put his hand in his pocket and drew out a moderately large, firmly sewn pouch of strong cordovan leather, held shut by two stout leather cords, and handed it to me. I put my hand in and drew out ten gold coins, and ten more and ten more and ten more. I quickly held out my hand to him. "Agreed; it's a bargain; for this pouch you have my shadow." He clasped it, and then without further delay knelt down before me and I saw him gently loosen my shadow from head to foot out of the grass with an admirable dexterity, lift it up, fold it and finally put it in his pocket. He stood up, bowed once more to me and then withdrew to the rosebushes. It seemed to me that I heard him laughing softly to himself there. But I held the pouch tightly by the cords; round about me the world was bright in the sun and I had not yet come to my senses.

2

I finally regained my senses and hastened to leave that place, with which I hoped I would have no further concern. First I filled my pockets with gold, then I tied the cords of the pouch tightly about my neck and hid the pouch itself on my chest. I got out of the park unnoticed, reached the highway and made my way back to the city. As I was approaching the gate, lost in thought, I heard someone shouting behind me: "Young man, hey, young man, stop a moment!" I looked around. An old woman called after me: "Do look out, sir, you've lost your shadow." "Thanks, mother." I threw her a gold coin for her well-intentioned advice and stepped under the trees.

At the city gate I had to listen to the same words from the sentry: "Where did you leave your shadow, sir?" And immediately after that, from several women: "Good Lord! The poor man has no shadow!" This began to annoy me and I took great care not to step into the sunlight. But it couldn't be managed everywhere. For instance, on Broad Street, which I had to cross immediately, and moreover, to my misfortune, at an hour when the boys were going home from school. A confounded hunchbacked rascal—I can still see him—noticed at once that I had no shadow. With a mighty shout he betrayed me to all the literary street urchins of the suburbs, who promptly began to criticize and throw dirt at me. "Regular people usually take their shadows with them when they go into the sun." To keep them at bay I threw handfuls of gold among them and, helped by some sympathetic souls, sprang into a cab.

As soon as I found myself alone in the moving vehicle, I began to weep bitter tears. The suspicion was already forcing itself upon me that, in the same degree as gold outweighs merit and virtue on earth, the shadow is valued above gold; and just as I had formerly sacrificed wealth to my conscience, so I had now given away my shadow for mere money. What was going to happen to me on earth?

I was still in a very disturbed state when the cab pulled up in front of my hotel; I was frightened at the idea of going up to that poor attic room. I had my things brought down to me, was handed the wretched bundle with contempt, threw down a few gold coins and gave orders to be taken to the most expensive hotel. The place had a northern exposure, so I had no cause to fear the sun. I dismissed the cabdriver with gold, asked to be shown the best room facing the front of the hotel and locked myself in it as soon as I could.

What do you think I did now? Oh, my dear Chamisso, it makes me blush to confess it even to you. I drew the unlucky bag from my bosom and, with a sort of fury which grew within me by its own power like a flaring flame, I drew out the gold and gold and gold and still more gold and scattered it over the carpet and walked over it and let it clatter and kept throwing more and more of the metal against the metal, feasting my poor heart on the glitter, until I fell back in exhaustion on the luxurious couch and rolled over and over in it in revelry. In this way the day and the evening passed. I did not open my door. Night found me lying on the gold, and then sleep overpowered me.

Then I dreamed of you; it was as if I were standing behind the glass door of your little room, and I saw you sitting there at your desk between a skeleton and a bundle of wilted plants; Haller, Humboldt and Linnaeus were open before you, and on your sofa lay a volume of Goethe and the *Magic Ring*. I studied you a long time and then every object in your room, and then you again; but you did not stir, nor did you breathe; you were dead.

I awoke. It still seemed to be very early. My watch had stopped. I felt crushed and thirsty and hungry too. I had eaten nothing since the previous morning. Peevishly and with a feeling of surfeit, I thrust away this gold with which I had shortly before satiated my foolish heart; now in my annoyance I did not know what to do with it. It could not remain lying there, so I tried to see whether the pouch would swallow it again. No. None of my windows opened out to the sea. I had to yield and drag the gold painfully and with bitter sweat to a large clothespress which stood in a closet and pack it in there. I left only a few handfuls lying about. After I had finished this task, I stretched out in exhaustion on an easy chair and waited till the people in the hotel began to stir. As soon as it was possible I had some food brought me and called for the landlord.

With him I discussed the future arrangement of my apartment. For personal service I selected a certain Bendel, whose loyal and intelligent face won my trust at once. It is he whose attachment has since then accompanied me and given me comfort through the misery of life and who has helped me to bear my sad lot. I spent the whole day in my rooms with temporary servants, shoemakers, tailors and merchants. I set my apartment in order and, merely to get rid of some of the stored-up gold, bought many precious objects and jewels, but it did not seem to me as if the pile of gold could be diminished.

Meanwhile I was in a state of great anxiety about my condition. I did not dare to step out of my room, and in the evening I had forty wax candles lit before I dared to emerge from the shadows. I recalled in horror the fearful scene with the schoolboys. I decided to test public opinion once more, though it required considerable courage to do so. —At that time the nights were moonlit. Late in the evening I put on an ample cloak, pressed my hat down over my forehead and stole trembling out of the house, like a criminal. Only when I reached a distant square did I venture to step out of the shadow of the houses, in whose protection I had come this far, into the moonlight, prepared to hear my destiny from the lips of the passersby.

Spare me, dear friend, the painful repetition of all that I had to endure. Women often showed the very deep sympathy that I inspired in them; there were remarks that pierced my soul no less than the mockery of youth and the arrogant contempt of men, especially those stout, corpulent men who themselves cast a broad shadow. A beautiful sweet girl apparently accompanying her parents, who were cautiously looking down at their feet, turned her shining eyes on me by chance. She was visibly frightened when she noticed that I had no shadow, hid her beautiful face in her veil, let her head droop and walked silently by.

I could bear it no longer. Salty rivers burst from my eyes, and with my heart sundered I withdrew, tottering into the dark. I had to hold onto the houses in order to steady my steps, and reached my apartment slowly and late.

I spent a sleepless night. The next day my first concern was to have the man in gray searched for everywhere. Perhaps I might succeed in finding him again, and how lucky it would be if he should regret the foolish bargain as I did. I sent for Bendel, for he seemed to have skill and dexterity. I gave him an exact description of the man who had in his possession a treasure without which my life was only a torment. I told him the time and place where I had met the man in gray, described to him all the people present and even added the clue that he was to make precise inquiries about a Dollond telescope, a Turkish carpet embroidered with gold, a splendid pleasure-tent and finally, black horses, whose history was somehow intertwined with that of the mysterious man, who had seemed to be insignificant to everyone, but whose appearance had disturbed the peace and happiness of my life.

When I had finished talking I brought out some money, as heavy a pile as I could carry, and added jewels and precious stones to it to give it greater value. "Bendel," I said, "this will smooth many paths and will make much that looked impossible easy. Don't be stingy with it, as I am not, but go and bring your master the joyful news on which alone his hope now rests."

He went. He came back late and dejected. None of Mr. John's people, none of his guests—he had spoken to them all—could even remotely remember the man in the gray coat. The new telescope was there, but no one knew where it had come from. The carpet, the tent were still there, spread out over the same hill; the servants boasted of their master's wealth and not one of them knew how these new treasures had come to him. He himself enjoyed them and was not in the least concerned about their source. The young gentlemen had the horses, which they had ridden, in their stables, and they praised the generosity of Mr. John, who had given them the horses that day. That much was clear from Bendel's detailed account. Though he had failed, his swift zeal and intelligent management received their merited praise from me. I motioned sadly for him to leave me alone.

"I have," Bendel began again, "given you a report, sir, about this matter which was so important to you. There still remains a message for me to deliver, which was given me early this morning by someone I met outside the door when I went out on the business in which I failed. The man's very words were: 'Tell Mr. Peter Schlemihl that he will not see me here again, because I am going overseas and a favorable wind calls me to the harbor now. But at the end of a year I shall have the honor of seeking him out myself and proposing another bargain, which will perhaps be acceptable to him. Give him my most humble regards and assure him of my gratitude.' I asked him who he was, but he said you 'would know who he was.'"

"What did the man look like?" I cried, full of foreboding. And trait by trait, word for word, precisely as he had described the man when he was looking for him, Bendel described to me the man in the gray coat.

"Unhappy man!" I cried, wringing my hands. "That was the very man himself!" and the scales fell from his eyes. —"Yes, it was he, it really was!" Bendel exclaimed in fright. "And I, blind, stupid fool, did not recognize him, did not recognize him, and have betrayed my master!"

Shedding tears, he broke into the bitterest reproaches against himself, and fell into a despair which inspired me with sympathy. I comforted him, assured him repeatedly that I did not doubt his loyalty in the least, and soon sent him to the harbor to pursue the man's steps if possible. But that very morning many ships, which had been held back in the harbor by adverse winds, had sailed each in a different direction, each destined for some other coast, and the gray man had vanished like a shadow, leaving no trace behind him.

3

What good would wings be to a man bound in iron chains? He would be in despair, in terrible despair. I lay there, like Fafnir beside his treasure, far from all human intercourse, starving amidst all my gold; but my heart was not with the gold; and I cursed that for the sake of which I saw myself cut off from all life. Nursing my gloomy secret all by myself, I was afraid of my lowliest servant, whom I was compelled to envy; for he had a shadow and dared to show himself in the sun. I passed the days and nights in my rooms in lonely mourning, and grief gnawed at my heart.

Another person was wasting away under my very eyes. My loyal Bendel did not stop tormenting himself with silent reproaches for having betrayed the confidence of his kind master by failing to recognize the man he had been sent out to find and with whom he must think my sad destiny stood in a close bond. But I could not blame him; I recognized in the event the fabulous character of that unknown man.

To leave no stone unturned, I once sent Bendel with a precious diamond ring to the most famous painter in the city, whom I invited to visit me. He came, I sent my servants away, locked the door, sat down beside the man, and after I had warmly praised his art, I came to the point with a gloomy heart—but not until I had sworn him to the strictest secrecy.

"Professor," I asked, "could you possibly paint an imitation shadow for a man who in the most unlucky way in the world has lost his own?"—"You mean a shadow cast by light?"

"Precisely." "But," he asked, "what clumsiness, what negligence made him lose his shadow?"—"How it happened," I replied, "is a matter of no importance. But this much," I lied to him shamelessly, "I must say. In Russia, where he was traveling last winter, his shadow once froze to the ground in an unusual cold spell, so that he was unable to tear it loose again."

"The imitation light-shadow that I could paint for him," the professor replied, "would really be only of the sort which he would lose again at the slightest movement. Especially a man who was so little attached to his own natural shadow, as would appear to be the case from your story. A man who has no shadow does not go into the sun—that's the most sensible and safest course." He got up and went away, after giving me a piercing look which I was unable to meet. I sank back in my easy chair and hid my face in my hands.

This is the state Bendel found me in when he entered. He saw his master's grief and wanted to withdraw silently, reverently. I looked up. Crushed beneath the burden of my sorrow, I had to share it with him. "Bendel," I cried to him, "Bendel, you incomparable man, you who see my suffering and respect it, you who don't seek to probe into it but seem to sympathize silently and piously, come to me, Bendel, and be the person closest to my heart. I have not locked the treasures of my gold from you, nor will I lock the treasures of my grief from you. Bendel, the world has judged and rejected me, and you, too, will perhaps abandon me when you learn my terrible secret. Bendel, I am rich, generous, kind, but—in God's name!—I have no shadow!"

"No shadow?" the good youth exclaimed in fright, and the tears poured from his eyes. "Woe is me that I was born to serve a master without a shadow!" He was silent and I covered my face with my hands.

"Bendel," I added after some time, trembling, "now that you have my secret, you can betray it. Go and give testimony against me." He seemed to be passing through a severe inner struggle, until finally he fell down before me and took my hand, which he moistened with his tears. "No," he exclaimed, "whatever the world may say, I will not forsake my kind master for the sake of a shadow, I will act justly, not prudently. I will stay with you, lend you my shadow, and help you where I can. And where I cannot help you, I will weep with you." I threw my arms about his neck, astonished by such an unusual attitude; for I was convinced that he was not doing it for money.

After that my fate and my way of life changed somewhat. It is unbelievable how zealous Bendel was to conceal my failing. Everywhere he was in front of me and beside me, anticipating everything, making arrangements and, where danger threatened unexpectedly, covering me swiftly with his shadow, for he was bigger and stronger than I. So again I ventured into society and began to play a role in the world. Of course, I had to assume many peculiarities and eccentricities. But these suit a rich man, and as long as the truth remained concealed, I enjoyed all the honor and respect my gold merited. I looked forward more calmly to the visit promised by the strange unknown man at the end of the year.

I knew very well that I must not stay long in the place where I had already been seen without my shadow and where I might easily be betrayed. Perhaps I only remembered the figure I had cut before Mr. John and the memory of it depressed me. For that reason I merely wanted to hold a rehearsal there, so that I might play the role elsewhere more easily and with more confidence. However, what kept me here for a time was my vanity: this is the element in man in which the anchor finds the most solid ground.

None other than the beautiful Fanny, whom I met again in another house, granted me some of her attention, without realizing that she had met me before, for now I possessed wit and intelligence. When I talked, people listened; and I myself did not know how I had acquired the art of carrying on or dominating a conversation with such ease. The impression I realized I had made on the beautiful woman made a fool of me, which is just what she wished, and after that time I followed her wherever I could, with a thousand efforts through shadow and twilight. I was vain only in order to make her vain about me, and with the best will in the world I could not force the intoxication out of my head and into my heart.

But why repeat to you at length the whole commonplace story? You yourself have told it to me often enough about other worthy people. But, to be sure, the old, well-known drama, in which I had good-naturedly taken a stale role, was given a denouement made especially for it, unexpected by me, by her and by everyone else.

One beautiful evening when, as usual, I had invited some people to an illuminated garden party, I was strolling arm in arm with the lady at some distance from the other guests, working hard to turn pretty phrases for her. She looked modestly down at her feet and gently returned the pressure of my hand. At that point the moon unexpectedly emerged from the clouds behind us and she saw only her own shadow cast before her. She started, looked at me in consternation, and then gazed down at the ground again, her eyes searching for my shadow. What went on in her mind was painted so strangely on her features that I would have broken into loud laughter had not an ice-cold shudder run down my back.

I released her from my arm and she fainted. Like an arrow I shot through the rows of horrified guests, reached the door, threw myself into the first carriage I found stationed there, and rode back to the city, where this time, in anticipation of my misfortune, I had left the cautious Bendel. He was frightened when he saw me and one word revealed everything to him. Post-horses were fetched on the spot. I took only one servant with me, a weathered scoundrel named Raskal, who had been able to make himself indispensable to me through his cleverness, and who could have no suspicion of what had happened that day. I drove thirty miles that same night. Bendel remained behind to liquidate my household, to give out gold and to bring me what I needed most. When he caught up with me the following day, I threw myself into his arms and swore to him, not that I would commit no more follies, but that I would be more cautious in the future. We continued our journey without delay, over the border and the mountains, and only in a nearby, little-frequented bathing spot on the other side of the mountains, separated from that unlucky place by that lofty bulwark, did I allow myself to be persuaded to rest from the distress I had experienced.

4

I shall have to pass rapidly over a period on which I should like to dwell, if I could conjure up its living spirit in my memory. But the color which animated it and which alone can reanimate it, has faded within me; and when I try to find again in my heart what moved it so powerfully at that time—both pain and happiness, the pious illusion—I strike in vain at a rock which no longer yields a living spring, and God has forsaken me. How different it looks to me now, that past time!—Badly rehearsed, and a novice on the stage, I was supposed to play a tragic role in that watering place. I gape at a pair of blue eyes and forget the play. The parents, disappointed by the game, stake their all on setting the whole action swiftly, and the common farce ends in derision. And that is all, all!—It seems silly to me and in bad taste, and again it seems frightful that something that once moved my heart so luxuriously and grandly can now appear to me in that light. Minna, as I wept then, when I lost you, so I weep now for having lost you in myself as well. Have I then become so old? O mournful reason! Only one more pulsebeat from that period, one moment of that delusion—but no! Alone on the high, desolate sea of your bitter flood; out of the last cup of champagne, the elf has vanished long ago.

I had sent Bendel ahead with some golden sovereigns to arrange an apartment for me according to my needs. He had thrown much money about and some vague information about the distinguished stranger whose servant he was, for I did not want my name to be known, which caused the good people to have strange thoughts. As soon as my house was ready, Bendel came to take me there and we set out on our journey.

About an hour from the place, on a sunny field, our road was barred by a crowd in holiday dress. The carriage stopped. Music, the music of bells, and cannon shots were heard; a loud *hurrah* penetrated the air; and before the door of the carriage there appeared a chorus of maidens of exceptional beauty in white dresses, but who faded before one of their group as the stars of the night fade before the sun. She stepped out from amidst her sisters; the tall, delicate figure kneeled down before me, blushing modestly, and held out to me on a silken cushion a wreath, twined from laurel, olive and roses, while she spoke a few words about majesty, reverence and love, which I did not understand but whose magical silver sound intoxicated my ears and heart—it seemed to me that this heavenly figure had already passed me once before. The chorus joined in and sang the praise of a good king and the happiness of his people.

And this scene, my dear friend, in full sunlight! She was still kneeling two feet from me and I, without a shadow, could not bridge the abyss, could not in turn fall on my knees before the angel. Oh, what would I have given at that point for a shadow! I had to conceal my shame, my anxiety, my despair, deep in the recess of my carriage. Bendel finally took thought on my behalf; he leaped out the other side of the carriage. I called him back and, from the little box which lay beside me, handed him a diamond-studded crown which had been meant to adorn the beautiful Fanny. He stepped forward and, in the name of his master, who could not and would not accept such signs of honor, said there must be a mistake. However, the good inhabitants of the city were thanked for their good will. Meanwhile he took the wreath from her hands and put the diamond crown in its place; then he reverently gave the beautiful maiden his hand, helped her to her feet, and with a gesture dismissed the clergy, the magistrates and all the deputations. No one was admitted beyond that point. He commanded the crowd to part and make way for the horses, mounted the carriage again, and we went on at a steady gallop, under a gateway made of foliage and flowers, toward the town. The cannon was fired energetically over and over again. The carriage stopped before a house. I leaped swiftly to the door, parting the crowd that had collected with the desire to see me. The mob shouted "Hurrah" under my window, and I let double ducats rain out of it. In the evening the city was spontaneously illuminated.

And still I did not know what all this was supposed to mean and whom I was taken for. I sent Raskal out to inquire. He learned that the townsfolk had reliable news that the good King of Prussia was traveling through the country under the name of a count; that my adjutant had been recognized and that he had betrayed himself and me; that their joy had been great when they were certain that I was there personally. Of course they realized now, since I obviously wished to preserve the strictest incognito, how wrong they had been to lift the veil so importunately. I had been so benignly, so graciously angry; I would certainly have to pardon their good hearts.

My scamp was so amused by the affair that he did his utmost, by words of blame, to strengthen the people in their belief for the present. He gave me a very comical account of the matter and, seeing me cheered by it, regaled me with an account of his own tricks. Must I admit it? I was really flattered to be taken for the reverend sovereign, if only under these circumstances.

I had a party arranged for the next evening under the trees which shaded the ground in front of my house and invited the whole town to it. The mysterious power of my purse, Bendel's efforts and Raskal's nimble inventive skill even succeeded in conquering time. It is truly astonishing how magnificently and beautifully everything arranged itself in those few hours. The splendor and luxury which were created there and the ingenious illumination were so wisely distributed that I felt myself quite secure. There was nothing left for me to add. I had to praise my servants.

The evening grew dark. The guests appeared and were presented to me. The phrase "Your Majesty" was heard no more, but with deep reverence and humility they addressed me as "Count." What was I to do? I accepted the title of count, and from that moment on I was called Count Peter. In the midst of the festive whirl my soul yearned only for one person. She appeared late, she who was the crown and wore it. She followed her parents modestly and did not seem to know she was the most beautiful woman there. The forest inspector, his wife and their daughter were presented to me. I was able to say many pleasant and obliging things to the old man; but before the daughter I stood like a boy who has been spanked, unable to stammer a word. Finally I begged her hesitatingly to dignify this festive occasion, to wield the office whose symbol adorned her. With a touching look in her eyes she modestly begged to be excused; but more abashed in her presence than she was herself, as her first subject, I brought her homage in profound reverence. The nod of the count became a command to all the guests and everyone joyfully strove to obey it. Majesty, innocence and grace, allied to beauty, dominated the happy festivity. Minna's happy parents believed that their child was being exalted only in their honor; I myself was in an indescribable state of intoxication. Everything I still had of the jewels I had brought along—to get rid of the load of gold, all the pearls and all the diamonds—I had put in two covered bowls and distributed at dinner in the name of the queen among her friends and all the other ladies. Meanwhile gold was being constantly cast among the exulting crowd in amounts exceeding all reasonable bounds.

Next morning Bendel revealed to me confidentially that the suspicion he had long nursed about Raskal's honesty had now become a certainty. Yesterday Raskal had embezzled full bags of gold. "Let us not begrudge the poor rogue the little bit of plunder," I replied, "I gladly give to everyone, why not to him too? Yesterday he and all the new people you gave me served me honestly, they helped me celebrate a happy festivity."

We talked no more of the matter. Raskal remained the first of my servants, but Bendel was my friend and confidant. He had grown accustomed to regard my wealth as inexhaustible, and he did not snoop about as to its source; but rather, entering into my spirit, he helped me invent opportunities to show it off and to squander gold. Of the unknown gray man, the pale sneaky fellow, I knew only this much: he alone could release me from the curse which weighed on me, and I feared the man upon whom my sole hope rested. For the rest, I was convinced that he could find me anywhere, but I could find him nowhere; for this reason I stopped all useless searching and waited for the promised day.

The splendor of my party and my behavior at it at first confirmed the very credulous inhabitants in their preconceived notion. It was soon learned from the newspapers, of course, that the whole fabulous journey of the King of Prussia had been a mere unfounded rumor. But I was a king once and for all, and a king I simply had to remain; and, moreover, I was one of the wealthiest and most royal kings there ever was. Only they did not really know which. The world has never had cause to complain of a lack of monarchs, least of all in our days. The good people, who had never seen one with their own eyes, guessed now this one, now that one, with equal success—Count Peter remained what he was.

Once there appeared among the resort guests a merchant who had gone bankrupt to enrich himself, who enjoyed general respect, and cast a broad, though somewhat pale, shadow. Here he wished to display the fortune that he had accumulated, and it even entered his mind to compete with me. I applied myself to my bag and soon had the poor devil at a point where, in order to rescue his reputation, he had to go bankrupt again and retreat beyond the mountains. In this way I got rid of him. I created many good-for-nothings and idlers in this region.

Amidst the royal splendor and squandering by which I made everyone subject to me, I lived very simply and in retirement in my house. I had made it a rule to observe the greatest caution; no one beside Bendel was to enter the rooms I inhabited, under any pretext whatsoever. As long as the sun shone I kept myself locked up there with him and it was believed that the count was working in his study. This labor was connected with the frequent couriers whom I sent out and received concerning every trifle. I received company only in the evening under my trees or in my drawing room, which was, under Bendel's direction, lavishly and skillfully illuminated. When I went out, on which occasions Bendel constantly had to watch me with the eyes of an Argus, it was only to the forester's garden and for the sake of her alone; for the innermost heart of my life was my love.

Oh, my good Chamisso, I will hope that you have not yet forgotten what love is. I leave much here for you to fill in. Minna was really a good, lovable, pious child. I had tied her whole imagination to myself. In her humility she did not know what she had done to deserve my interest in her, and she repaid love with love, with the full youthful power of an innocent heart. She loved like a woman, sacrificing herself completely, devotedly loving only him who was her life, unconcerned even if she herself should be destroyed; that is, she really loved.

But I—oh, what frightful hours—frightful and yet worth longing for again—I spent weeping on Bendel's shoulder when, after my first senseless intoxication, I reflected, looked at myself sharply, I without a shadow, who was destroying this angel with malicious selfishness, stealing this pure soul with lies. At such times I resolved to reveal myself to her; then again I vowed with solemn oaths to tear myself from her and to flee; and finally I broke into tears again and arranged with Bendel how I was to visit her in the forester's garden that evening.

At other times I deceived myself with great hopes of the impending visit of the unknown gray man, and wept again when I sought in vain to believe it. I had calculated the day on which I expected to see the frightful man again, for he had said in a year, and I believed him.

Minna's parents were good, respectable old people who loved their only child very much. The whole relationship took them by surprise when it was already in existence, and they did not know what to do about it. They had not dreamed that Count Peter could even think about their child, and now he actually loved her and was loved in return. The mother was probably vain enough to think of the possibility of a union and to work toward one; but the common sense of the old man left no room for such harebrained notions. Both were convinced of the purity of my love; they could do nothing but pray for their child.

A letter has fallen into my hands, which I still have from Minna from those days. Yes, it is her writing. I will copy it for you.

"I'm a weak, silly girl and I would like to think that my lover, because I love him deeply, deeply, would not hurt a poor girl like me. Oh, you are so good, so inexpressibly good; but don't misunderstand me. You must not sacrifice—or wish to sacrifice—anything for me; oh Lord, I could hate myself if you did that. No, you have made me infinitely happy, you've taught me to love you. Go thou forth! I know my fate, Count Peter belongs not to me but to the world. I'll be proud when I hear: that was *him*, and that was *him* too, and *he* did that; there they worshiped *him* and there they idolized *him*. Behold, when I think this, I am angry with you for forgetting your lofty destiny for a simpleminded child. Go thou forth, else the thought will yet make me unhappy, I who am so happy, so blissful through you. Have I not twined an olive branch and a rosebud into your life, too, as into the wreath that I was permitted to present to you? I have you in my heart, my beloved, do not fear to leave me—I shall die, ah, so happy, so unspeakably happy through you!"

You can imagine how deeply these words cut into my heart. I explained to her that I was not what people seemed to take me for; I was only a rich but infinitely miserable man. A curse rested on me, which was to be the only secret between her and me, because I was not without hope yet that the curse would be lifted. This was the poison of my life: that I might drag her down with me into the abyss, she who was the only light, the only happiness, the only heart of my life. Then she wept again because I was unhappy. Ah, she was so full of love, so good! To spare me but one tear, she would have sacrificed everything, and with what happiness!

However, she was far from interpreting my words correctly. She merely surmised that I was some prince upon whom a severe exile had been imposed, some lofty, outlawed brigand, and her imagination vividly pictured her lover in heroic colors.

Once I said to her: "Minna, the last day of next month may change and decide my destiny. If it does not, then I must die because I don't want to make you unhappy." Weeping, she hid her face on my breast. "If your destiny changes, just let me know that you are happy. I have no claim on you. But if you are wretched, then bind me to your misery so that I may help you to bear it."

"Darling, darling, take back those rash, foolish words which escaped your lips. Do you know this misery, do you know this curse? Do you know who your lover . . . what he . . . ? Don't you see me shuddering convulsively before you, hiding a secret?" She fell sobbing at my feet and repeated her request, swearing an oath.

The forest inspector entered and I declared to him that it was my intention to ask for his daughter's hand on the first day of the following month. I fixed that time because much might happen before then that could influence my destiny. Only my love for his daughter was unalterable.

The good man was properly frightened upon hearing such words from the lips of Count Peter. He threw his arms about me and then was quite abashed at having forgotten himself. Now it occurred to him to doubt, to weigh and to inquire. He spoke of a dowry, of security, of a future for his dear child. I thanked him for reminding me of this. I told him that I wished to settle in this region, where I seemed to be liked, and to lead a carefree life here. I asked him to buy the finest estates that were available in the country in the name of his daughter and to send the bill to me. In this way a father could best serve the suitor. This gave him much trouble, for everywhere some stranger had anticipated him, and so he only bought estates for about a million.

Occupying him in this way was basically an innocent stratagem to get him out of the way, and I had already used similar devices with him, for I must confess that he was something of a nuisance. The good mother, on the other hand, was a little deaf and not, like him, eager for the honor of entertaining the count.

The mother arrived and the happy people urged me to spend more of the evening with them. I dared not stay another minute: I already saw the rising moon half lighting the horizon. My time was up.

Next evening I went to the forester's garden again. I had thrown my cloak loosely over my shoulders and pushed my hat far over my eyes; I was walking toward Minna. As she looked up and caught sight of me, she made an involuntary gesture; once more there stood clearly before my mind the scene of that gruesome night when I had shown myself in the moonlight without a shadow. It was really she. But had she, too, recognized me now? She was silent and thoughtful. A hundred-pound weight lay on my chest. She threw herself on my breast weeping silently. I went.

Now I found her frequently in tears. My heart grew more and more somber, and only the parents swam in excessive bliss. The fateful day was approaching, fearful and dull as a storm cloud. The next to last evening was there and I could scarcely breathe any longer. By way of precaution, I had filled a few chests with gold and I sat up waiting for the twelfth hour. It struck.

Now I sat there, my eyes fixed on the hands of the clock, counting the minutes, the seconds, like dagger thrusts. At every sound I started. Day broke. The leaden hours crowded each other, midday came, evening, night; the handle of the clock moved, my hope faded; it struck eleven and no one appeared, the last minutes of the last hour came and no one appeared, the first stroke of the twelfth hour struck and I sank back on my couch shedding hopeless tears. Tomorrow I was to ask for the hand of my beloved—I who was permanently without a shadow. Toward morning an anxious sleep closed my eyes.

5

It was still early when I was awakened by voices raised in a violent altercation in my anteroom. I listened. Bendel refused access to my door, Raskal asserted adamantly that he would not take orders from the likes of him and insisted on getting into my room. The kind Bendel reproved him: such words, if they should come to my ears, would lose him his profitable job. Raskal threatened to lay hands on him if he barred the entry to me any longer.

I had half dressed, pulled the door open in anger and advanced on Raskal. "What do you want, you rogue?" He took two steps backward and answered quite coldly: "To ask you most humbly, Count, to let me see your shadow. The sun is shining so beautifully on the courtyard right now."

I stood there thunderstruck. It was a long time before I could speak again. "How dare a servant!" Calmly he interrupted me: "A servant can be a very honest man and not be willing to serve a man without a shadow. I demand to be dismissed." I had to pluck other strings. "But Raskal, dear Raskal, who put this unhappy idea into your head, how can you believe. . . ?" He continued in the same tone: "People are saying you have no shadow. Show me your shadow or give me my discharge."

Bendel, pale and trembling but more collected than I, made a sign to me. I tried gold, which soothes everything; but gold, too, had lost its power and he threw it at my feet. "From a shadowless man I take nothing." He turned his back on me and, whistling a ditty, with his hat on his head, went slowly out of the room. Motionless, my mind a blank, as if turned to stone, I stood there with Bendel, looking after him.

With a deep sigh and death in my heart I prepared to redeem my promise and to appear in the forester's garden like a criminal before his judges. I arrived in the dark arbor, which was named after me, and where she must have expected me this time too. The mother came toward me, carefree and joyful. Minna sat there, pale and beautiful like the first snow which sometimes kisses the last flowers in the autumn and at once melts into bitter water. The forest inspector was walking up and down excitedly, holding a written paper in his hand. He seemed to be suppressing many emotions which painted themselves on his normally impassive face in alternating flushes and pallor. He came up to me as I entered and in halting phrases asked to speak to me alone. The walk on which he invited me to accompany him led to an open, sunny part of the garden; I sat down silently on a chair and a long silence followed, which even the good mother did not dare interrupt.

The forest inspector was still storming up and down the arbor at an uneven pace. Suddenly he was standing before me, looking at the paper he had in his hand. He asked me with a searching look: "Is it possible, Count, that you are not unacquainted with a certain Peter Schlemihl?" I was silent.—"A man of excellent character and of special gifts—" He expected an answer.—"And suppose I were that man myself?"—"Who," he added vehemently, "has lost his shadow!" "Oh, my foreboding, my foreboding!" cried Minna. "Yes, I've known a long time, he has no shadow!" And she threw herself into the arms of her mother, who was terrified and clasped her convulsively to her breast, reproaching her for keeping such a secret to her own misfortune. But she, like Arethusa, had been transformed into a spring of tears, which flowed more copiously at the sound of my voice and burst into a storm at my approach.

"And you," the forest inspector began again furiously, "you have not hesitated, with unheard-of insolence, to deceive her and me; and you pretend to love the girl whom you have brought so low? See how she weeps and wrings her hands. Oh horrible, horrible!"

I had so completely lost control of myself that, talking as in a fever, I began: "After all, a shadow is nothing but a shadow; one can get along without it and it isn't worth raising such a fuss about it." But I myself felt so keenly what nonsense I was talking that I stopped of my own accord and he did not think I deserved an answer. I added: "What one has lost once, one can find another time."

He burst out angrily: "Confess, my dear sir, confess. How did you lose your shadow?" I had to lie again: "A rough man one day stepped so heavily on my shadow that he tore a big hole in it. I've merely sent it in for repairs, for gold can accomplish much; I was supposed to get it back yesterday."

"Good, my dear sir, very good!" the forest inspector replied. "You are courting my daughter. Others are doing the same. As a father it is my duty to look after her. I give you three days' time to look about for a shadow; if you appear before me within three days with a well-fitted shadow, you will be welcome. But on the fourth day—this much I can tell you—my daughter will be another man's wife." I wanted to say a word to Minna, but she clung tighter to her mother, sobbing more vehemently, and the mother silently motioned to me to go. I staggered away, feeling as if the world were closing behind me.

Separated from Bendel's loving care, I roamed through the woods and fields in confusion. The sweat of anxiety was dripping from my forehead, a hollow groan was wrung from my breast, madness raged within me.

I don't know how long this had lasted, when I suddenly found myself on a sunny heath with someone tugging at my sleeve. I stopped and looked about me. It was the man in the gray coat and he seemed to have lost his breath running after me. He began to speak at once: "I had announced my arrival for this day, but you could not wait. However, things can still be remedied. Take my advice, trade your shadow in again—it's at your disposal—and turn right back. You'll be welcome in the forester's garden and the whole thing will have been only a joke. I shall take care of Raskal, who betrayed you and who is courting your fiancée. The fellow is ripe."

I still stood there as though in sleep. "Announced yourself for today?" I reviewed the chronology again; he was right, I had been out by one day all the time. I searched for the little bag on my chest with my right hand. He guessed my intention and retreated two steps.

"No, Count, it's in good hands. You keep it." I looked at him with staring, wonder-filled eyes. He continued: "I ask for only a trifle as a memento. You will be good enough to sign this note." On the parchment were the words:

"By virtue of this, my signature, I bequeath my soul to the bearer after its natural separation from my body."

In mute astonishment I gazed alternately at the document and at the unknown gray man. I had scratched my hand on a thorn; from this scratch he caught a drop of blood on a freshly cut pen, which he now held out to me.

"But who are you?" I finally asked him. "What does it matter?" he replied. "And can't you tell from looking at me? A poor devil, a sort of scholar and doctor, who reaps poor thanks from his friends for excellent services, and has no other joy on earth except a bit of experimentation. But do sign. Down below at the right: Peter Schlemihl."

I shook my head and said: "Excuse me, sir, I'm not going to sign that." "No?" he repeated in astonishment. "And why not?"

"It really seems to me a bit risky to stake my soul on a shadow." "That so? That so? Risky," he repeated, and he broke into loud laughter. "And, if I may ask, what is this thing, your soul? Have you ever seen it, and what do you expect to do with it when you are dead? You should be happy that you have found an amateur who is willing to pay you while you are still alive for the bequest of this X, this galvanic force or polarizing effect or whatever else the silly thing may be, with something real, namely with your bodily shadow, through which you may obtain the hand of the girl you love and the fulfillment of all your wishes. Would you rather deliver the poor young creature to that rogue Raskal? No, you really must see it with your own eyes. Come, I'll lend you this vanishing cap here"—he pulled something out of his pocket—"and we'll make an unseen pilgrimage to the forester's garden."

I must confess that I felt very much ashamed at being ridiculed by this man. I hated him from the bottom of my heart, and it was this personal repugnance rather than principles or prejudices that kept me from buying my shadow, however much I needed it, with the signature he desired. Besides, the thought of undertaking the journey he proposed in his company was unbearable. It revolted my deepest feelings to see this ugly sneak, this sneering kobold, step mockingly between me and my beloved, between our two torn, bleeding hearts. I looked on what had happened as an act of fate, my misery as unalterable, and, turning to the man, I said to him:

"Sir, I have sold you my shadow for this little bag, which is in itself most excellent, and I have regretted it enough. Can the deal be canceled, in Heaven's name?" He shook his head and made a very gloomy face. I continued: "Then I will not sell you anything else that I possess, even if it is at the price of my shadow, and so I will sign nothing. I may conclude from this that the disguise you have invited me to assume would turn out to be incomparably more amusing for you than for me. So consider this a refusal, and since it just can't be otherwise, let us part."

"I regret, Monsieur Schlemihl, that you stubbornly reject the proposal I have offered you as a friend. However, I may be luckier another time. I'll see you again soon. By the way, do permit me to show you that I don't allow the things I buy to grow moldy, but respect them, and that they are well taken care of with me."

He promptly drew my shadow out of his pocket and, skillfully unfolding it, threw it on the heath, and spread it out at his feet on the sunny side in such a way that he walked between the two attendant shadows, mine and his; for mine had to obey him also, and direct and accommodate itself to his movements.

When I saw my poor shadow once again after such a long time, and found it being humiliated into doing such base service, I was in boundless distress. My heart was sore and I began to weep bitterly. The hated man strutted about with the plunder he had snatched from me and renewed his insolent proposal:

"You may still have it; one stroke of the pen and you will deliver poor, unhappy Minna from the claws of the rogue into the arms of the highly honored count. As I said, only one stroke of the pen." My tears flowed with renewed force, but I turned and beckoned to him to leave.

Bendel, who in great anxiety had followed my steps to this spot, appeared at this moment. When the faithful, good soul found me weeping and saw my shadow—for it was unmistakable—in the power of the gray stranger, he resolved at once to restore my property to me, even if it required force to do so. Since he did not know how to attack the delicate thing, he attacked the man himself with words, and without much questioning he ordered him peremptorily to let me have at once what belonged to me. Instead of answering, the man turned his back on the innocent boy and went. Bendel raised the buckhorn club he carried and, following on his heels, let him feel the full force of his sinewy arm accompanied by repeated commands to give up the shadow. The other bowed his head as if he were used to such treatment, arched his shoulders and silently went his way over the heath with calm steps, abducting both my shadow and my faithful servant. For a long time still, I heard the muffled sound echo through the wilderness, until finally it was lost in the distance. As before I was alone with my misfortune.

6

Left on the desolate heath, I gave rein to my boundless tears, relieving my poor heart of a nameless, anxious burden. But I saw no limits, no end, no goal to my excessive misery, and with especially grim fury I sucked at the new poison which the stranger had poured into my wounds. When I conjured up Minna's image in my mind and the beloved, sweet figure appeared to me pale and in tears, as I had last seen her in my disgrace, Raskal's phantom insolently and mockingly stepped between her and me. I hid my face in my hands and fled through the desert, but the ghastly phantom would not give me rest, but pursued me at a run, until I sank breathlessly to the ground and moistened the earth with a new spring of tears.

And all this for a shadow! And this shadow I could have regained by a stroke of the pen. I thought over the strange proposal and my refusal. I was desolate—I had lost all sanity and judgment.

The day passed, I stilled my hunger with wild fruits, my thirst in the nearest mountain stream. Night descended and I lay down under a tree. The damp morning awakened me from a heavy sleep, in which I heard myself panting as though in a death rattle. Bendel must have lost track of me and I was glad to think that he had. I didn't want to go back among human beings, from whom I had fled in terror like the frightened mountain game. In that way I lived for three anxious days.

On the morning of the fourth I found myself on a sandy plain on which the sun shone. I sat on some rocky ruins bathed in its rays, for I was now eager to enjoy the sight of the sun after being so long without it. Silently I nourished the despair in my heart. Then I was frightened by a gentle noise. Ready for flight, I cast my eyes about me but saw no one, except that a human shadow, not unlike my own, came gliding by me on the sunny sand; walking by itself, it seemed to have lost its master.

At that a mighty impulse stirred within me. "Shadow," I thought, "are you seeking your master? I will be he." And I leaped over to take possession of it; I thought that if I succeeded in stepping into its traces, so that it met my feet, it would remain attached to them and in time become used to me.

At my movements the shadow took flight, and I had to begin a strenuous hunt for the nimble fugitive; only the thought of being delivered from my fearful predicament supplied me with enough strength to pursue it. It was fleeing toward the forest some distance away, in whose shade I would surely lose it. As I saw this, terror shot through my heart, kindled my desire and gave wings to my feet. Clearly I was gaining on the shadow, I was gradually coming closer to it, I must reach it. Now it suddenly stopped and turned toward me. Like the lion at his prey, I sprang at it with a mighty leap, to take possession of it. Unexpectedly I met with hard, physical resistance. Invisibly I received the most violent blows in the ribs that it was ever the lot of man to feel.

The effect of my terror was to make me lower my arms convulsively and to press firmly whatever it was that stood invisibly before me. In the swift action I fell forward, stretched out on the ground; but below me, on his back, was a man, whom I held in my embrace and who only now became visible to me.

And now the whole phenomenon became intelligible to me in a very natural way. The man must have carried and then thrown away the invisible bird's nest which renders the person who holds it, but not his shadow, invisible. I peered about me and soon discovered the shadow of the invisible nest itself. I leaped up and seized the precious booty. Invisible and shadowless, I held the nest in my hands.

The man stood up swiftly, looked about for his successful conqueror, but on the spacious sunny plain saw neither him nor the shadow, for which he was especially searching. He had not had time to observe before this that I was without a shadow, nor could he have suspected such a thing. When he had convinced himself that every trace was lost, he turned his hand against himself in the greatest despair and tore his hair. But this treasure which I had gained gave me the opportunity and the desire to mingle among men once more. I lacked no pretexts for justifying my vile robbery, rather, I needed no such pretexts, and in order to avoid any such problem I hurried away, not looking back at the unfortunate man, whose anxious voice echoed behind me a long while. At least that is how all the circumstances of this event appeared to me at that time.

I burned with the desire to go to the forester's garden and learn for myself the truth of what the hated gray man had told me; but I did not know where I was. To get my bearings I climbed the nearest hill. From its peak I saw the nearby town and the forester's garden lying at my feet. My heart pounded and tears of another sort than those I had shed before came into my eyes: I was to see her again. Anxious longing hastened my steps down the best path. Unseen, I passed several farmers who were coming from the city. They were talking about me and Raskal and the forester; I wanted to hear nothing and hurried by.

I came into the garden, all the thrills of expectation in my heart. Something like laughter came toward me and I shuddered; I cast a swift glance about me, but I could discover no one. I went on; I thought I heard the sound of human steps near me, but I could see nothing and I believed my ears were deceiving me. It was still early, there was no one in Count Peter's Arbor, the garden was still empty. I roamed through the well-known paths and approached the house. The same sound pursued me more audibly. With an anxious heart I sat down on a bench in the sunny space opposite the house. I seemed to hear the unseen kobold sit down beside me with a mocking laugh. The key was turned in the lock, the door opened and the forester came out, holding some papers in his hand. I felt a sort of mist over my head. I looked about and—horror—the man in the gray coat was sitting near me, studying me with his satanic smile. He had pulled his vanishing cap over his head and mine. At his feet his shadow and mine lay peacefully alongside each other. He was playing carelessly with the familiar parchment he held in his hand and, while the forester was walking up and down the arbor, absorbed in his papers, he bent over confidentially and whispered in my ear:

"So you did accept my invitation and here we are, two heads sitting under one cap. Very good, very good. But now give me back my bird's nest. You don't need it any longer and you're too honest a man to want to keep it from me. But you needn't thank me, I assure you, for I was glad to loan it to you." He took it out of my hand without any resistance from me and put it in his pack, once more laughing at me so loudly that the forester looked about for the source of the noise. I sat there as though petrified.

"You will surely admit," he continued, "that such a cap is much more convenient. It covers not only the man but his shadow, too, and as many others as he wants to take with him. Look, today I have two more with me." He laughed again. "Mark this, Schlemihl, what you refuse to do voluntarily at first, you are finally compelled to do. I should think you'd buy the thing from me, take your fiancée back, for there is still time, and we'll let Raskal swing on the gallows. That will be easy, as long as there's no shortage of rope. Listen, I'll throw in my cap into the bargain."

The mother came out and the conversation began. "What's Minna doing?" "She's crying." "Simple child! The situation can't be altered." "Of course not. But to give her to another man so soon. Oh, my husband, you are cruel to your own child." "No, Mother, you see things in a false light. Even before she's through shedding these childish tears, she'll find herself the wife of a very rich and honored man, and she'll awaken out of her pain, comforted, as though from a dream, and thank God and us, you'll see." "Heaven grant it." "True, she has a considerable estate right now; but after the sensation caused by the affair with the adventurer, do you believe another match as suitable as this Mr. Raskal will turn up? He has property here in the country worth six millions, free from all encumbrances, paid for in cash. I have had the deeds in my own hands. He was the man who snatched everything from me; and besides, he has in his portfolio notes against Thomas John for about three and a half million." "He must have stolen a lot." "What sort of talk is this again? He saved wisely where others squandered." "A man who has worn livery." "Nonsense! And he has an impeccable shadow." "That's true, but . . ."

The man in the gray coat laughed and looked at me. The door opened and Minna came out. She was leaning on a maid's arm. Silent tears rolled down her beautiful pale cheeks. She sat in an easy chair which had been set up for her under the linden trees, and her father took a chair beside her. He took her hand tenderly and talked to her gently as she began to sob violently:

"You are my good, dear child, and you will be sensible too. You won't wish to sadden your old father, who wants only your happiness. I can well understand, dear heart, that you've been deeply shaken, you've miraculously escaped from your misfortune. Before we discovered this shameful deception you were deeply in love with this unworthy fellow. Look, Minna, I know it and don't blame you for it. I myself, my dear child, loved him too, as long as I took him to be a prominent man. But now you yourself realize how everything has changed. Why, every poodle has his shadow, and my only precious child shall marry a man. . . ? No, you're not even thinking of him anymore. Listen, Minna, now you're being courted by a man who is not afraid of the sun, an honored man, who is, to be sure, not a prince, but who owns ten millions, ten times more than you do, a man who will make my precious child happy. Don't answer me. Don't resist. Be my good, obedient daughter. Let your loving father care for you. Dry your tears. Promise me you'll give your hand to Mr. Raskal. Say it, will you promise me this?"

She answered in a faint voice: "I have no will, no further wish on earth. Let the will of my father be my fate." At that moment Mr. Raskal was announced and insolently joined the party. Minna lay in a swoon. My hated companion looked at me angrily and whispered to me swiftly, "And you can bear this? What substitute for blood do you have in your veins?" With a swift movement he scratched a slight wound in my hand; some blood flowed, and he continued: "Real red blood! Then sign!" I had the parchment and the pen in my hand.

7

I shall expose myself to your judgment, dear Chamisso, and not attempt to prejudice it in my favor. For a long time I have judged myself sternly, for I have nourished the gnawing worm in my heart. This earnest moment perpetually hovered before my mind, and I was able to face it only with a dubious eye, with humility and contrition. Dear friend, anyone who lets his foot wander frivolously from the straight and narrow path is led unexpectedly into other paths, which draw him downward, ever downward. In vain he sees the guiding stars shine in the sky; there is no choice left him, he must continue irresistibly down the slope and sacrifice himself to Nemesis. After the precipitate error which had put the curse on me, I had through love flagrantly forced my way into the destiny of another being. What was left for me but to jump blindly in to rescue where I had sown destruction, where swift help was demanded of me? For the final hour had struck. Don't think me so base, Adelbert, as to believe that any price demanded of me would have seemed too high, that I would have been stingy with anything I had, more than with mere gold. No, Adelbert; but my heart was filled with an unconquerable aversion for this mysterious sneak on crooked paths. Perhaps I was doing him an injustice, but all association with him was revolting to me. Here, too, as so often in my life, and as so often happens in history, an event took the place of an action. Later I became reconciled with myself. First I learned to respect necessity, and what is more substantial than the deed which has been done, the event which has occurred, which is the property of necessity? Then I learned to revere that necessity as a wise providence which permeates the whole great machine of which we are mere driving and driven wheels; what must be, must be; what was to happen, happened; and not without that Providence which I finally learned to revere in my own destiny as in those affected by mine.

I don't know whether to ascribe it to the tension of my mind under the stress of such powerful emotions, or to the exhaustion of my physical powers, weakend by unaccustomed starvation during the last days, or finally to the disturbing turmoil which the presence of this gray monster aroused in my whole being. In any case, as I reached to sign the paper, a deep swoon came over me and I lay for a long time as though dead.

The stamping of feet and cursing were the first sounds that reached my ears as I regained consciousness. I opened my eyes. It was dark. My hated companion was angrily busying himself about me. "Isn't this behaving like an old woman! Pull yourself together and do what you've resolved to do! Or have you changed your mind and prefer to whine?" I sat up with difficulty and looked silently about me. It was late evening. From the brightly lit forester's house festive music could be heard. Groups of people were walking along the garden paths. A few approached, engaged in conversation, and sat on the bench where I had been sitting. They were talking about the union, solemnized that morning, of the rich Mr. Raskal with the daughter of the house. So it had happened.

I brushed the vanishing cap from my head, so that the stranger promptly vanished, and, silently plunging into the deepest darkness of the bushes, I took the road through Count Peter's Arbor and hurried toward the garden gate. But, invisibly, my tormenting spirit pursued me with sharp words. "So, Monsieur with the weak nerves, this is the way you thank me for the trouble I've taken to look after you the whole day long. And I'm to act the fool in the play. Very well, you stubborn fellow, just you try to run away from me; we're inseparable. You have my gold and I, your shadow. That will leave neither of us in peace. Has anyone ever heard of a shadow abandoning its master? Yours will draw me after you until you accept it again with grace and I'm rid of it. What you have failed to do energetically and willingly, you'll have to make up for, only too late, in surfeit and boredom. One does not escape one's fate." He went on and on in the same tone. I fled in vain; he did not yield but was always there, talking sneeringly of gold and shadow. I was unable to be alone with my own thoughts.

I had taken a path to my house through streets empty of people. When I stood before it I could scarcely recognize it. Behind the shattered windows no lamps were lit; the doors were shut; there were no servants stirring within. Beside me the stranger gave a loud laugh: "Yes, yes, that's the way it is. But you'll find your Bendel at home indeed. Recently he was providentially sent home so tired that he's probably been guarding your house ever since." He laughed again. "He'll have tales to tell. Well then, good night for today. See you again soon."

I rang the bell repeatedly until light appeared. From inside Bendel asked who was ringing. When the good man recognized my voice, he could hardly control his joy. The door flew open and we stood weeping in each other's arms. I found him greatly altered, weak and ill; but then my hair had turned quite gray.

He led me through the desolate rooms to an inner chamber which had been spared; he brought food and drink, we sat down and he began to cry again. He told me that he had thrashed the lean man dressed in gray whom he had met with my shadow, so long and for such a distance that he himself had lost trace of me and had collapsed with weariness. Later, unable to find me, he had returned home, where the mob, at Raskal's instigation, had soon stormed the house, smashed the windows and satisfied its lust for destruction. That is how they had behaved toward their benefactor. My servants had scattered and fled. The local police had banned me from the city as a suspicious character and given me twenty-four hours to leave the region. Bendel was able to add much to what I already knew about Raskal's wealth and his betrothal. This villain, who had prompted all the mischief done to me here, must have known my secret from the beginning. Apparently, attracted by the gold, he had been able to force his way to me and, even at that early time, had procured a key to the safe full of gold, where he had laid the foundation for the fortune which he could now scorn to increase.

All this Bendel told me with frequent tears, and then wept to see me once more and to have me back again, and because, having long suspected to what state my misfortune might have reduced me, he saw me bear it calmly and resolutely. For this is the form which despair had taken in me. I saw my misery before me, gigantic, unalterable; I had shed tears until they would flow no more. Not another cry would be pressed from my heart; I now met my misfortune with bared head, cold and indifferent.

"Bendel," I began, "you know my lot. A severe punishment has been visited on me, not without former guilt on my part. You shall not, innocent man, tie your fate to mine any longer; I won't have it. I'm going to leave this very night. Saddle a horse for me. I'll ride alone. You stay here. I insist. There must be a few more chests of gold here. Keep them. I'll wander alone in the world. But whenever a serene hour smiles upon me again, and fortune looks upon me in reconciliation, I'll think of you loyally, for I have wept on your faithful breast in heavy, painful hours."

With a broken heart the honest fellow had to obey his master's last order, which pained his soul. I was deaf to his requests and entreaties, blind to his tears. He brought my horse, I pressed the weeping boy once more to my breast, leaped to the saddle and, under the cloak of night, left the grave of my life, heedless of what road my horse might take, for I had no further goal on earth, no wish, no hope.

8

I was soon joined by a pedestrian who, after walking beside my horse for a while, asked if I would let him put his cloak on my horse's back, since we were going the same way. I allowed him to do so in silence. He thanked me with easy grace for the slight favor, praised my horse, and took the opportunity to laud the fortune and the power of the rich and, I hardly know how, entered upon a sort of soliloquy, in which I was merely the audience.

He developed his views about life and the world and very soon turned to metaphysics, from which he demanded the solution to all riddles. He analyzed the problem with great clarity and went on to its solution.

You know, my friend, that I have clearly recognized, ever since I went through the school of the philosophers, that I have no aptitude for philosophical speculation, and I have completely abandoned this field. Since then I have left many things alone, have renounced the hope of knowing and understanding much and, as you yourself advised me to do, I have as far as possible followed the voice within me on the road it took, trusting my common sense. Now, this word artist seemed to erect, with great talent, a tight structure which rose by itself on its own foundation and stood up as though through an inner necessity. Only, I wholly missed in it the very thing I would most have liked to find; so the structure became for me a mere work of art, whose graceful compactness and perfection served to delight the eye alone. But I listened gladly to this eloquent man who had diverted my attention from my sufferings to himself, and I would cheerfully have yielded to him had he claimed my soul as well as my intelligence.

Meanwhile time had passed and imperceptibly the dawn had brightened the sky. Startled, I suddenly looked up and saw the splendid colors unfolding in the east, announcing the approach of the sun. Against it there was no protection at this hour, when shadows preen themselves at their full length; no rampart was visible in the open country. And I was not alone. I cast a glance at my companion and was startled again. It was none other than the man in the gray coat.

He smiled at my confusion and, without giving me a chance to speak, continued: "Do let our mutual interests unite us for a while, as is the custom in the world; we always have time to part. This highway along the mountain range is, after all, the only one you can sensibly take; though this may not have occurred to you, you must not go down into the valley, and you will want even less to return over the mountains from which you have come. This happens to be my road too. I see you already blanching before the rising sun. I will lend you your shadow for the time we are together, and in return you will put up with my presence. Since you don't have your Bendel with you any more, I'll serve you well. You don't like me, I'm sorry about that, but you can use me all the same. The devil isn't as black as he is painted. It's true you annoyed me yesterday, but I don't resent that today; and I have already shortened the way for you so far, you must admit that yourself. Why don't you try on your shadow once more?"

The sun had risen and people were passing us on the road, so I accepted his offer, though with inner revulsion. With a smile he let my shadow glide to the ground, and it soon assumed its place by the horse's shadow and merrily trotted along beside me. I felt very strange. I rode past a troop of country folk, who respectfully made way, their heads bared, before a man of means. I rode on and with eager eye and pounding heart looked down sideward from my horse at what had formerly been *my* shadow. I had now borrowed it from a stranger, from an enemy in fact.

The latter walked along beside me unconcerned, whistling some ditty. He on foot, I on my horse. I was seized with a dizziness, the temptation was too great, and I suddenly jerked the reins, dug my spurs into the horse and took a side road at full speed. But I did not take my shadow away with me, for, as I turned, it glided from the horse and waited on the road for its lawful owner. I had to turn back in shame; after he had finished his tune the man in the gray coat laughed at me, put my shadow back in place again, and informed me that it would only consent to cling to me and stay with me if I possessed it as my legal property. "I'm holding on to you by your shadow," he continued, "and you can't escape me. A rich man like you simply must have a shadow, there's no other way; your only fault is that you haven't recognized this before."

I continued my journey on the same road; all the comforts of life and even its splendors returned to me; I could move freely and easily now that I possessed a shadow, though it was only a borrowed one; and I inspired respect everywhere, the respect which wealth commands. But I had death in my heart. My strange companion, who announced himself as the unworthy servant of the richest man in the world, was extraordinarily helpful, exceedingly dexterous and skillful, the very model of a valet for a rich man; but he would not leave my side and talked incessantly, always manifesting the greatest confidence that in the end I would conclude the bargain about the shadow, if only to get rid of him. He was as much a nuisance to me as he was objectionable. I was really afraid of him. I had made myself dependent on him. After leading me back to the glory of the world from which I was fleeing, he clung to me. I had to suffer his eloquence and almost began to feel that he was right. A rich man must have a shadow in this world, and if I wanted to maintain the position which he had again seduced me into assuming, there was only one possible outcome. But on this point I stood firm; after sacrificing my love, after my life had turned stale, I was not going to sell my soul to this creature, even for all the shadows in the world. I did not know how it was to end.

One day we were sitting in front of a cave which is visited by tourists who travel in the mountains. You can hear the roar of subterranean rivers rising from boundless depths, and when you throw a stone, no bottom seems to check it in its reverberating fall. As he often did, the man in gray painted for me, with exaggerated imagination and the iridescent charm of the most brilliant colors, careful, detailed pictures of what I might achieve in the world by virtue of my little bag, if only I had my shadow in my power again. Supporting my elbows on my knees, I hid my face in my hands and listened to the perfidious fellow, my heart divided between his blandishments and the stern will within me. I could not last with such an inner cleavage and began the decisive struggle.

"You seem to forget, sir, that while I have allowed you to remain in my company under certain conditions, I have reserved full freedom for myself." "If you give the word, I'll pack up." This was his usual threat. I was silent. He sat down at once and began to roll up my shadow. I turned pale but let him go on. A long silence followed. He spoke first:

"You can't bear me, sir, you hate me, I know; but why do you hate me? Is it perhaps because you attacked me on the open highway and tried to rob me violently of my bird's nest? Or is it because you thievishly sought to snatch my property, the shadow, which you thought was entrusted to you on your honor alone? I for my part don't hate you for this; I find it quite natural that you should try to make the most of your advantages, cunning and force; besides, the fact that you have the very strictest principles and think like the very soul of honesty is a whim I have nothing against. In point of fact I don't think as strictly as you; I merely act as you think. Have I ever applied my thumb to your throat to take possession of your most valuable soul, which I happen to fancy? Have I ever let a servant loose against you to regain my bartered purse? Have I attempted to abscond with it?" I had no answer to this. He continued: "Very well, sir, very well. You can't bear me; I can understand that very well too, and I don't resent it. We must part, that's clear, and you, too, are beginning to bore me. To rid yourself completely of my humiliating presence, I advise you once more: buy the thing from me." I held the purse out to him: "At this price." "No." I gave a deep sigh and spoke again: "Well then. I insist upon it, sir, let us part; don't block my path any longer in a world which I trust has enough room for both of us." He smiled and replied: "I am going, sir, but first I want to inform you how you may ring for me if ever you should feel the need for your most humble servant. You need only shake your purse so that the everlasting gold coins in it jingle; the sound will attract me instantly. Everyone in the world thinks only of his own advantage; but you see that I am concerned with yours too, for I am obviously making new power available to you. Oh, this purse! And even if the moths had already eaten your shadow, that purse would still form a strong bond between us. Enough, you control me through my gold. Command your servant even from a distance; you know that I can show myself helpful enough to my friends, and that the rich are in especially good standing with me. You've seen this yourself. But your shadow, sir—let me tell you—will never again be yours save on one single condition."

Figures out of the old days appeared before my mind. I asked him quickly, "Did you have a signature from Mr. John?" He smiled. "With such a good friend it wasn't necessary." "Where is he? By heaven, I must know." He slowly put his hand in his pocket and from it dragged out by the hair the pale, crippled form of Mr. Thomas John; his blue, corpselike lips moved to form the heavy words: *"Justo judicio Dei judicatus sum; justo judicio Dei condemnatus sum."* (By the just judgment of God I am judged; by the just judgment of God I am condemned.) I was horrified and, swiftly throwing the ringing purse into the depths, I spoke my last words to him: "I beseech you in God's name, frightful man, get thee hence and never let me set eyes on you again." He arose morosely and promptly disappeared behind the masses of rock which formed the boundary of the savage, overgrown place.

9

I sat there without a shadow and without money; but a heavy weight had been lifted from my chest and I was serene. If I had not lost my love as well, or if I had had no guilt about the loss, I believe I could have been happy, but I did not know what to do. I searched my pockets and found a few more gold coins in them; I counted them and laughed. My horses were down below at the inn, and I was ashamed to return there; I had at least to wait for the sunset, and the sun was still high in the sky. I lay down in the shadow of the nearest trees and fell quietly asleep.

In a sweet dream, pleasant pictures merged into a merry dance. Minna, a wreath of flowers in her hair, floated past and gave me a friendly smile. The honest Bendel was adorned with flowers too, and hurried past with a friendly greeting. I saw many more figures and it seems to me I saw you too, Chamisso, in the distant crowd; a bright light shone but no one had a shadow, and what is stranger still, this did not look at all bad—flowers and songs, love and joy, under palm groves. I would neither detain nor interpret the mobile, lovely forms that flitted quickly by; but I know that I enjoyed dreaming this dream and took care not to awaken. I was really already awake, but still had my eyes closed in order to retain the vanishing forms a little longer.

I finally opened my eyes; the sun still stood in the sky, but in the east; I had slept through the night. I took this as a portent not to return to the inn. I lightly gave up the possessions I had there and decided to go on foot along a side road that led through the densely wooded base of the mountain, leaving Fate to decide what to do with me. I did not look behind me and did not think of turning to Bendel—whom I had left behind me a rich man—as I could, of course, have done. I reflected on the new character that I was to assume in the world. My clothes were very modest. I had on an old black Russian jacket I had worn in Berlin and which had turned up again on this journey, I don't know how. In addition I had a traveling cap on my head and a pair of old boots on my feet. I got up, cut a knotty stick at that spot as a memento of it and set off at once on my wanderings.

In the forest I met an old peasant, who greeted me in a friendly way and with whom I fell into a conversation. Like a curious traveler I inquired from him first about the way, then about the region and its inhabitants, the products of the mountains and so on. He replied to my questions talkatively and with intelligence. We came to the bed of a mountain stream which had spread desolation over a large strip of forest. I shuddered inwardly at the sunny expanse; I let the peasant precede me. But in the midst of the dangerous spot he stopped and turned around to tell me the story of this desolation. He soon noticed what I was lacking and broke off in the middle of his sentence: "But how does it happen that you have no shadow, sir!" "Alas, alas!" I replied with a sigh. "During a long, serious illness, I lost my hair, nails and shadow. You see, father, at my age, the hair that I have gotten back is quite white, and my nails are short, but my shadow still refuses to grow back." "Oh, oh!" the old man replied, shaking his head, "no shadow, that's bad. That was a bad illness you had, sir." But he did not resume his story and, at the next crossroad we came to, he left me without saying a word. Bitter tears once more trembled on my cheeks and my serenity was gone.

I continued my way with a sad heart, and no longer sought any man's company. I kept to the darkest forest. Sometimes I had to wait for hours at a sunny spot until there was no human eye to forbid my passage. In the evening I sought shelter in the villages. I was really making for a mine in the mountains, where I thought I would find work underground; for, apart from the fact that my present situation made it necessary for me to support myself, I had realized that only strenuous work could now protect me from my destructive thoughts.

A few rainy days helped me considerably on my way, but at the cost of my boots, whose soles had been made for Count Peter, not for the servant on foot. I was already walking on my bare feet. I had to get myself a pair of new boots. The following morning I attended to this business with due solemnity in a spot where there was a church fair, and where one of the booths had old and new boots for sale. I chose a pair and haggled about them for a long time. I had to give up the idea of a new pair, which I very much wanted; the high price frightened me off. I therefore contented myself with some old boots, which were still good and strong. The handsome, fair-haired boy who ran the booth handed them to me with a friendly smile in return for cash payment, wishing me luck on my way. I put them on at once and left the place by the northern gate.

I was deeply absorbed in my thoughts and scarcely saw where I set foot; for I was thinking of the mine, which I hoped to reach that evening, and where I did not really know how to announce myself. I had not gone two hundred feet when I noticed that I had lost my way; I looked about for it but found myself in a desolate, ancient pine forest, which seemed never to have been touched by an axe. I pressed forward a few more feet and saw that I was in the midst of desolate rocks, which were overgrown with moss and lichens and between which lay snow and ice fields. The air was very cold. I looked about me, the forest had vanished behind me. I took a few more steps; around me the stillness of death prevailed; the ice on which I stood extended as far as the eye could reach. A heavy mist hung over it; the sun stood bloody on the edge of the horizon. The cold was unbearable. I did not know what had happened to me; the congealing frost compelled me to hasten my steps, and I heard only the roar of distant waters; one step more and I was at the icy shore of the ocean. Countless herds of seals hurled themselves noisily into the waters. I followed this shore again; I saw naked rocks, land, forests of birch and pine; I continued straight ahead for some minutes more. I was stifling hot. I looked about me; I was standing under mulberry trees between beautifully cultivated rice fields. I sat down in the shade of the trees and looked at my watch; I had left the marketplace not more than fifteen minutes before; I thought I was dreaming and bit my tongue to wake myself; but I was awake. I shut my eyes in order to compose my thoughts. Before me I heard strange, nasal syllables. I looked up and two Chinamen, whose Asiatic features would have made them unmistakable even if I had utterly disregarded their clothing, addressed me in their native tongue with the traditional greetings of their country. I stood up and took two steps backward. I saw them no more; the landscape was totally altered: trees and forests instead of rice fields. I studied these trees and the vegetation around me; the ones I knew were southeastern Asiatic plants. Wanting to go up to one tree, I took a step and again everything was changed. I now marched like a recruit at drill and strode along with slow, measured steps. Strangely changing lands, fields, meadows, mountain ranges, steppes and dunes rolled past my astonished eyes. There was no doubt about it, I had seven-league boots on my feet.

10

I fell to my knees in mute devotion and shed tears of gratitude, for my future suddenly was clear to me. Cut off from human society by a youthful guilt, I had by way of compensation been thrown back on nature, which I had always loved. The earth had been given me as a rich garden; study was to be the direction and strength of my life, with science as its goal. It was not a resolve I made. What appeared before my inner eye then as a clear and perfect model, I have since then merely sought to depict faithfully with quiet, strict, unremitting diligence, and my satisfaction has depended on the congruence of what I have depicted with that model.

· I roused myself to take immediate possession of the field which I was to harvest in the future by making a rough survey of it. I was standing on the heights of Tibet, and the sun, which had risen a few hours before, was already setting in the evening sky. I wandered through Asia from east to west, overtaking the sun in its course, and entered Africa. I looked about curiously, measuring it repeatedly in all directions. In Egypt, as I was gazing at the old pyramids and temples, I saw in the desert, not far from Thebes and its hundred gates, the caves in which Christian hermits had formerly dwelt. Suddenly it struck me: here is your house. As my future abode I chose one of the most hidden caves, which was at once spacious, comfortable and inaccessible to jackals. Then I continued on my way.

I crossed over to Europe at the Pillars of Hercules and, after viewing its southern and northern provinces, I went from northern Asia over the polar glacier to Greenland and America, and roamed through both parts of that continent. The winter, which had already set in in the south, drove me north from Cape Horn.

I lingered until day came in eastern Asia and continued my wandering only after a period of rest. Through both Americas I followed the chain of mountains which constitutes the highest known irregularity on our globe. I walked slowly and cautiously from peak to peak, now over flaming volcanoes, now over snow-covered domes, often breathing with difficulty. I reached Mount St. Elias and jumped across the Bering Straits into Asia. There I followed the eastern coast in its manifold windings and studied with special attention which of the islands situated there were accessible to me. From the Straits of Malacca my boots carried me to Sumatra, Java, Bali and Lomboc; by way of the smaller islands and rocks which teem in this sea, I attempted, often in the face of danger but always in vain, to find a northwest crossing to Borneo and other islands of this archipelago. I had to abandon hope. I finally sat down on the extreme point of Lomboc and, my face turned toward the south and east, I wept as if I had firmly locked the gate of my prison, because I had reached my limit so soon. New Holland, that remarkable country, so essential for an understanding of the earth and its sunwoven cloak, of the plant and animal world, and the South Sea with its zoophyte islands, were forbidden to me; and so everything that I was to collect and cultivate was condemned from its very inception to remain a mere fragment. Oh, my Adelbert, how vain are man's efforts!

Often in the severest winter of the Southern Hemisphere I attempted to take those two hundred steps which separated me from Van Diemen's Land and New Holland, from Cape Horn westward by way of the polar glacier, quite unconcerned about my return, or whether that land should close over me like the lid of my coffin. I took desperate steps with foolish daring over the drifting ice and braved the cold and the sea. But all in vain. I have not been in New Holland to this day; I always came back to Lomboc and sat down on its extreme point and wept again, my face turned toward the south and the east, as though at the securely locked gate of my prison.

I finally tore myself away from this spot and went once more with a sad heart into the interior of Asia; I continued to roam through it, following the morning twilight westward, and arrived that very night at my predetermined house in the Thebaid, which I had touched the previous afternoon.

As soon as I had rested a little and it was day over Europe, I made it my first concern to procure everything I needed. First of all, brakes; for I had learned how inconvenient it was not to be able to shorten my steps in order to investigate nearby objects comfortably, except by taking off my boots. A pair of slippers over them did the job. Later on I even carried two pairs about with me, because I often threw a pair off when lions, humans or hyenas frightened me during my botanizing and I had no time to pick them up. My very good watch was an excellent chronometer for the short duration of my walks. In addition I needed a sextant, some instruments and books.

To obtain all these things, I took a few wretched walks to London and Paris, which were conveniently covered by fog. When the remainder of my magic gold was used up, I produced as payment some African ivory, which I easily found, though I had to choose the smallest tusks so as not to overtax my strength. I was soon provided and equipped with everything, and immediately began my new way of life as a private scholar.

I roamed about the earth, one time measuring its heights, another time, the temperature of its springs and of the air, now observing animals, or again investigating plants. I hurried from the equator to the pole, from one world to the other, comparing experience with experience. My usual food was the eggs of African ostriches or northern sea birds, and fruits, especially bananas and those of tropical palms. In lieu of happiness I enjoyed nicotianas, and in place of human bonds and sympathy, the love of a faithful poodle, who watched over my cave in the Thebaid and, when I returned to him laden with new treasures, leaped up at me in joy and gave me the human feeling that I was not alone on earth. One more adventure was to lead me back among men.

11

One day, when I was collecting lichens and algae on the shores of Norway, with the brakes on my boots, a polar bear unexpectedly came toward me from behind a rock. I threw my slippers away and was about to step on an island that lay before me; a naked rock projecting from the water formed a transition to it. I stepped firmly on the rock with one foot, but fell into the sea on the far side of it, because the slipper was still on that foot.

The intense cold gripped me; I survived with great effort. As soon as I was on land again, I rushed as fast as I could to the Lybian desert to dry myself in the sun. But the sun was so hot and beat so strongly down on my head that I staggered back north very ill. I tried to find relief in vigorous movement and ran with swift, unsteady steps from west to east and from east to west. I was in daylight at one moment, in the dark of night the next, sometimes in summer and soon in the cold of winter.

I don't know how long I staggered over the earth this way. A burning fever raged in my veins, and I feared that I was losing my sanity. My bad luck would have it that in my careless running about I stepped on someone's foot. I may have hit him; for I received a powerful blow and fell down.

When I regained consciousness, I was lying comfortably in a good bed among many others in a spacious and handsome room. Someone was sitting at my head; people were going through the room from bed to bed. They reached mine and talked about me. They called me Number Twelve, and yet on the wall at my feet there was certainly a black marble tablet—it was no illusion, I could read it clearly!—with large golden letters which spelled my name

PETER SCHLEMIHL.

On the tablet under my name there were two more rows of letters, but I was too weak to make them out. I closed my eyes again.

I heard something, in which Peter Schlemihl was mentioned, being read loud and clearly, but I could not grasp its meaning. I saw a very friendly man and a very beautiful woman in black appear before my bed. The forms were not alien to me, yet I could not recognize them.

Some time passed and I regained my strength. My name was Number Twelve, and Number Twelve was taken for a Jew because of his long beard, though he was cared for no less because of that. No one seemed to have noticed that he had no shadow. My boots, I was assured, were with everything that had been found on me when I was brought here; they were in good and secure custody and would be returned to me after my recovery. The place in which I lay ill was called the *Schlemihlium;* what was recited daily about Peter Schlemihl was an exhortation to pray for him as the founder and benefactor of this institution. The friendly man whom I had seen at my bed was Bendel; the beautiful woman was Minna.

I recovered in the *Schlemihlium* without being recognized and learned still more. I was in Bendel's native city, where he had built this hospital in my name with the remainder of my otherwise unlucky gold and supervised the place himself. Minna was a widow; a criminal trial had cost Mr. Raskal his life and most of her fortune. Her parents were no longer alive. She lived here as a devout widow, doing works of mercy.

She once had a conversation with Mr. Bendel at the bed of Number Twelve: "Why, noble lady, are you willing to expose yourself so often to the bad air here? Is it possible that Destiny is so harsh to you that you want to die?" "No, Mr. Bendel, ever since my long dream came to an end and I awoke to my true self, I have been satisfied; I no longer wish death, nor do I fear it. I think of past and future with serenity. Don't you, too, now serve your master and friend in a blessed way with a quiet, inner happiness?" "Thank Heaven, yes, noble lady. Things have gone strangely for us; we have heedlessly drunk much good and much bitter woe from the full cup. Now it is empty; now one would like to think that all of it was merely a rehearsal and that, equipped with true insight, one may expect the beginning of reality. The beginning of reality is something different; one does not wish the earlier hocus-pocus to return and yet, on the whole, one is glad to have experienced it. Also I am confident that things must be better for our old friend than they were then." "I too," replied the beautiful widow, and they went on.

This conversation had made a profound impression upon me; but I did not know whether to reveal my identity or to leave the place unrecognized. I made my decision. I asked for paper and pencil and wrote the words:

"Your old friend, too, is now better off than he was then, and if he is atoning, it is the atonement of reconciliation."

After this I asked permission to dress, as I felt stronger. They brought the key for the little closet that stood near my bed. I found in it everything that belonged to me. I put on my clothes, hung my botanical box, in which, to my joy, I found my northern lichens again, about my neck over my black Russian jacket, put on my boots, placed the note on my bed and, as soon as the door opened, I was already far on the road to the Thebaid.

As I was traveling the road along the Syrian coast which I had taken the last time on my way from home, I saw my poor Figaro coming toward me. This excellent poodle seemed to want to follow the track of his master, whom he may have long been expecting. I stopped and called to him. He leaped up at me, barking with a thousand touching expressions of his innocent, high-spirited joy. I took him under my arm, for of course he could not follow me, and brought him home with me.

I found everything in order and gradually, as I regained my

strength, I returned to my former occupations and to my old way of life. Except that for a whole year I kept away from the polar cold, which had become unbearable to me.

And so, my dear Chamisso, I live to this day. My boots do not wear out, as the very learned work of the famous Tieckius *De Rebus Gestis Pollicilli** had at first led me to fear. Their power remains unimpaired; only my strength is fading, but I am comforted by the fact that I have used it for a steady purpose and not fruitlessly. I have, as far as my boots would allow, explored more thoroughly than any man before me the earth, its shape, its elevations, its temperature, its atmospheric changes, the phenomena of its magnetic power, and the life on it, especially the plant kingdom. In several works I have noted and arranged the facts with the most painstaking precision and I have set down my desultory conclusions and views in a few treatises. I have established the geography of the interior of Africa and of the northern polar regions, of the interior of Asia and of its eastern coasts. My *Historia stirpium plantarum utriusque orbis*† stands as a large fragment of the *Flora universalis terrae* and as a part of my *Systema naturae*. I believe that I have not only increased the number of known species by more than a comfortable third, but have also contributed something to the knowledge of nature and the geography of plants. I am working very diligently at my fauna. I shall see to it that before my death my manuscripts are deposited with the University of Berlin.

And I have chosen you, my dear Chamisso, to be the trustee of my strange story, so that it may perhaps serve as a useful lesson for many of the earth's inhabitants when I have vanished. But you, my friend, if you want to live among men, learn to respect first your shadow, then your money. But if you want to live only for yourself and for your better self, oh, then you need no counsel.

Translated by Harry Steinhauer

---

* According to Ludwig Tieck's play *The Life and Deeds of Little Tom Thumb* seven-league boots carry the wearer one mile less every time they are repaired.

† The Latin titles mean respectively: *History of the Stems of Plants of Both Worlds; Flora of the Whole Earth; System of Nature*. Chamisso himself published a work entitled *Views on the Science of Plants and the Realm of Plants*.

The Story of Good Caspar and Fair Annie

Clemens Brentano

I t was early summer. The nightingales had just begun to sing, but on this cool night they were silent. The breath of distant storms was in the air. The night watchman called out the eleventh hour. Homeward bound I saw before the door of a large building a group of men, all sorts of young fellows, just out of the taverns, gathered about someone sitting on the doorsteps. The bystanders seemed to be showing such lively concern that I sensed some mishap and joined the group.

An old peasant woman was sitting on the steps. Despite the concern of the young men, she turned a deaf ear to all questions and good-natured suggestions. There was something rather uncanny, indeed something imperious, about the way the good old woman knew just what she wanted, the way she settled down to sleep under the open sky, as little abashed by her audience as though she were at home in her own bedroom. She threw her apron about her as a cloak, drew her big black lacquered hat down over her eyes, placed her bundle of belongings under her head and refused to answer all questions.

"What's the matter with this old woman?" I asked one of the onlookers. Replies came from every hand: "She's walked eighteen miles from the country, she's worn out, she doesn't know her way about the city, she has friends at the other end of town but doesn't know how to get there." "I was going to take her," said one, "but it's a long way and I don't have my housekey with me. Besides, she wouldn't know the house she's looking for."—"But she can't stay here overnight," interjected a newcomer. "She absolutely insists upon it," replied the first. "I told her right away I'd see her home, but she just talks nonsense; she must be drunk."—"I think she's simpleminded. At any rate, she can't stay here," repeated the former, "the night is cool and long."

During all this chatter the old woman, just as if she were deaf and blind, had calmly finished her preparations for the night. When the last speaker again stressed his point: "She certainly can't stay here," she replied in a strangely deep and earnest tone:

"Why shouldn't I stay here? Isn't this a ducal house? I'm eighty-eight years old, and the duke certainly won't drive me from his threshold. Three of my sons have died in his service and my only grandson has taken his leave.—God will surely forgive him, and I don't want to die until he lies in an honorable grave."

"Eighty-eight years old and walked eighteen miles!" exclaimed the bystanders. "She's tired and childish; you grow weak at that age."

"But, mother, you might catch cold here and take sick, and you'll be lonesome too," said one of the group, bending down to her.

The old woman spoke again in a deep voice, half-entreating, half-commanding:

"Oh leave me in peace and be sensible! I'm in no need of a cold, I'm in no need of being lonesome. It's already late, I'm eighty-eight years old, morning will dawn soon, then I'll go to my friends. If you're a believer and have a cross to bear and can pray, you can surely live through these few short hours as well."

The crowd had gradually dispersed, and the last ones still standing about now hastened away, too, because the night watchman was coming down the street and they wanted him to unlock their doors for them. I was the only one left. The street noises died away. I began pacing thoughtfully back and forth under the trees of the square lying opposite. The manner of the peasant woman, her positive, serious way of expressing herself, her self-reliance despite her years, which she had seen roll round in their seasons eighty-eight times: all this made it seem that she considered this long life only as a vestibule to a sanctuary. I was greatly moved. What were all the pangs, all the desires of my heart? Unmindful, the stars continue in their course. To what end did I seek meat and drink, and from whom and for whom did I seek them? Whatever I may strive for here, whatever I may love and gain, will it ever teach me to spend the night on a doorstep with as much composure as this good pious soul? And there await the morrow? Will I ever find my friend, as she is certain to find hers? Oh, I'll not even reach the city but collapse footsore and exhausted in the sands before the gates, or fall into the hands of robbers. Such were my thoughts. When I walked beneath the linden trees toward the old woman again I heard her praying aloud to herself with bowed head. Strangely affected, I stepped up to her and said: "Good mother, pray a little for me too!" With these words I tossed a silver thaler into her apron.

Perfectly composed the old woman said: "A thousand thanks, my dear Master, you have heard my prayer."

I thought she was speaking to me and said: "Mother, did you ask me for something? I wasn't aware of it."

The old woman started in surprise and spoke: "Good sir, do go home, say your prayers and lie down to sleep. Why are you roaming the streets at this hour? That is no good for young fellows, for the enemy goeth about and seeketh where he may seize upon you. Many a one has come to grief running around at such hours of the night. Who are you looking for? The Lord? He is in the hearts of men, if they are righteous, and not in the streets. But if you seek the enemy, rest assured, he's with you already. Just go home and pray to be rid of him. Good night."

With these words she quietly turned on her other side and put the thaler in her traveling sack. Everything the old woman did made a peculiar, serious impression on me. I addressed her again: "Good mother, what you say is true, but it's you that keep me here. I heard you praying and wanted to ask you to include me in your prayers."

"That's been done," she said. "When I saw you walking there under the lindens, I prayed God to give you good thoughts. Now have them and go to bed!"

Instead, I sat down on the steps beside her, grasped her withered hand and said: "Let me sit here with you through the night, and you tell me where you're from and what you're looking for here in the city. You have no one to stand by you, at your age one is nearer to God than to men. The world has changed since you were young."

"Not that I've noticed," she replied. "My whole life long I've found it pretty much the same. You are still young and at your age everything seems new and strange. I have lived and relived so much that I now look upon life only with joy, because God is so faithful in all things. But one should never turn goodwill away, lest the good friend fail to appear another time when he would be most welcome. Stay where you are, perhaps you can be of some help. I will tell you what has brought me these long miles into the city. I never thought I'd see this place again. Seventy years ago I served as a maid in this very house where I'm now sitting on the doorstep. Since then I've never been back. How time flies! Like the wink of an eye. How often I used to sit here of an evening seventy years ago waiting for my sweetheart, who was in the Guards. This is where we became engaged. If he—but hush, here comes the nightwatch."

Then she began to sing in a subdued voice, the way young girls and servants do on bright moonlit nights before the doors, and I listened with delight to this lovely old song from her lips:

> When the Judgment Day shall be,
> The stars will fall on land and sea.
> Ye dead, ye dead shall rise and meet
> To stand before the Judgment Seat.
> You shall there approach the height
> Where lovely angels sit so bright;
> God in His glory awaits you there,
> A beauteous rainbow round His chair.
> There those false Jews shall trembling stand
> Who gave our Lord into Pilate's hand.
> Tall trees shed a radiance round,
> By hardest stones hard hearts are ground.
> If you can say this simple prayer,
> Say it but once a day,
> Then the soul shall pass God's test
> When we enter heaven and final rest.
>
> > Amen.

When the watch approached the old woman exclaimed: "Oh, today is the sixteenth of May, everything's just the same, just like it was then, only they wear different headgear and don't have pigtails. What difference, if the heart is pure?" The officer of the watch stopped beside us and was just asking us our business here at this late hour when I recognized in him an acquaintance, the lieutenant, Count Grossinger. I explained the situation briefly, and he replied, singularly stirred: "Here's a thaler for the old woman and a rose too"—he was holding it in his fingers—"old peasants are fond of flowers. Tomorrow ask her to repeat the song so that you can write it down for me. I've searched far and wide for it and never come across a complete version." Then we parted, for from the nearby guardpost toward which I had accompanied him across the square the sentry called: "Who goes there?" As he turned to leave Grossinger told me he was in command of the guard at the castle and that I should look him up there. I went back to the old woman and gave her the rose and the thaler.

She seized the rose with touching impetuousness and fastened it to her hat, while in a soft voice and almost weeping, she recited:

> Roses the flowers on the hat I wear,
> If I had lots of money I'd have no care,
> Roses and my dear one.

I said to her: "Why, mother, you're growing quite merry," and she returned:

> Merry, merry,
> Reckless, very,
> Much did dare he,
> High did fare he,
> Then miscarry.
> Wherefore stare ye?

Then she said: "See, my friend, isn't it a good thing I stayed here on the doorstep? Everything's the same, believe me. Seventy years ago today I was sitting here. I was a bright young thing and liked to sing all kinds of songs. I was just singing the song about Judgment Day that I sang tonight, when the watch went by. A grenadier threw a rose into my lap as he passed—I still have the petals between the leaves of my Bible. That was the beginning of my acquaintanceship with my husband, God rest his soul! Next morning I wore the rose to church; he saw me there, and soon we were on good terms. That's why I was so pleased to get a rose tonight. It's a sign that I'm to come to him, and I look forward to that with all my heart! Four sons and a daughter have gone before me, day before yesterday my grandson took his leave—God help him and have mercy on him!— Tomorrow another good soul will leave me. But why do I say tomorrow, isn't it already past midnight?"

"The clock has indeed struck twelve," I replied, puzzled by her words.

"God grant her comfort and peace these four short hours to come!" said the old woman and fell silent, folding her hands. I too was silent, gripped by her words and her manner. But since the silence became prolonged and the thaler the officer had given her still lay in her apron, I said to her: "Put the thaler away, Mother, you might lose it."

"This one I'll not put away, I'll give it to my friend in her last great need," she replied. "The first one I'll take home with me tomorrow, it belongs to my grandson, he shall have the use of it. You see, he was always a splendid fellow, with a deal of pride in his person and in his soul—oh God, in his soul!—The whole long way to the city I prayed for him. The dear Lord will surely have mercy on him. Of the lads at school he was always the neatest and the most hardworking, but the astonishing thing was his sense of honor. His lieutenant always said too: 'If my squadron has any sense of honor, then Caspar Finkel's responsible.' He was a lancer. The first time he came back from France he had all kinds of fine stories to tell, but they always concerned honor. His father and his stepbrother served with the militia and were always quarreling with him about honor, for where he had too much of it, they had too little. God forgive me my great sin, I don't want to speak evil of them, everyone has his cross to bear; but my dear dead daughter, Caspar's mother, worked herself to death for her sluggard of a husband, and still she never managed to pay off his debts.

"So the lancer told his stories about the French, and when his father and his stepbrother tried to run them down he would say: 'Father, you don't understand, they have a great sense of honor!' Then the stepbrother would get nasty and say: 'How can you keep babbling to your father about honor? Wasn't he a corporal? He ought to know more about honor than a private like you!'—'Yes,' old Finkel would chime in, 'you bet I was a corporal and I let many an insolent fellow have a taste of the lash. If I'd had Frenchmen under me, they'd have felt it even sharper, with their sense of honor!' Remarks like these mortified the lancer. One day he said: 'I'll tell you a little story about a French sergeant that I like better. Under the last king corporal punishment was to be introduced into the French army. An order of the minister of war to this effect was proclaimed at a grand review in Strasbourg, and the rank and file heard it in grim silence. Now at the close of the ceremony a private overstepped some regulation and his sergeant was ordered to advance and administer him twelve blows. He had to obey this stern command. But when he was through he took the musket of the man he had beaten, placed the butt on the ground before him and discharged the piece with his foot. The ball pierced his brain and he sank down dead. The incident reached the ears of the king, who immediately ordered that corporal punishment be discontinued. There, father, was a man with a real sense of honor!'—'He was a fool,' said the brother. 'Eat your honor if you're hungry,' muttered the father. Then my grand-son took his saber and left the house and came to my cottage and told me everything and shed bitter tears. I couldn't cheer him up, and though I was somewhat taken by the story of the French sergeant, in the end I could only say to him: 'To God alone be honor!' I gave him my blessing, for his furlough expired the next day and he intended to ride a couple of miles to the place where a godchild of mine was in service on an estate. He thought a lot of this girl and wanted to see her once more.—They'll soon be united, if God hears my prayers. He has already taken his leave and my godchild will get hers today. I've already got her dowry together, there won't be any wedding guests but me." Here the old woman lapsed into silence and seemed to be praying. I was mulling over all kinds of thoughts about honor and wondering whether a Christian should consider the deed of the French sergeant noble. I wish somebody would clear me up on this point!

When the night watchman sang out one o'clock, the old woman said: "Two hours more! Oh, are you still there? Why don't you go home to bed? You won't be able to work tomorrow and you'll get into trouble with your employer. What is your trade, by the way?"

The idea of explaining to her that I was an author caused me some embarrassment. I couldn't say, "I am a scholar," without lying. It's a remarkable thing that a German always feels a bit ashamed to call himself an author *(Schriftsteller)*, and he is especially wary of using this term when speaking to the lower classes, because it so readily calls to their mind the scribes and Pharisees of the Bible. The term *Schriftsteller* has not been so generally accepted among the Germans as *homme de lettres* among the French. In France there exists a kind of authors' guild; in their works one sees more of a professional tradition and even hears the question: *Où avez vous fait votre philosophie?* (Where did you take your degree?). Well, a Frenchman does have more of a made man about him. But it isn't this un-German custom alone that makes it embarrassing to pronounce the word when they ask your occupation at the city gate. A certain inner shame makes us so reticent, the feeling that comes over those who barter in free spiritual capital, the immediate gifts of heaven. Scholars are less embarrassed than poets; for they as a rule have paid their tuition and are usually state officials. They split thicker logs or work in shafts where there's a lot of water to pump out. But a so-called poet is in a bad way, because he has generally played truant to climb Parnassus. And there really is something suspicious about a poet by vocation; perhaps if poetry were only one's avocation it would be a shade better. It's an easy matter to reproach the professional poet with the words: "Sir, every mother's son has some poetry in his makeup, just as he has a brain, heart, stomach, spleen, liver and so on, but he who feeds to excess, pampers or fattens one of these organs, and develops it at the expense of the others, or even goes to the length of making it a means of livelihood has cause to be ashamed of himself vis-à-vis the rest of himself. One who lives by poetry has lost his balance—an enlarged goose liver, no matter how delicate the taste, presupposes a sick goose." Everyone who does not earn his bread by the sweat of his brow must feel a measure of humiliation. And this humiliation is particularly keen when one is not completely bathed in ink and has to admit that he is a *Schriftsteller*. Such thoughts passed through my head as I pondered what my reply to the old woman should be. She was surprised at my hesitancy, looked me in the face, and said:

"What's your trade? I ask. Why don't you tell me? If it's not honest, then apprentice yourself properly: an honest trade has its own reward. I hope you're not a hangman or a spy who's on my trail. For my part, be what you will, just tell me who you are! If you were lounging about this way by day, I'd think you were a loafer or a do-nothing, a fellow who props himself against the wall, so as not to fall over from laziness."

At that a word came to me that might bridge the gap between us: "Good mother," I said, "I am a clerk."—"Well," she replied, "you should have said so right off. So you're a man of the pen. For that you need a good head, nimble fingers and a good heart. A clerk, eh? In that case you can write a petition to the duke for me, but one that will be sure to come to his notice and find favor with him, not just get shoved aside with a lot of others."

"Of course I can write a petition for you," I said, "and I'll take great pains to make it as forceful as possible."

"That's good of you," she replied, "God reward you for it. May you live to be older than I am and in your old age may God grant you such a calm spirit and such a lovely night with roses and thalers and also a friend to write a petition for you, if you need one. But go home now, my friend, get some paper and write my petition. I'll wait here one more hour, then I'm going to my godchild. You can go along, she'll be happy about the petition. Her heart is pure, but God's judgments are hard to understand."

After these words the old woman again fell silent, bowed her head and seemed to be praying. The thaler was still lying in her lap. She was weeping. "Dear mother, what's the matter?" I asked. "What's grieving you so? Why are you crying?"

"Why shouldn't I cry? I'm crying because of the thaler, because of the petition, everything. But what good does it do? The world is still much, much better than we deserve, and tears as bitter as gall are still too sweet. Just look at that golden camel over there, the apothecary's sign! How strange and glorious God has created everything! But we aren't mindful of it, and a camel like that can sooner pass through the eye of a needle than a rich man enter the kingdom of heaven.—But why are you still sitting there? Why don't you go get your paper and bring me the petition?"

"Good mother," I said, "how can I frame the petition, if you don't tell me what you want in it?"

"I have to tell you that? Then petition writing's not much of a trick," she replied, "and I'm not surprised that you were ashamed to call yourself a clerk, if I have to tell you everything. Well, I'll do my best. Put into the petition that two lovers are to be laid side by side and that one of them is not to be dissected but left so that his limbs are all together at the cry: 'Ye dead, ye dead, arise and meet to stand before the Judgment Seat!' " Then she began to weep bitterly again.

I had a foreboding that a great sorrow must be weighing on her but that with the burden of her years she felt it only at intervals. She wept, but without complaint; her words were always calm and dispassionate. Once more I begged her to tell me the full purpose of her mission to the city, and she replied:

"My grandson, the lancer, the one I told you about, was very fond of my godchild, as I mentioned, and was constantly talking to fair Annie—that's what they called her because of her smooth features— about honor. He kept telling her that she must cherish her honor and his too. As a result, the girl began to take on fine airs in her looks and dress. She was more delicate and better mannered than other girls of her class. Everything touched her more closely, and if a fellow clasped her a bit roughly at a dance or swung her higher than the bridge of the bass fiddle, she would come to me in tears, always saying that it offended her honor. Oh, Annie was always a peculiar girl. Sometimes, before anyone knew what was going on, she would grab her apron with both hands and tear it from her body, as though it were afire, and then burst into terrible tears. But there was a reason for that: teeth were tearing at her, the fiend never rests. If only the girl had not been possessed with honor and had put stronger trust in our dear Lord, never abandoning Him in all her tribula tions, and borne shame and contempt for His sake, instead of laying such store by worldly honor! The Lord would have had mercy. He still will. Oh, they will surely meet again. God's will be done!

"The lancer had returned to France. He had not written for a long time and we almost gave him up for dead and often wept for him. But he was lying in a hospital recovering from a dangerous wound, and when he returned to his squadron and was made a noncommis-sioned officer, he remembered that two years before his stepbrother had insulted him, calling him nothing but a private, while his father was a corporal. He also thought of the story of the French sergeant, and how he had talked to Annie so much about honor when he left home. Then he had no more peace; he became homesick, and when his captain asked him what was bothering him, he said: 'Sir, I feel as though I was being drawn home by teeth!' They gave him leave to ride home on his horse, for all the officers trusted him. He got a three-month furlough and was to return with the remounts. He hastened as fast as he could without harming his mount, which he took better care of than ever because it was entrusted to him. One day he was feeling terribly anxious to get home. It was the day before the anniversary of his mother's death, and he seemed to see her running along in front of his horse, crying: 'Caspar, do me the honor!' Ah, that very day I was sitting alone beside her grave and thinking: if only Caspar were here too! I had made a wreath of forget-me-nots and hung them on the sunken cross. I measured the space round about and thought to myself: 'I'd like to lie here, and Caspar shall lie there, if God grants him a grave at home. Then we'll all be together when the call comes: "Ye dead, ye dead, arise and meet to stand before the Judgment Seat!" ' But Caspar didn't come, and I didn't know he was so close and could have come. He felt a great urge to hasten there, for in France he had often thought about this day and had brought along a wreath of marigolds to decorate his mother's grave, and also a wreath for Annie that she was to keep against her day of honor."

Here the old woman grew silent and shook her head; but when I repeated her last words: "that she was to keep against her day of honor," she continued: "Who knows, perhaps they'll grant it to me still. Oh, if I could only wake the duke!" "Why?" I asked. "What do you want with him, Mother?" She answered earnestly: "Oh, what would there be to life if it didn't end; what would there be to life if it weren't eternal!" Then she went on with her story:

"Caspar could easily have been in our village by noon, but that morning the innkeeper had pointed out to him that his mount had a saddle sore and said: 'My friend, that does a horseman no honor.' Caspar felt deeply the justice of these words, loosened the girth and treated the wound, then continued his journey on foot, leading his horse. Late in the evening he arrived at a mill some three miles from our village. The miller was an old friend of his father. He put up there for the night and was received as a welcome guest from foreign parts. Caspar led his horse into the stable, put the saddle and his knapsack in a corner and went into the living room. He asked the miller about his family and was told that I, his old grandmother, was still alive and that his father and stepbrother were well and prospering. Yesterday they had brought grain to the mill. The father had taken to trading in horses and oxen and was doing well. As a result, he now had some regard for his honor and didn't go around so patched and ragged any more. Caspar was much pleased to hear that. When he asked about fair Annie, the miller said he didn't know her, but if he meant the girl who had been a servant at Rose Farm, she, so he'd heard, had taken service in the city, because she could get more experience there and there was more honor connected with it. A hand at Rose Farm had told him this a year ago. This also pleased Caspar, and though he was sorry he wouldn't get to see her right away, he hoped to find her in the city soon, pretty and neat, so that it would be a real honor for him, a corporal, to go walking with her of a Sunday.

"Then he told the miller a number of things about France, they ate and drank together, Caspar helped him pour grain in the hopper, then the miller took him upstairs to bed, while he himself lay down on some grain sacks below. The clatter of the mill and his longing to be home kept Caspar, weary as he was, from sleeping soundly. Restless, he thought of his dead mother and of fair Annie and of the honor that would be his when he returned to his family as a corporal. At last he dropped into a light slumber, but often sat up with a start out of disturbing dreams. Several times it seemed to him that his dead mother came up to him, wringing her hands and begging for help. Then he thought that he had died and was being buried, but that he himself was walking along as a corpse in his own funeral procession, fair Annie at his side. He wept bitterly that his comrades did not accompany him, and when he got to the churchyard he saw that his grave was beside his mother's. Annie's grave was there too, and he gave Annie the wreath he had brought for her and hung the wreath for his mother on the cross over her grave. Then he looked around and saw nobody there but me and Annie. Someone had grabbed her by the apron and pulled her into her grave. He then climbed into his grave and asked: 'Is there no one here who will do me the last honors and shoot into my grave, as becomes a brave soldier?' Then he drew his pistol and shot himself into the grave.

"At the report of the shot he started up in great fright; it seemed to him he heard the windows rattle. He peered about the room, then he heard another shot, then a tumult in the mill and cries through its clatter. He jumped out of bed and seized his saber. At that moment his door opened and he saw in the full moonlight two men with blackened faces rushing at him with raised cudgels. He defended himself and struck one of them a blow on the arm. Both fled, bolting the door, which opened outwards, behind them. Caspar tried in vain to pursue them. Finally he managed to kick out a panel of the door. He crept through the hole and ran down the stairs, where he heard the miller whimpering as he lay tied and gagged among the sacks of grain. Caspar released him and rushed to the stable to look after his horse and knapsack. Both were gone. In great anguish he hurried back to the miller and lamented his misfortune: all his belongings were gone, the mount entrusted to him had been stolen. It was this that drove him to distraction. But the miller showed him a big bag of money he had fetched from a cupboard in the upper room and said: 'Be content, Caspar, I owe it to you that I didn't lose all my savings. The robbers had laid their plans to make off with this money, which was in your room. I owe everything to your brave defense; I have lost nothing. The ones that took your horse and knapsack must have been lookouts; they fired warning shots because they probably realized when they saw your equipment that I had a cavalryman in the house. You'll not come to grief if I can help it. I'll spare no money and no pains to find your mount again and if I can't, I'll buy you another, cost what it may.' Caspar replied: 'I don't want any presents, that's against my honor, but if you'll advance me seventy thalers, I'll give you my note to return the sum in two years.' This was agreed. The lancer took his leave and hastened toward his village to report the matter to a magistrate who represented the local gentry. The miller stayed behind to wait for his wife and son who had gone to a wedding in the vicinity. As soon as they returned he meant to follow the lancer and make his statement to the magistrate also. You can well imagine, my dear Mr. Clerk, with what a heavy heart poor Caspar hastened on his way to our village, on foot and poor, when it had been his aim to ride in proudly. He had been robbed of fifty-one thalers he had gained as booty, of his patent as a noncommissioned officer, of his furlough and the wreaths for his mother's grave and for fair Annie. He was desperate. In this state of mind he arrived in the village at one o'clock in the morning and immediately knocked at the door of the magistrate, who lives in the first house as you come in. He was admitted and made his deposition, listing all that had been stolen from him. The magistrate advised him to go at once to his father, who was the only peasant in the place who kept horses. He could then patrol the region with his father and his stepbrother, to see if they could find some trace of the robbers. Meanwhile he, the magistrate, would send others out on foot and question the miller for any further evidence. Caspar left for his father's farm. His way led past my cottage and through the window he heard me singing a hymn. I hadn't been able to close an eye for thinking of his dear, dead mother, so he tapped on my window and said: 'Praise be to Jesus Christ, dear Grandmother, Caspar is here.' Oh, how those words struck me to the marrow. I ran to the window, opened it, and kissed him and embraced him with endless tears. He hurriedly told me his misfortune and mentioned the magistrate's commission to his father, which had to be carried out at once. The sooner they got on the trail of the thieves, the better, for his honor depended on the recovery of his mount.

"That word 'honor' made me tremble—I knew the trials he would have to face. 'Do your duty, and to God alone be honor!' I said, and he left me to hurry away to Finkel's farm at the other end of the village. When he was gone I sank to my knees and prayed God to protect my Caspar. Oh, I prayed with such fervor as never before and said over and over: 'Lord, thy will be done, on earth as it is in heaven.'

"Caspar ran to his father's place filled with terrible anxiety. He climbed over the garden wall, heard the creaking of the pump, a neighing in the stall. His blood ran cold. He stood stock-still. By the light of the moon he saw two men washing themselves at the pump and thought his heart would break. One of them said: 'This confounded stuff won't come off!' The other said: 'Let's go into the stall first and bob the nag's tail and cut its mane. Did you bury the knapsack deep enough in the manure pile?'—'Yes,' replied the other. Then both went into the stable, and Caspar, mad with grief, rushed up, locked the stable door behind them and cried: 'Surrender in the name of the duke! If you resist, I'll shoot!' He had caught his father and stepbrother as horse thieves. 'My honor, my honor's gone!' he cried, 'I'm the son of a horse thief!' When the two heard these words they had a sinking feeling. 'Caspar, dear Caspar,' they called, 'for God's sake don't bring ruin upon us! We'll give back everything, Caspar. For your dear mother's sake, who died this day, have mercy on your father and brother!' But Caspar was desperate. He kept crying out: 'My honor, my duty!' Then, when they tried to force the door and were kicking a hole in the clay wall in an attempt to escape, Caspar fired his pistol into the air and shouted: 'Help,

help, thieves, help!' The peasants that the magistrate had roused out of bed were just coming up in order to make plans as to how best to pursue the men who had broken into the mill. At the sound of the shot and the cries they rushed to the scene. Old Finkel was still pleading with his son to open, but Caspar said: 'I am a soldier and must act as the law demands.' The magistrate came up, followed by the peasants. Caspar cried: 'God's mercy, sir, my own father, my brother are the thieves. Oh, I wish I had never been born! I've locked them in the stable, my knapsack's buried in the manure pile.' The peasants ran into the stable, bound old Finkel and his son and dragged them to the house. Caspar dug up his knapsack, took out the two wreaths, but didn't go into the house. He went to the churchyard to his mother's grave. It was just getting light. I had been out in the meadow and bound two wreaths of forget-me-nots for Caspar and myself. I thought: 'We'll decorate his mother's grave together when he comes back from his ride.' Then I heard all sorts of strange noises in the village, and since I don't like a hubbub and prefer to be alone, I went around the village toward the churchyard. I heard a shot, saw smoke curling up, and hurried to the churchyard.—Oh Lord of Heaven, have mercy on him! Caspar lay dead on his mother's grave. He had put a bullet through his heart. He had shot himself through the wreath he had brought for Annie, which he had fixed on a button over his heart. The wreath for his mother he had already hung on her cross. I felt as though the earth were yawning under my feet when I saw him. I threw myself on his lifeless body and kept crying out: 'Oh Caspar, my poor boy, what have you done? Who told you the extent of your misery? Oh, why did I let you go before I had told you everything? What will your poor father, your brother say when they find you like this?' I didn't know he had taken this step on account of them; I thought he had a quite different reason. But there was worse in store. The magistrate and the peasants brought old Finkel and his son bound with ropes. Misery made me dumb, I couldn't utter a sound. The magistrate asked me whether I had seen my grandson. I pointed to where he lay. He went up to him; he thought he was crying on his mother's grave. He shook him and blood gushed from his wound. 'Jesus and Mary!' he cried, 'Caspar has done away with himself!' At these words the two prisoners looked at each other in horror. They took up Caspar's body and carried it along beside his father and brother to the magistrate's house. The whole village was filled with lamentation. Some peasant women led me along after the others. Oh, that was the most terrible walk of my life!"

The old woman again fell silent and I said to her: "Good Mother, your sorrow is great, but God loves you. Those he tries most sorely are his dearest children. Tell me now, what induced you to make the long journey here, and what is the purpose of your petition to the duke?"

"Oh, you must know by now," she said calmly. "To get an honorable grave for Caspar and fair Annie. This wreath I brought with me for her day of honor—it's all drenched with Caspar's blood, just look!"

She drew a little wreath of gold tinsel out of her bundle and showed it to me. By the faint light of dawn I could see that it was blackened by powder and splattered with blood.

My heart ached at the misfortune of this good old woman, and the dignity and steadfastness with which she bore it filled me with awe. "Oh, dear mother," I said, "how will you tell poor Annie the extent of her misery in such a way that she doesn't sink down dead with fright? And what kind of a day of honor is that for which you are bringing her this woeful wreath?"

"Good sir," she said, "you just come along with me, you can go with me to her. I can't walk very fast, so we'll reach her just in time. On the way I'll tell you everything."

Then she rose, said her morning prayer with great composure, and arranged her clothing. She hung her bundle on my arm. It was two o'clock in the morning, day was just beginning to break as we walked through the quiet streets.

"You see," she continued her story, "when Finkel and his son were locked up, the magistrate summoned me to his court. Caspar's body was laid on a table, covered with his lancer's cloak, and carried into the room, and I had to tell the justice all I knew about him, and what he had said to me that morning at the window. Every word of mine went down on paper. Then he looked through the notebook they had found on Caspar. There were various records of expenses in it and several stories about honor, including the one about the French sergeant, and just after it something written in pencil." Here the old woman handed me the notebook; I read these last words of the unhappy Caspar:

"I too cannot outlive my disgrace. My father and brother are thieves, they have even robbed me. It broke my heart, but I had to turn them over to the law, for I am a soldier of my sovereign and my sense of honor allows me no leniency. I have given my father and my brother over to vengeance for honor's sake. Oh, may everyone pray that I may be granted an honorable burial here next to the grave of my mother, where I have fallen. I ask my grandmother to send fair Annie the wreath through which I shot myself, and my greetings too. I am sorry for her from the bottom of my heart, but she must not marry the son of a thief, for she has always held honor dear. Sweet fair Annie, I hope you won't take my death too hard; it has to be, and if you were ever a little fond of me, don't speak evil of me now! My disgrace is not my doing. I tried so hard all my life to live honorably. I was already a noncommissioned officer and had a fine reputation in my company. I would surely have become an officer one day, and Annie, truly I would not have left you to court some grand lady—but the son of a horse thief, one who for honor's sake must hand his own father over to the law for judgment, cannot outlive his disgrace. Annie, dear Annie, do accept the little wreath; I have always kept faith with you, as God is my witness! I give you back your freedom, but do me the honor never to marry anyone who might be considered inferior to me. And if it is in your power, intercede for me that I may have an honorable burial beside my mother, and should you die in the village, ask that your grave be beside ours. My good grandmother will come to us too, then we'll all be together. I have fifty thalers in my knapsack; have them put out at interest for your first child. The pastor is to have my silver watch, if I receive an honorable burial. My horse, my uniform, and my arms belong to the duke; the notebook is for you. Farewell, my dear sweetheart, farewell, dear grandmother! Pray for me, and to all farewell—God have mercy upon me—my despair is great!"

I could not read these last words of an assuredly noble and afflicted human being without shedding bitter tears.—"Caspar must have been a very good person, mother," I said to the old woman. She stopped and pressed my hand, then said, deeply moved: "Yes, he was the best person on earth. But he shouldn't have written those last words about despair; they'll cheat him of his honorable burial, they'll put him on the dissecting table. Oh, dear Mr. Clerk, if you could only help us in this!"

"How, dear mother?" I asked. "What can these last words matter?"—"Oh, they do," she replied, "the magistrate told me so himself. An order has gone out to all the courts: only suicides out of melancholy are to have an honorable burial, those who lay hand on themselves out of despair are to be sent to the dissecting table, and the magistrate told me he'd have to send Caspar there, because he had admitted his despair in so many words."

"That's certainly a strange law," I said, "for in the case of every suicide a suit could be brought as to whether it arose from melancholy or despair, and that could last so long that the judge and the lawyers would themselves fall into melancholy or despair and end up on the dissecting table. But cheer up, mother, our duke is a kind and just ruler; if the matter is brought to his attention, he'll certainly allow Caspar a place beside his mother."

"God grant it!" she replied. "You see, dear sir, when the magistrate had noted down all the evidence, he gave me the notebook and the wreath for fair Annie, and so I walked all the way yesterday to bring her this comfort on her day of honor. Caspar died just in time; if he had known everything, he would have gone mad with grief."

"Well, what is this now about fair Annie?" I wanted to know. "First you say she has only a few more hours, then you speak of her day of honor, and say she'll be comforted by your sad news. Tell me straight out: is she marrying someone else, is she dead, is she ill? I have to know everything so that I can put it in the petition."

To this the old woman replied: "Oh, my dear Mr. Clerk, these are the facts, God's will be done! You see, when Caspar returned I wasn't as happy as I might have been; when he took his life I wasn't as sad as I should have been. I couldn't have survived if God in His mercy had not sent me a greater sorrow. It was a stone placed before my heart like an icebreaker piling before a bridge, and the sorrows rushing upon me like ice floes would surely have torn my heart away, but they broke against the stone and drifted coldly by. I'll tell you something very sad:

"When my godchild, fair Annie, lost her mother—she was a cousin of mine who lived twenty miles away—I was taking care of the sick woman. She was the widow of a poor peasant. In her youth she had loved a gamekeeper, but had rejected him because of his wild ways. The gamekeeper finally came to such a pass that he was jailed for murder and sentenced to death. The news reached my cousin on her sickbed and grieved her so deeply she grew worse every day. When she at last came to die she entrusted her dear fair Annie to me as my godchild and said with her parting breath: 'Dear Anne Margret, when you pass through the town where the gamekeeper is imprisoned send a message to him through the jailer that on my deathbed I entreat him to turn to God, and that in my last hour I have prayed for him and send him greetings.'—Soon after these words she died, and when she had been buried I took little Annie—she was three then—on my arm and started home.

"At the edge of the town I had to pass through I came to the house of the headsman, and because he was also famous as a veterinary our burgomaster had asked me to pick up some medicine for him. I went in and told him what I wanted and he told me to come with him to the attic where he kept his store of herbs and help him select. I left little Annie below in the living room and followed him to the attic. When we came back down the child was standing before a little cupboard on the wall and kept saying: 'Grandma, there's a mouse in there! Listen! There's a mouse in there!'

"At these words the headsman looked very serious. He tore open the cupboard and said: 'God have mercy on us!' for he saw his headsman's sword, which hung by itself in the cupboard, swaying to and fro. He took down the sword and I shuddered. 'Good woman,' he said, 'as you love your dear little Annie, don't be frightened if I take my sword and scratch the skin a bit all around her neck, for the sword swayed in her presence, it wanted her blood, and if I don't scratch her neck with it, great misery will befall the child.' He took hold of the girl; she began to cry terribly. I too cried out and clasped her to me. At that moment the local burgomaster came in. He was returning from the hunt and had brought a sick dog to be treated. He wanted to know the cause of the outcry. Annie screamed: 'He's going to kill me!' I was beside myself with horror. The headsman told the burgomaster what had happened. The latter reproved him sharply for his superstition, as he called it, and added some strong threats. But the headsman remained calm and only said: 'That's what my forefathers did, and that's what I do.' The burgomaster answered: 'Master Franz, if you thought that your sword moved because I was giving you notice, as I do herewith, that tomorrow morning at six you are to behead the gamekeeper Jürge, then I could see some reason in it, but when you draw conclusions regarding this child, that's senseless and crazy. A thing like that could drive a person to despair, if one found out later in life that it had occurred in one's childhood. Lead no one into temptation.'—'Nor any headsman's sword,' said Master Franz to himself, and hung the sword back in the cupboard. Then the burgomaster kissed little Annie and gave her a breadroll from his hunting pouch. He asked me who I was, where I came from, and where I was going. When I told him about the death of my cousin and her message to the gamekeeper Jürge, he said to me: 'You can deliver the message in person. I'll take you to him myself. He has a hard heart, it may be that the memory of that good woman who thought of him before she died will move him in his final hours.' The good gentleman then took us in his cart to his house.

"He told me to go into the kitchen, where we had a good meal, and toward evening he led me to the condemned man. When I told the gamekeeper my cousin's last words, he began to shed bitter tears and cried out: 'Oh God, if she had become my wife, I would never have ended like this!' Then he asked to see the pastor again, he wanted to pray with him. The burgomaster promised to send for him, praised Jürge for his change of heart and asked whether he had any last wish he could fulfill for him. The gamekeeper said: 'Yes, please beg this good old mother to be present tomorrow at my execution and to bring the little daughter of her deceased cousin with her. That will give me strength in my last hour.' When the burgomaster repeated to me this request, I couldn't refuse the miserable soul, as gruesome to me as it was. I had to give him my hand and make a solemn promise, then he sank back weeping on his straw. The burgomaster took me to his friend, the pastor, and I had to tell him the whole story before he visited the jail.

"I spent the night at the burgomaster's house. The next morning I took the hard road to the place of execution. I stood in the circle beside the burgomaster and watched him break the little staff. Then Jürge made a fine parting speech, all the people wept, and he looked at me and little Annie, who was standing in front of me, deeply moved. Then he kissed Master Franz, the pastor prayed with him, they blindfolded his eyes, and he knelt down. The headsman gave him the deathblow. 'Jesus, Mary and Joseph!' I screamed, for Jürge's head had flown right toward Annie and seized the child's apron with its teeth. She was shrieking with fear. I tore off my own apron and threw it over the grisly head. Master Franz ran up, tore the head loose and said: 'Mother, mother, what did I tell you yesterday? I know my sword, it's alive!'—I had sunk to the ground with fright; little Annie never stopped screaming. The burgomaster was quite unnerved and had me and the child driven to his house, where his wife gave us a change of clothing. That afternoon he gave us some money, and many people of the town, who were curious to see the girl, did likewise, so I came away with twenty thalers and many clothes for her. In the evening the pastor came and preached me a sermon about how I was to bring up Annie in the fear of the Lord and pay no heed to any evil omens, which were only snares of Satan that must be scorned. Then he gave me a handsome Bible for Annie, which she still has, and the next morning the kindly burgomaster had us driven nine miles toward home.—But, oh dear God, everything has still come to pass, just as predicted!" Here she fell silent.

A fearful premonition came over me; the old woman's story had completely cast me down. "In the name of God, mother," I cried, "what has become of poor Annie? Is there no help for her?"

"She was dragged to her fate by teeth," said the old woman. "Today she must die. But it was an act of despair; honor, honor was on her mind. Passion for worldly honor brought about her disgrace. She was seduced by a nobleman, he abandoned her, she smothered her child in the same apron that I threw over the head of Jürge, the gamekeeper. She had taken it from me secretly. Oh, she was dragged to it by teeth! She wasn't in her right mind. The seducer had promised to marry her and said that Caspar had fallen in France. Then she despaired and did the evil thing and gave herself up to the law. At four she's to be executed. She wrote me to come to her. That's what I'm about now. I want to bring her the wreath and poor Caspar's greetings and the rose I got tonight—that will comfort her. Oh, Mr. Clerk, if only you can bring it about through your petition that her body and Caspar's may be buried in our churchyard!"

"I'll do everything in my power, everything!" I cried. "I'll go to the castle at once. My friend, the one who gave you the rose, is in charge of the castle guard; I'll get him to waken the duke. I'll kneel before his bed and beg him to pardon Annie."

"Pardon?" said the old woman coldly. "She was dragged to it by teeth. Listen, dear friend, justice is better than pardon. What good is pardon on this earth? We must all be judged:

> Ye dead, ye dead, arise and meet
> To stand before the Judgment Seat.

She doesn't want a pardon. They offered her one if she would name the father, but she said: 'I murdered his child and want to die and not bring unhappiness upon him. I must suffer my punishment, so that I may be with my child, but it could ruin everything if I told his name.' So she was sentenced to die by the sword. But you go to the duke and beg him for an honorable grave for Caspar and Annie. Go. Go now! See there, the pastor's just coming to the jail. I'll ask him to take me with him to see fair Annie. If you hurry, you can meet us out at the place of execution and perhaps comfort us with the news of an honorable grave for Caspar and Annie."

We had now come up with the pastor. The old woman explained her relationship to the condemned girl and he readily allowed her to accompany him into the jail. I ran as never before to the castle. On the way I received a gleam of comfort; it seemed like a hopeful sign, as I dashed by the house of Count Grossinger, to hear from the open window of the gardenhouse a sweet voice singing to a lute:

> Though Mercy went a-wooing,
> Yet Honor watches well,
> Respectful love renewing,
> She breathes tonight farewell.
>
> If Love gives roses to her
> The veil let Mercy take,
> Then Honor greets the wooer
> With love for Mercy's sake.

And there were more good omens! A hundred paces further I found a white veil in the street; I picked it up, it was full of fragrant roses. With the veil in my hand I hastened on, thinking: "Oh God, this is Mercy." As I turned the corner I saw a man who drew his cloak about him as I passed and swiftly turned his back. He need not have done so: I saw and heard nothing. My sole thought was, "Mercy, Mercy!" I rushed through the iron gate into the courtyard of the castle. God be praised, the lieutenant, Count Grossinger, who was pacing up and down beneath the blossoming chestnut trees, came forward to greet me.

"Count," I cried impetuously, "you must take me to the duke immediately, right this instant, or it will be too late. All will be lost!"

This request seemed to embarrass him; he replied: "Are you in your right mind? You can't possibly see the duke at this hour. Return when he reviews the troops and I'll present you."

The ground was burning beneath my feet. "Now," I cried, "or never! You must! A life hangs in the balance."

"It's out of the question at this hour," replied Grossinger in a tone of finality. "My honor's at stake. I have strict orders to allow no one up tonight."

The word "honor" drove me to desperation. I thought of Caspar's honor, of fair Annie's honor, and said: "Hang honor! I have to see the duke as a last resort in a case where just such honor has brought ruin. Admit me at once, or I'll start shouting."

"If you make a move, I'll have you thrown in the guardhouse," said Grossinger sternly. "You're a dreamer, you have no sense of the realities."

"Oh, I know about realities, frightful realities!" I retorted. "I have to see the duke. Every moment is precious! If you won't announce me, I'll find my way alone."

And I was on the point of mounting the stairs leading to the duke's chambers when I espied the same muffled figure I had just encountered in the street hurrying in that direction. Grossinger forcibly turned me around so that I shouldn't see who it was. "What are you doing, you rash fool?" he whispered. "Hold your peace or you'll bring me to grief."

"Why didn't you stop that man who went up?" I asked. "His business can't be more urgent than mine. I *must* see the duke, I must! The fate of a poor, deluded, unhappy creature is at stake."

Grossinger hissed: "You saw that man go up. If you ever breathe a word about it, you'll face my blade. Precisely because *he* went up, *you* can't. The duke has business with him."

A light appeared in the duke's windows. "God, there's a light, he's up!" I cried. "I must speak to him. In heaven's name let me go or I'll cry for help."

Grossinger grabbed my arm and said: "You're drunk, come along to the guardhouse. I'm your friend, you can sleep it off and then recite for me the song the old woman was singing tonight on the doorstep when I passed by with the watch. That song interests me very much."

"It's precisely about the old woman and her kin that I have to speak to the duke!" I cried.

"About the old woman?" returned Grossinger. "Tell me about her; she won't interest the duke. Now come along to the guard-house."

He was trying to lead me away when the castle clock struck half past three. The sound pierced me like a cry of anguish and I shouted at the top of my lungs up at the duke's windows:

"Help! in God's name. Help for a miserable deceived creature!" Grossinger flew into a mad rage; he tried to clap his hand over my mouth, but I freed myself. He thumped me in the back of the neck, he cursed. I felt and heard nothing. He called the guard. A corporal hurried up with some soldiers to take me into custody, but at that instant the duke's window was thrown open and a voice called down:

"Lieutenant Grossinger, what's all the noise? Bring that person up here at once!"

I didn't wait for Grossinger to act but rushed up the stairs and fell at the feet of the duke, who looked at me with embarrassment and ill humor and told me to get up. He was wearing boots and spurs but had on his dressing gown, which he carefully drew together over his chest.

As briefly as possible I related all the old woman had told me of the suicide of the lancer and the story of fair Annie. I entreated him to delay the execution for at least a few hours and begged him to grant the two unfortunates an honorable grave, if no pardon was possible.—"Oh mercy, mercy!" I cried, drawing forth from my bosom the white veil filled with roses. "This veil that I found on the way to you seemed to give promise of mercy," I added.

The duke seized the veil impetuously; he seemed much moved. He pressed it between his palms and I continued: "Your Highness, this poor girl is a victim of false honor. A nobleman seduced her and promised her marriage, but she was so high-minded that she preferred to die rather than reveal his name—" He interrupted me, exclaiming with tears in his eyes: "Enough, for heaven's sake, enough!"—Then turning to Grossinger, who was standing at the door, he brusquely commanded: "Ride, both of you, as hard as you can, to the place of execution. You, Lieutenant, fasten this veil to the point of your sword, wave it and shout: Mercy! Mercy! I will follow."

Grossinger took the veil. An utter change had come over him—he looked like a ghost in his fear and haste. We ran into the stall, mounted, and were off at a gallop. He stormed out of the city gate like a madman. When he fastened the veil to his sword, I heard him exclaim: "Lord God, my sister!" I didn't know what he meant. He rose in his stirrups, waved the veil and kept shouting: "Mercy! Mercy!" On the hilltop we saw the crowd gathered for the execution. My horse shied at the streaming veil. I am a poor rider, I couldn't catch up to Grossinger, he flew like the wind; I bent every effort. Evil chance! An artillery company was holding morning practice nearby. The roar of the cannon drowned our cries and they could not be heard at a distance. Grossinger's horse stumbled, he was thrown. The crowd suddenly drew back and I could see into the circle about the place of execution. I caught the glint of steel in the early light—ah God, it was the headsman's sword!—I charged up, only to hear the lamentations of the bystanders. "Pardon! Pardon!" shouted Grossinger and lunged with the waving veil into the circle like a man possessed, but the executioner held up to him the head of fair Annie, dripping with blood and smiling at him dolefully. He cried out: "God have mercy on me!" and fell to the ground over the corpse. "Kill me, kill me, you people! I seduced her, I am her murderer!"

An avenging fury seized the crowd. The women and girls surged forward, tore him from the body and kicked at him. He did not defend himself. The guards could not hold the angry mob in check. Suddenly there was a shout: "The duke, the duke!"—He drove up in an open carriage; a youth with a hat deep in his face and wrapped in a cloak was sitting beside him. Grossinger was dragged into the duke's presence. "Lord Jesus, my brother!" the youthful officer exclaimed from the carriage in a very feminine voice. The duke, greatly embarrassed, bade him be still and sprang from the carriage. The young man was about to follow but the duke pushed him back, not too gently. This in turn led to the discovery that the young man was Grossinger's sister disguised as an officer. The duke gave orders for the battered, bleeding, unconscious Grossinger to be placed in the carriage. His sister threw all caution to the winds and cast her cloak over him, revealing herself in woman's apparel. The duke was clearly taken aback, but collected himself and ordered the carriage to turn back and take the countess and her brother to her dwelling. This incident had somewhat quelled the rage of the crowd. In loud tones the duke said to the officer in command: "Countess Grossinger saw her brother galloping past her house to bring the pardon. She wished to be present at this happy occasion. When I drove by, bent on the same mission, she was standing at her window and begged me to take her into my carriage. I could not refuse the kindhearted young woman. In order to prevent any stir, she donned her brother's cloak and hat and now, due to an unfortunate accident, she has given the whole matter the appearance of a romantic scandal. But why, Lieutenant, weren't you able to protect that luckless Count Grossinger from the mob? It's a terrible misfortune that he was thrown and came too late, but that's not his fault. I want the count's assailants arrested and punished."

A general outcry followed this speech: "He's a scoundrel, he seduced her, he's the murderer of fair Annie, he said so himself, the no-good wretch!"

When the accusations resounding from all sides were confirmed by the pastor, the commanding officer, and the court officials, the duke was deeply shaken. He kept repeating: "Shocking, shocking, oh, the miserable wretch!"

Pale as a ghost, the duke stepped into the circle to look at the corpse of fair Annie. She was lying on the green turf in a black dress trimmed with white ribbons. The old grandmother, who paid no attention to anything going on around her, had laid the severed head to the trunk and covered the terrible cleavage with her apron. She was now engaged in folding Annie's hands over the Bible the pastor had given her when she was a little child. She bound the tinsel wreath about her head and pinned on her breast the rose that Grossinger had given her that night, not knowing for whom it was to be.

When the duke saw what the old woman had done, he said: "Poor lovely Annie! Shameful seducer, you came too late!—Poor old mother, only you have remained faithful to her till death." His eyes fell upon me and he said: "You mentioned Corporal Caspar's last will. Do you have it with you?" I turned to the old woman: "Let me have Caspar's notebook, mother; His Highness wishes to read his last will."

The old woman, who had been intent only on her own affairs, said sullenly: "Are you here again? You might just as well have stayed at home. Do you have the petition? Now it's too late. I wasn't able to give the poor girl her last comfort and assure her that she and Caspar would lie in an honorable grave. Oh, I lied to her about it, but she didn't believe me."

The duke interrupted: "You didn't lie to her, mother. My messenger did all in his power. The fall from the horse was to blame for everything. She shall have an honorable grave beside her mother and Caspar, who was a brave fellow. The pastor shall preach them a funeral sermon on the text: 'To God alone be honor!' Caspar shall be buried as an officer candidate, his company shall shoot into his grave three times, and the sword of the seducer Grossinger shall be laid on his coffin."

With these words he took up Grossinger's sword that was still lying with the veil on the ground, removed the veil, covered Annie with it, and said: "This ill-fated veil, which was to bring her pardon, shall restore her honor. She died pardoned and in honor; it shall be buried with her."

Then he handed the sword to the commanding officer, saying: "Today at review I will give you further orders concerning the burial of the lancer and this poor girl."

He then read aloud Caspar's last words in a voice betraying deep emotion. The old grandmother embraced his knees with tears of joy, as though immeasurably blessed. The duke said: "Rest satisfied, mother! You shall have a pension until the end of your days. A monument shall be raised to the memory of your grandson and Annie." He then requested the pastor to drive the old woman and the coffin in which the body was laid to his house and later to escort her to her village and arrange the funeral.

Since the adjutant had arrived in the meantime, he told me in parting: "Give my adjutant your name, I'll send for you. You have shown splendid charitable zeal." The adjutant took down my name and bowed graciously. The duke galloped off toward the city, taking with him the blessings of the crowd. The good old grandmother and the body of fair Annie were brought to the house of the pastor, and the following evening he drove her back home. On that evening the commanding officer also arrived with Grossinger's sword and a troop of lancers.

Then good Caspar, with Grossinger's sword on his bier and his officer's patent, was buried next to fair Annie at the side of his mother. I had also hastened to put in an appearance and escorted the old grandmother, who was childish with joy but said little. As the lancers fired the third salute into Caspar's grave she fell back dead in my arms. She too has found her grave beside her kin. God grant them all a blessed resurrection!

> You shall there approach the height
> Where lovely angels sit so bright;
> God in His glory awaits you there,
> A beauteous rainbow round His chair.
> Then the soul shall pass God's test
> When we enter heaven and final rest.

> Amen.

When I returned to the city, I learned that Count Grossinger was dead. He had taken poison. On my desk I found a letter from him which read:

"I owe you much. You revealed my disgrace, which had long been eating out my heart. I well knew the song the old woman sang, Annie had recited it for me many a time. She was an incredibly noble being. I was a criminal—I had given her a written promise of marriage—she burned it. She was in service in the home of an old aunt of mine. She often suffered from melancholy. Through certain medicinal preparations that have a kind of magic effect I ensnared her soul.—God have mercy on me!—You have saved my sister's honor also. The duke loves her—I stood high in his favor—this affair has shaken him.—God help me, I have taken poison.

Joseph Count Grossinger."

Fair Annie's apron, to which the head of the gamekeeper Jürge clung at his beheading, is preserved in the ducal museum. It is said that the duke will elevate Count Grossinger's sister to a princess with the name, *Voile de Grace,* that is, Veil of Mercy, and make her his wife. At the next review near D—— the monument on the graves of the two ill-starred victims of honor in the village churchyard is to be dedicated. The duke and the princess will attend in person. The duke is much pleased with the monument. He and the princess are said to have worked out the design together. It sets forth True and False Honor. Both figures are bowing deeply on either side of a cross; Justice, with sword swung high, stands on one side, Mercy casting a veil on the other. Some find in the head of Justice a similarity to the duke, in the head of Mercy a likeness to the princess.

Translated by Carl F. Schreiber (revised by R. M. Browning)

The Madman of Fort Ratonneau

Achim von Arnim

On a cold and blustery October evening Count Durande, the
gallant old commander of the Marseilles garrison, sat shivering and alone before the ill-provided hearth of his imposing official
residence, dragging his chair closer and closer to the blaze as
carriages on their way to a grand ball rumbled past in the street
outside and his batman and choice companion, Basset, snored
loudly in the antechamber. It is not always warm, even in the South
of France, mused the old gentleman, shaking his head, and even here
people grow old, but the bustle of the social round heeds old age no
more than architects heed the winter. He, the commanding officer of
all the disabled and superannuated soldiers who at that time—it was
during the Seven Years' War—formed the garrison of Marseilles and
its surrounding forts—what should he with his wooden leg do at a
ball: even the lieutenants of his regiment would be precious little use
on the dance floor. Here by the fire, on the other hand, his wooden
leg came in most useful, for he employed it to thrust into the flames
at intervals the pile of green olive-branches which, not wishing to
rouse Basset, he had had placed ready by his side. A fire of this kind
has a fascination of its own. The crackling flames appear to be
interlaced with the fresh green foliage, the leaves, half-ardent and
half-verdant, seem like lovesick hearts. It set the old man thinking of
the splendors of his youth, and he immersed himself once more in
the devising of those firework displays which in times past he had
arranged at court, speculating on the novel and still more diverse

cascades and convolutions of many-colored flame with which he meant to astonish the good people of Marseilles on the occasion of His Majesty's birthday. His mind, to tell the truth, was rather less congested than the ballroom. But in the exhilaration of success, as he visualized the flaring, whizzing, crackling spectacle merging at last into the awe-inspiring silent radiance of the grand finale, he had kept on thrusting more and more olive branches into the fire and failed to notice that the wooden limb itself had caught alight and that a good third of it was already consumed. Only now, as he made to leap to his feet, his imagination fired and given wings by his vision of this grand finale, the simultaneous ascent of a thousand rockets, only now did he realize, on tumbling back into his easy-chair, that his wooden leg was much abbreviated and that the stump was still the seat of an alarming conflagration. Unable in this plight to stand up on the instant, he propelled his chair tobogganwise into the center of the room by means of the blazing member, calling at the same time for his servant and a bucket of water.

At this moment help arrived in the person of a young woman who tackled the blaze with determination. She had earlier been shown into the room and had been trying for some time, but in vain, to draw the commandant's attention to her presence by means of a discreet cough. She tried to smother the flames with her apron, but the smoldering wood ignited the material, and the commandant, now in dire straits indeed, shouted for someone to come to their rescue. Within moments passersby were crowding in from the street, and Basset had been roused. The sight of the blazing limb and the blazing apron set them all laughing, but the whole thing was extinguished by the first bucket of water that Basset fetched from the kitchen, and the onlookers duly took their leave. The poor woman was drenched to the skin and unable to recover at once from the shock. The commandant had her wrapped in his warm greatcoat, and she was offered a glass of good strong wine. She would take nothing, however, but simply sobbed over her "misfortune" and begged the commandant for a few words in private. He consequently dismissed his neglectful servant from the room and seated himself in a gingerly fashion beside the young woman. "Alas, it is my husband," she said in French that had an outlandish German accent. "My husband will go out of his mind if he hears of this. Oh, my poor husband, this must be another of those tricks that the Devil plays upon him."

The commandant asked her about her husband, and the woman told him that it was in fact on account of her dear husband that she had come to see him, bringing with her a letter from the colonel of the Picardy regiment. The commandant put on his spectacles, duly recognized his friend's seal, rapidly scanned the message, then said, "So you are the Rosalie he speaks of, formerly a Demoiselle Lilie from Leipzig, whom Sergeant Francoeur married while he was wounded and a prisoner there? Tell me about it, it sounds like an uncommon love affair! What of your parents, did they place no obstacle in your way? And what sort of comic fancies has your husband conceived as a result of the head-wound that made him unfit for active service—although it seems he was considered the smartest and the handiest sergeant of the lot, the very life and soul of his regiment?"

"Oh, sir," replied the young woman with a renewed access of grief, "my love is to blame for all our misfortunes, it is I and not his wound that brought my husband into disgrace. It is my love that put the Devil into him so that the Evil One plagues him and muddles his wits. Instead of drilling his men he is sometimes prompted by the Devil to prance about like a maniac in front of them, and he orders them to copy him, or else he pulls such dreadful faces that they are terrified almost out of their wits, and yet he orders them not to move so much as a finger. And not so long ago—and this was the last straw—he dragged the general in command from his horse when he ordered the regiment to retreat during a skirmish, then Francoeur mounted the general's horse himself and carried the enemy battery at the head of his regiment."

"A devil of a fellow, indeed!" cried the commandant. "If only such devilment were to get into all our generals, then we need not fear a second Rossbach. If your love can manufacture devils of that sort, then I wish you would make love to every man jack in the army!"

"I fear it is the curse my mother put upon me," sighed the young woman. "I never knew my father. My mother had many men to visit her, and I was made to wait upon them. That was all the work I had to do. I was a dreamy girl and took no notice of the amiable remarks of these men. My mother shielded me from their importunities. The war had scattered most of these gentlemen who used to visit my mother and gamble secretly at her lodging; much to my mother's annoyance we now perforce lived a secluded life. That was why she hated friend and foe alike, and would not let me give to the wounded and the hungry who passed by our house. This made me very unhappy, and once I was all by myself and busy preparing our midday meal when a long train of carts went past bearing wounded whom I recognized from their speech as Frenchmen taken prisoner by the Prussians. I wanted so much to run down to them with the food I had made ready, yet I was afraid of my mother. But when I caught sight of Francoeur, with his head bandaged, lying on the last of the carts—I don't know what came over me. All thought of my mother vanished, I snatched up the soup and a spoon and, without even pausing to lock the doors, I hastened after the carts as they entered the Pleissenburg fortress. I found him. He had already climbed down from the cart, and I boldly addressed the man in charge and was able to secure the best palliasse for the wounded man. And when he had been laid upon it, what bliss it was to offer the hot soup to the sufferer! His eyes lit up and he swore to me that I had a halo round my head. I replied that it was simply the brim of my bonnet which had been pushed up in the course of my hurried ministrations. He said that the divine light shone from my eyes! Ah, I could not forget those words ever, and had he not already won my heart, I must surely have given it to him in that instant."

"Well and truly spoken!" said the commandant, and Rosalie continued: "That was the finest hour of all my life, I gazed on him with ever greater ardor, for he declared that it did him good for me to look at him, and when at last he slipped a little ring upon my finger I felt myself rich as never before. Into our silent rapture burst my mother, cursing and scolding. I cannot repeat what she called me, and in any case I felt no shame, for I knew that I was guiltless and that he would not believe evil of me. She tried to drag me away, but he held me fast and told her that we were betrothed, that I was already wearing his ring. What a dreadful change came over my mother's face! It seemed to me as if a searing flame sprang from her throat, and her eyes appeared to turn inwards, so that only the whites could be seen. She called down a curse on me and solemnly consigned me to the Devil. And just as a brilliant light had dazzled my eyes the instant I caught sight of Francoeur that morning, so now a black bat seemed to have laid its murky wings across my vision. The world seemed somehow half removed from me, and somehow I did not feel quite real. My heart was in despair but yet I could not help bursting into laughter. 'You hear that? The Devil's laughing in you already,' cried my mother and swept off triumphantly as I fell into a swoon.

"When I came to myself again I could not go to her and leave the wounded man alone, for the incident had much affected him. Indeed, I was secretly angry with my mother on account of the harm she had done the poor fellow. It was not until three days later that I crept home in the evening without saying a word to Francoeur. I dared not knock on the door, but after a while a woman who had been our maid came out and told me that my mother had hastily sold up all her things and gone off, no one knew whither, with a strange gentleman who was said to be a gambler. And so I was now cast off by all the world and I was glad to sink into my Francoeur's arms, freed from all my cares and burdens. Not even the young girls whom I knew in the town now wished to have anything to do with me, so that I was able to devote myself entirely to him and the nursing that he needed. I labored for his sake: until that time I had merely toyed with lace-making for the sake of adorning my own person, but now I was not ashamed to sell the work of my hands, for it brought him comfort and refreshment. But again and again, whenever he was not entertaining me with some merry tale or other, I could not help thinking of my mother. She appeared in my mind's eye, all in black with her eyes blazing, cursing me over and over again, and I could not rid my mind of her. I did not wish to say anything to Francoeur for fear of upsetting him; I complained of headaches that I did not have, of toothaches I did not feel only so that I could weep as I had to. Oh, if only I had put more trust in him then, I should not have brought about his ruin, but every time I made to tell him I believed I was possessed of the Devil because of my mother's curse, then the Devil sealed my lips. And I was afraid, too, that if I told him, he would not be able to love me any more, and I could not bear even the thought of that. This torment of mind, and perhaps also the unremitting work I forced myself to do, at last undermined my constitution; violent convulsions that I tried to hide from him seemed like to suffocate me, and it appeared that medicine only made the illness worse.

"Barely had Francoeur recovered than he arranged the wedding. An elderly parson made a solemn speech in which he enjoined Francoeur to take to heart all that I had done for him, how I had given up my homeland, well-being and friends for his sake and had even brought a mother's curse upon myself. All these tribulations and misfortunes he must bear and share with me. I saw my husband tremble at these words, but he spoke his assent audibly enough and we were wed. ——

"The first few weeks were blissfully happy. I felt relieved of half my suffering and did not at once realize that half the curse had been passed on to my husband. Soon, however, he was complaining that the preacher in his black cassock was always there in front of his eyes and threatening him. In consequence he conceived such a furious antipathy to parsons, churches and sacred images that he felt constrained to curse them, and yet he did not himself know why. And to rid himself of this idea he gave way to any and every whim, capering and carousing so that through the commotion of the blood he might feel better. I put it all down to his captivity, although I knew in my heart of hearts that it was the Devil that was plaguing him.

"Through the good offices of his colonel, who had doubtless missed his services, for Francoeur was no common soldier, my husband was released in an exchange of prisoners. We departed from Leipzig with light hearts, and in our talk we pictured a splendid future for ourselves. But hardly had we passed from the struggle for daily sustenance to the comfortable life of a well-provisioned army in winter quarters than my husband's violent behavior reached new heights. He would beat on a drum for days on end, and to distract his mind would argue and pick quarrels with all and sundry. The colonel could not make him out. It was only with me that he was as gentle as a child. When the campaign was reopened I was delivered of a son, and with the pangs of birth the Devil that had plagued me seemed banished for good. Francoeur, on the other hand, grew more and more headstrong and violent. The colonel wrote to say that he was courageous to the point of madness, but so far had been lucky enough to escape unscathed. His comrades believed he was really out of his mind at times, and the colonel feared he would have to post him to the sick reserve. The colonel had a certain respect for me, he took heed of my pleas until Francoeur's wild behavior towards the general that I have already told you about led to his arrest. The surgeon explained that he was suffering from a dementia due to the head-wound that had been neglected during his captivity, and that he would have to spend a few years at least with a reserve regiment in a warm climate to see whether the root of his disorder might not be eliminated thus. He was told that he was being relegated to the reserve as a punishment for his offence, and he departed cursing from his regiment.

"I begged the colonel for this letter and resolved to tell you all this in confidence, so that Francoeur may be judged not by the rigor of the law but with due allowance for his infirmity, of which my love was the sole cause, and so that you might station him for his own good in some small, out-of-the-way place, rather than that he should become the subject of idle gossip in this great city. But, gracious sir, a woman who had today rendered you some slight service may perhaps ask you on your word of honor to preserve inviolate the secret of his malady, which he himself little suspects and which, should it become public, would offend his pride." "There's my hand on't," cried the commandant, who had listened to the young woman's fervent words with approval. "And what is more, I will listen to your intercession three separate times, supposing Francoeur should take it into his head to play his crazy tricks. It would be best to avoid this altogether, however, and I shall therefore send him forthwith as relief to a fort that requires a garrison of no more than three men. There you will find comfortable quarters for yourself and your child, he will have little occasion for folly, and any crazy tricks he does get up to will never come to light."

The woman thanked him for his kind and prudent offer, kissed the old gentleman's hand, and in return he lighted the way for her as she descended the staircase with many a curtsy. This puzzled old Basset, the commandant's batman, and he wondered what had possessed his master to show her such respect: whether perhaps he had begun an affair with the blazing woman that might have some prejudicial effect on his own influence.

Now it so happened that the old gentleman had the habit, when he could not sleep of an evening, of musing aloud in bed on everything that had occurred during the day, as though he were obliged to make his confession to the bedpost. And while the carriages rumbled past on their way back from the ball and kept him awake, Basset eavesdropped in the next room and heard the monologue from beginning to end. The matter seemed to him all the more worthy of note because Francoeur came from his own part of the country and they had borne arms in the same regiment, although he was much the elder. And now he suddenly thought of a friar he knew who had rid a number of people of devils, and he resolved to take Francoeur to this man as soon as might be. He had a great weakness for charlatans of this sort and looked forward eagerly to seeing yet another devil cast out.

Rosalie, much pleased with the success of her visit, had slept well; in the morning she purchased a new apron, and having tied it on went to meet her husband as he led his weary old pensioners into the city to the accompaniment of an excruciatingly tuneless marching song. He kissed her, swung her into the air and said, "You reek of the fires of Troy: I have you once again, my fairest Helen!" Rosalie grew pale and felt it necessary to explain to him, when he asked her about it, that she had been to see the commandant about their quarters, that his wooden leg had happened to be on fire and that her apron had been burned as well. He was displeased that she had not waited for his arrival, but he soon forgot this in a thousand witticisms about the burning apron. He then presented his men to the commandant, extolling all their physical infirmities and intellectual virtues with such charm and verve that he at once won the good opinion of the old gentleman, who thought to himself: the girl is in love with him, but she is German and cannot be expected to understand Frenchmen; every Frenchman has a bit of the devil in him. He bade the sergeant come inside so as to make his closer acquaintance, found him well instructed in the art of fortification, and—which delighted him even more—discovered in Francoeur a zealous pyrotechnician who had devised all kinds of fireworks displays while he was with his regiment. The commandant expounded to him his latest project for a grand display on the king's birthday, the plan, in fact, which had been so rudely interrupted the previous day when his leg caught fire, and Francoeur entered into his schemes with sparkling enthusiasm. The old gentleman then informed him that he and two of his old soldiers were to relieve the little garrison of Fort Ratonneau. There was a plentiful store of gunpowder there, and he and his two men were to busy themselves filling rockets, winding catherine wheels and tying up firecrackers. Just as the commandant was on the point of handing over the key of the powder magazine, however, along with the inventory, it suddenly occurred to him what the woman had said, and still grasping the key, he remarked: "I trust the Devil doesn't plague you so that you won't get up to any mischief." "Speak of the Devil and he will appear," replied Francoeur with a certain jauntiness. This restored the commandant's confidence and he at once handed over the key, the inventory and the order for the present garrison to stand down. And so Francoeur was dismissed, and there in the hall stood Basset who fell on the sergeant's neck. They had recognized each other at once, and each gave a brief account of what had befallen him since they last met. But Francoeur, who was most strict in all military matters, quickly tore himself away and invited Basset to come on the succeeding Sunday—provided he could obtain leave—to Fort Ratonneau as the guest of its commander, which post he himself had the honor to occupy.

The entry of the relief garrison into the fort was a cheerful occasion for all concerned: the departing garrison had had their fill of the fine prospect of Marseilles, and the relieving party were delighted by the selfsame view, with the well-laid-out defenses, the comfortable quarters and beds. They purchased from the departing troops a number of goats, a pair of pigeons, a dozen fowl and sundry devices by means of which they might indulge in a quiet bit of poaching at the cost of the game in the surrounding countryside, for soldiers with idle hours are inveterate huntsmen. When Francoeur had formally taken over command he at once ordered his two privates, Brunet and Tessier to come with him and open the powder magazine, check through the list of stores and then carry a certain quantity of powder into the workshop for the purpose of manufacturing fireworks. The list of stores was correct in every item, and the sergeant at once set one of his two men to work on the fireworks. Accompanied by the other he made a tour of the cannons and mortars, polishing the bronze pieces and painting black the cast-iron guns. Soon he had charged a sufficient store of bombs and shells, and he then trained the entire armament so that it bore upon the sole approach to the fort. "The fort is impregnable!" he cried over and over again. "I can hold it, even though the English should land and seek to storm it with a hundred thousand men! But things were indeed in a sorry state up here!" "It's like this in all the forts and batteries," remarked Tessier. "The old commandant can't get around so easily, what with his peg leg and all, and the English, thank God, have never taken it into their heads to make a landing." "We'll change all that," cried Francoeur. "I'd rather have my tongue burned out than suffer our enemies to reduce Marseilles to ashes, or even admit that we have reason to fear them."

His wife was made to assist him in clearing the ramparts of grass and moss, in whitewashing the walls and ventilating the provisions that were stored in the casemates. During the first few days there was scarcely time to sleep, so relentlessly did the untiring Francoeur drive them on to work, and his skillful hands achieved in this space what another might have needed a month to do. In the midst of all this bustle his wild whims left him in peace; he was brusque in his manner, but it was always to a particular purpose, and Rosalie blessed the day that had brought him to these higher altitudes where the Devil no longer seemed to have power over him. The weather, too, had grown milder and brighter with the veering of the wind, so that they seemed to experience a renewed summer. Every day ships entered the harbor, saluting the forts along the coast and being saluted by them in turn. Rosalie, who had never lived by the sea, felt herself transported into a different world, and her little boy reveled in the freedom of the fort's walled garden after being so much shut up in baggage wagons and inn parlors. This garden the former occupants of the fort, after the manner of soldiers, particularly gunners, had embellished with highly complex mathematical figures executed in boxwood hedges. High over the little stronghold fluttered the banner with the fleur-de-lis, Francoeur's pride (an auspicious emblem of his wife, who had been christened Lilie), and the child's favorite diversion.

Thus arrived the first Sunday, gratefully welcomed by one and all, and Francoeur enjoined his wife to prepare some specially tasty dish for the midday repast, as he was expecting his friend Basset. He had a particular wish for a good omelette, since the hens in the fort were laying well, and he also furnished the kitchen with a number of wildfowl that Brunet had shot. In the midst of these preparations Basset came puffing up the hill and was delighted with the transformation of the fortress. He enquired on behalf of the Commandant concerning the fireworks and was astounded at the great number of completed rockets and star shells. Francoeur's wife now went about her work in the kitchen, the two privates set off on an expedition to fetch fruit for their meal, all of them determined to spend the day in leisurely content, and to have read out to them the newspaper that Basset had brought up with him.

In the garden Basset sat opposite Francoeur and gazed at him long and hard in silence. Francoeur asked him why he was staring at him thus. "It seems to me you look as fit as ever, and you behave perfectly sensibly, too." "And who might doubt it, pray?" enquired Francoeur, his temper rising. "That's what I should like to know!" Basset tried to change the subject, but there was something terrifying in Francoeur's bearing, his dark eyes blazed, he tossed his head back and thrust out his lips. Poor gossiping Basset's heart fell into his boots, and he began to speak, in a voice as high-pitched as a fiddle, of rumors that he had heard in the commandant's house, namely that Francoeur was possessed by the Devil, and of his own well-meaning plan to have Francoeur exorcised by a member of the monastic order, Father Philip, whom he had for this purpose invited to come up to the fort before they sat down to table, under the pretext that he celebrate Mass in the chapel there for the benefit of the garrison, who were too far removed to attend regular services. On hearing this, Francoeur flew into a rage, swearing that he would take a bloody revenge on anyone who spread such lies about him. He knew nothing of the Devil, and it was all the same to him whether there was any such thing or not, for he had never had the honor to make his acquaintance. Basset said that it was in no way his fault, he had simply overheard the story as the commandant recited it aloud to himself, and anyway it was this demon that was the reason for Francoeur being transferred from his regiment. "And who told the commandant about that," demanded Francoeur, trembling all over. "It was your wife," replied Basset, "but she only meant it for the best, so as to excuse you if you got up to any mischief." "We are no longer man and wife," shrieked Francoeur, striking his forehead. "She has betrayed me, ruined me, she has secrets with the commandant. She has suffered no end of hardship for me, there is no limit to what she has done for me, and she has done me infinite harm, I owe her nothing more, we are parted for good!"

Little by little he seemed to grow outwardly calmer, the more the turmoil within him grew; once again he had a vision of the black-clad parson, as the victim of a mad dog imagines he can still see the dog before his eyes. Just at that moment Father Philip entered the garden. Francoeur strode up to him and asked him his business. Father Philip felt the time had come to administer his exorcism, he adjured the evil spirit with great vehemence, repeatedly making the sign of the cross over Francoeur. All this infuriated the latter even more; as commander of the fort he ordered Father Philip to leave the place at once. But the doughty friar strove ever more manfully against the devil in Francoeur, and when he went so far as to raise his staff, Francoeur's martial pride could not tolerate the threat. With the strength of a madman he seized the diminutive Philip by his habit and tossed him over the iron grille that protected the entrance to the fort, and had it not been for the good man's clothing catching on the spikes that surmounted it he would have suffered a heavy fall down the stone steps.

Close by the iron gate stood the table already laid for their meal, and this reminded Francoeur of food. He called for his dinner, and Rosalie brought it, a little flushed from the fire but very cheerful, for she did not catch sight of the friar outside the gate: he, having scarcely recovered from his initial fright, was praying silently that no further peril might befall him. Rosalie scarcely noticed that both her husband and Basset were staring at the table, the one morosely, the other in acute discomfiture. She asked about the two soldiers, but Francoeur replied: "They can have theirs afterwards. I am so hungry I could tear the whole world to shreds." Thereupon she served the soup, giving Basset the larger helping out of politeness, and returned to the kitchen to cook the omelette. "And how did the commandant like my wife?" asked Francoeur. "Very much," answered Basset, "He wished he had been as well off as you when he was a prisoner." "Then he shall have her!" rejoined the sergeant. "She asked about the two soldiers who are not here, but she never asked what was the matter with me. Because you're the commandant's servant she's trying to get you on her side. That's why she filled your plate to the brim. She gave you the largest glass of wine, and just you watch, she'll bring you the largest helping of omelette too. If she does, then I shall simply get up, you can take her away and leave me here by myself." Basset was about to reply, but at that moment Rosalie appeared with the omelette. She had already cut it into three pieces, and she went up to Basset and pushed a piece on to his plate with the words, "You won't find a better omelette at the commandant's: you must admit I'm a first-rate cook." Gloomily Francoeur peered into the dish in her hand—the gap was indeed almost as large as the two remaining pieces put together. He rose to his feet and exclaimed: "So that's the way of it! We are no longer man and wife!" So saying, he strode off to the powder-magazine, opened the iron door, went inside and closed it behind him. His wife gazed after him in consternation and let fall the dish: "Dear God, it is the Evil One plaguing him again. I only hope he does no mischief in the magazine." "Is that the magazine?" yelled Basset. "He'll blow himself to kingdom come! Save yourself and the child!" With these words he took to his heels; even the monk did not venture inside again, but followed Basset's example. Rosalie darted into the house to fetch her baby, snatched it up as it lay sleeping in its cradle, scarcely knowing what she did. As she had once risen and followed Francoeur in a trance, so she now fled from him, saying to herself: "My child, it is only for your sake; for my part, it would be better to die along with him. Hagar, you did not suffer as I do, for I am casting myself out into the wilderness!"

Bemused by such thoughts she descended the wrong path and found herself on the marshy riverbank. She was too weary to go any further and therefore seated herself in a small rowing boat, which being only a little way drawn up on to the bank, could easily be thrust into the stream, and so she allowed herself to drift down the river. She did not dare to look back, for every time a shot was fired down by the harbor she believed the fortress had been blown up and half her life along with it. By and by she relapsed into a dull and feverish doze.

Meanwhile the two soldiers, laden down with apples and grapes, had arrived back at the fort, only to be halted in their tracks by the stentorian voice of Francoeur as he fired a musket shot over their heads: "Get back!" He then called to them through a speaking trumpet: "I will talk to you by the curtain wall. I alone am in charge here, and I mean to live alone here as long as the Devil pleases." They could not imagine what all this meant, but they had no choice but to comply with the sergeant's will. They clambered down to the sheer slope known as the curtain wall, and barely had they arrived there when they saw Rosalie's bed and the child's cradle descending at the end of a rope, to be followed by their own bedding and kit. Francoeur called through his speaking trumpet: "Take what is yours, and bring the bed, the cradle and my runaway wife's clothes to the commandant's house, that's where you'll find her. Tell her, Satan has sent them, along with this old flag to cover up the shame she shares with the commandant!" With these words he threw down the great French ensign that had floated over the fort and continued: "I hereby declare war on the commandant. He has until nightfall to prepare his weapons, then I shall open fire. Let him give no quarter, for, Devil take me, I shall show him none. He can do what he likes, but he shall not lay a finger on me: he gave me the key to the magazine, and I mean to use it. The instant he thinks he has me, I shall blow him and myself to kingdom come and back again into the pit of hell—that will make the dust fly!"

Brunet at last found the courage to speak and called up: "Think of our most gracious king. Remember you are his subject; don't say you mean to take up arms against him." To this Francoeur retorted: "Inside me I have the king of all kings on this earth; inside me I have the Devil himself, and in the Devil's name I tell you: say not another word, or I will dash you to pieces!" At this threat the two men silently gathered up their belongings and left the rest where it was. They knew that up there were piled masses of boulders that could be dislodged to smash anything at the foot of the curtain wall.

When they reported to the commandant in Marseilles they found him already busy with preparations, for Basset had informed him of all that had passed. He dispatched the two men to the fort with a cart so that they might recover the woman's belongings before the threatening rain began to fall. At the same time he sent out men to search for the woman and her baby. Meanwhile he summoned his officers in order to discuss what measures might be taken. This council of war was concerned above all about the potential loss of a fine fortress, supposing it should be blown up. Shortly, however, an emissary arrived from the city, where the rumor had already spread, and pointed out that the finest part of the town was quite certain to be demolished in this event. It was generally agreed that force could not be employed, for there was no honor to be gained in combat against a single man, whereas immeasurable loss might be averted by a compromise. In the long run, sleep was bound to overpower Francoeur's madness, and when that happened a party of determined men should scale the fort and seize him. Scarcely had this decision been arrived at when the soldiers who had retrieved Rosalie's bed and chattels were brought into the room. They had a message from Francoeur to deliver, namely that the Devil had made known to him that they proposed to take him prisoner while he was asleep, but for the sake of a number of his old comrades in devilment who might be employed in this enterprise he would warn them that he meant to sleep peacefully in the barred and bolted magazine with muskets by his side, and long before they could break down the door he would be awake and would blow the magazine to smithereens by firing a shot into the powder barrels. "He is right," said the commandant. "He can choose no other course of action. We shall have to starve the fellow out." "He has had the whole of our provisions for the winter taken up there," remarked Brunet. "We should have to wait for six months at least, and anyway he said he would levy a handsome toll on the ships sailing in to supply the city, otherwise he would sink them on the spot. And just to show that no one should try to run the blockade by night he would take occasion to let fly a few cannonballs across the river during the hours of darkness." "It's true, he has opened fire!" cried one of the officers, and everyone present ran to a window on the top floor. What a sight! At every angle of the fort the cannons opened their fiery jaws, the balls whistled through the air, and the crowds in the streets fled screaming for cover—apart from a few individuals who chose to demonstrate their courage by boldly observing the perilous spectacle. And richly rewarded for it they were: with a blinding flash Francoeur discharged a bundle of rockets into the air from a howitzer, along with a cluster of star shells from a mortar, followed by numberless other projectiles fired from muskets. The commandant averred that the effect was capital. He himself had never dared to discharge fireworks as projectiles from artillery pieces, but the artifice produced an effect that was well-nigh meteoric, and Francoeur deserved a pardon for this alone.

The nocturnal illuminations had a further consequence that was intended by no human design: it saved the lives of Rosalie and her child. The two of them had fallen fast asleep as they drifted peacefully in the rowing boat, and in her dreams Rosalie seemed to see her mother consumed by lurid inward flames, and she asked her why she had to suffer like this. It seemed as if a loud voice resounded in her ears: "My curse is burning me as it burns you, and if you cannot redeem it, then I must remain enthralled by the Evil One." She seemed about to say more, but Rosalie had already started out of her slumber, she saw high above her the climactic brilliance of Francoeur's star shells and heard a sailor hailing hard by: "Port your helm, or we shall run down a boat with a woman and a baby in it." And in that same moment the bow of a great river-barge passed close astern like the yawning maw of a whale, veered off to port, but dragged the frail craft sideways along with it. "Save my poor child!" she cried, and a boat hook linked her with the larger vessel, which at once cast anchor. "If it hadn't been for those fireworks going up from Fort Ratonneau," called one of the sailors, "I should never have sighted you, and we should have run you down all unawares. What are you doing out on the river all by yourself and so late? Why didn't you hail us?" Rosalie answered their questions rapidly and begged them urgently to take her to the commandant's residence. Taking pity on her, the boatman sent off his boy to guide her thither.

At the commandant's house she found everything in turmoil. She asked him to be mindful of his promise to pardon her husband three separate escapades. He denied that he had meant escapades of this order, the previous complaints had been of practical jokes and crazy delusions, but this was devilishly serious. "Then it is you who are in the wrong," said Rosalie, for now she saw clearly the path she must follow. "What is more, I told you of my poor husband's condition, and nevertheless you entrusted him with such a perilous position. You vowed to keep my secret, and yet you told the whole story to your servant Basset, who has plunged us all into this calamity through his harebrained schemes and his meddling. It is not my poor husband who is to blame for the disaster, but you, and it is you who must answer to the king for it." The commandant defended himself against the accusation that he had ever said anything to Basset, but the latter confessed that he had overheard his mono-logue, so the whole of the blame must fall on him. The old officer swore that he would get himself shot in front of the fort the very next day so as to pay with his life for the dreadful debt he had incurred towards his monarch, but Rosalie begged him not to be too hasty, telling him to bear in mind that she had already rescued him from the flames once. She was given a room in the commandant's residence and put her child to bed there, pondering on the whole affair as she did so, and praying to God that He might show her how to redeem her mother from the flames and her husband from the curse.

But even as she knelt there she fell into a deep slumber and awoke in the morning with no awareness of any dream or divine revelation.

The commandant, who had already attempted an assault on the fort early in the morning, returned in ill humor. To be sure, there had been no losses among his men, but Francoeur had shown such skill in sending countless balls and bullets whizzing narrowly to the right and left of them and close over their heads that clearly they owed their lives only to his forbearance. He had blockaded the river with warning shots, and no one might drive along the highroad: in short, all traffic with the city was blocked for the day, and the authorities were threatening that, if the commandant did not go about the business with the utmost caution but attempted to besiege the fort's occupant as though this were enemy territory, then they would mobilize the citizenry and give very short shrift to his decrepit veterans.

For three days the commandant allowed himself to be held thus at arm's length, and every evening was made resplendent by a firework display, and every evening Rosalie reminded him of his promise to be lenient. On the third evening he informed her that the assault was timed for noon on the following day; the city had acquiesced because all traffic was utterly disrupted and there was a risk of eventual famine. He would lead an assault on the main gate while another party attempted to make their way up secretly from the far side in the hope of taking their man from the rear before he could run for the powder magazine. It would cost lives, the outcome was uncertain, but he was resolved to wipe out the disgrace of having, by his faintheartedness, allowed a madman to think in his arrogance that he could defy an entire city. The direst catastrophe would be preferable to any such suspicion. He had put his affairs in order, both in regard to the world and his Maker, Rosalie and the child would find that they had not been overlooked in his will. Rosalie threw herself at his feet and inquired what the fate of her husband would be, supposing he were taken alive in the assault. The commandant turned away and said in subdued tones: "It is bound to be death. No court-martial would return a verdict of insanity, there is too much discernment, prudence and intelligence in his mode of behavior. The Devil cannot be brought to book, and so Francoeur must suffer in his stead." After a flood of tears Rosalie composed herself and said: supposing she could deliver the fortress into the commandant's hands without bloodshed or danger, would Francoeur's offense then be pardoned on grounds of insanity? "Yes, indeed, I swear it!" cried the commandant. "But it is useless, he hates you more than anyone, and yesterday he shouted to our outposts that he would hand over the fort if we sent him his wife's head." "I know him," said the young woman. "I will cast out the devil in him and bring him peace. I would die in any case if he did, so I have nothing to lose supposing I die by the hand of him to whom I am wedded by the most sacred of vows." The commandant bade her consider it well, questioned her on her intentions, but could resist neither her pleading nor the prospect of escaping by this means a catastrophe which otherwise seemed inevitable.

Father Philip made his appearance in the house and related that the madman Francoeur had now hoisted a large white flag on which he had painted a picture of the Devil, but the commandant was little inclined to listen to his tale and desired him to go at once to Rosalie as she wished to make her confession. After she had done this with all the serenity of a devout mind she asked Father Philip to bear her company as far as the shelter of a stone rampart where no bullet could possibly reach him. There she would give into his keeping her child together with a sum of money sufficient to provide for its upbringing, for she could not bear to part with her beloved son yet. After making enquiries in the house as to whether he would indeed be safe from shot and shell in the place she mentioned he promised her this with some trepidation. For he had entirely lost faith in his power to cast out devils and readily conceded that what he had hitherto cast out might well not have been Satan himself but some lesser spirit.

With many a tear Rosalie attired her baby once more in white with red ribbons, then she took him in her arms and silently descended the stairs. The old commandant was standing at the foot of the staircase and could do no more than squeeze her hand before averting his face, abashed that he should shed tears in front of onlookers. And so she stepped into the street. No one knew what she meant to do; Father Philip hung back and would gladly have been relieved of his perilous duty, and the pair were followed by a crowd of idlers asking the friar what they were about. Many people cursed Rosalie because she was Francoeur's wife, but this curse left her unmoved.

In the meantime the commandant was leading his men by concealed paths to the points from which the assault was to be launched, supposing the sergeant's wife could not abate his mania.

At the city gate the crowd deserted Rosalie, for Francoeur was firing desultory shots across the open ground before the gates. Father Philip complained of feeling weak and said he must sit down for a space. Rosalie commiserated with him and pointed out the rocky rampart where she would suckle the child once more before laying it down wrapped in her cloak. There they might look for it, and it would be perfectly safe, supposing she should fail to return. Father Philip seated himself behind a rock and began to pray, while Rosalie continued with firm steps to the rampart, where she suckled the baby, gave it her blessing, wrapped it in her cloak and lulled it to sleep. Then she left it with a sigh that dispersed the dark clouds within her, so that blue sky and the radiance of the sun filled her heart and gave her strength. Now, as she stepped from behind the wall, she was visible to her obdurate husband. A blinding flash darted out by the gate, a blast of air that all but hurled her off her feet, a thunderous bang accompanied by a rushing noise told her that death had brushed her by. But she no longer felt fear, a voice within her told her that naught that outlived this day could ever perish, and love for her husband, for her baby, stirred anew in her heart as she glimpsed the former standing on the breastwork to reload and heard her child crying behind her. She felt more pain and sorrow for the two of them than for her own plight, and the arduous path before her was not the thought that most exercised her mind. A fresh shot deafened her and sent dust and splinters flying in her face, but she prayed and looked up to Heaven. And so she entered the narrow defile cut in the rock that, like a prolongation of the gun barrels, was designed to restrict with venomous thrift the grapeshot charge of two cannons and direct its lethal mass against approaching attackers. "What can you see, woman?" bellowed Francoeur. "It's no use looking up in the air, your angels will not come to your aid, here stand death and the Devil!" "Neither death nor the Devil can keep me from you any longer," she said with serene confidence and walked on up the great steps. "Woman," he screamed, "you have more courage than the Devil himself, but it will not help you." He blew on the spluttering linstock to revive it, sweat glistened on his brow and cheeks, it seemed as though two natures were warring within him. And Rosalie, not wishing to curb the conflict nor to anticipate the issue, of which she now began to be confident, proceeded no further, but knelt down on the steps no more than three paces distant from the guns at the very point where their lines of fire must cross. Gasping for air, he ripped open his tunic and waistcoat at the throat, clutched at his tangled dark locks and tore out his hair in fury. In wild agitation he pounded repeatedly with his fists on his forehead, and so opened the wound; tears and blood put out the burning fuse, a sudden gust of wind swept the powder from the touchholes and ripped the Devil's flag from the turret. "The chimney sweep is trying to get out, he is crying up the chimney," shouted Francoeur, covering his eyes with his hands. All at once he came to himself, threw open the iron gates, staggered towards his wife, lifted her to her feet, kissed her and said at length: "The black miner has burrowed his way out, light is pouring into my head again, the air is blowing through it, and our love will once more kindle a flame so that we shall never again feel the cold. Oh God, what crimes have I done in these last days! Let us waste no time, they will not grant me many hours. Where is my child, let me kiss him as long as I am still at liberty. But what is it—to die? Did I not die once when you left me, and now you are back, and your coming gives me more than your going ever took from me, a boundless sense of my own being, the fleeting moments of which are themselves enough for me. Now I could gladly live with you, even though your guilt were greater than my despair, but I know the laws of war, and thank God, I can at least die a repentant Christian."

In her rapture, well-nigh choked with tears, Rosalie could scarcely say that she forgave him, that she was free from all guilt, and that her child was nearby. She hastily bound up his wound, then led him down the steps to the rampart where she had left the child. There they found the worthy Father Philip with the baby. He had crept up to it, taking cover behind one rock after another, and as they approached, the child let something fly out of its hands as it stretched them out to greet its father. As all three of them embraced, Father Philip related how a pair of doves had fluttered down from the fort and played gently with the child. They had allowed the baby to touch them and had, so to speak, comforted it in its desolation. When he saw that, Philip had dared to approach the child. "They used to be like guardian angels, my child's favorite playmates at the fort. They sought him out faithfully and they will surely return and never leave him." And sure enough, the doves flew amicably round and round them, bearing green leaves in their beaks. "Our sin has departed from us," said Francoeur. "Never again will I rail against peace, I feel its comfort now."

In the meantime the commandant and his officers had approached, he having observed the happy outcome through his telescope. Francoeur surrendered his sword. The commandant informed him that he was pardoned in consideration of his wound having robbed him of reason, and gave orders that a surgeon should examine the wound and dress it more effectively. Francoeur sat down and submitted to everything, gazing all the time at his wife and child. The surgeon was astonished that he gave no sign of pain, and extracted from the wound a splinter of bone that had produced suppuration all round it. It seemed that Francoeur's powerful constitution had gradually and continuously worked to expel the splinter until at last external force, indeed his own desperate agency, had caused it to pierce the surface. The surgeon assured the onlookers that, but for this providential chance, an incurable dementia would have devoured the hapless Francoeur. So that no undue exertion might harm him, the sergeant was laid upon a cart, and his entry into Marseilles, amidst a populace that has always esteemed audacity higher than benevolence, was like a triumphal procession. The women threw laurel wreaths on to the cart, and all and sundry crowded forward to catch a glimpse of the high-spirited miscreant who had imposed his will on so many thousands of people for three entire days. The men, however, offered their garlands of flowers to Rosalie and her child, extolling her as their liberator and promising her and her son a rich reward for saving their city from destruction.

After a day like this there is seldom anything else in the life of one individual that would be worth the telling, although it was only in later and more placid years that the couple, restored to their former happiness and freed from the curse, realized the full measure of the good fortune they had won. The worthy old commandant adopted Francoeur as his son, and although he could not bestow on him his own name, he did nevertheless leave him his blessing and a part of his estate. Something that affected Rosalie even more profoundly, however, was the news, gleaned some years later from an acquaintance of her mother's in Prague, that the wretched woman had repented of the curse she had cast on her daughter every day throughout a pain-racked year; longing for the dissolution of her body and the release of her soul, a burden to herself and those around her, she had lived on until the day when Rosalie's devotion and her absolute trust in God had been triumphantly crowned. On that selfsame day, comforted it seemed by an inner illumination, and professing her faith in the Savior, she had passed peacefully to her rest.

> Grace will break the curse of sin,
> Love will cast the Devil out.

Translated by M. M. Yuill

Memoirs of a
Good-for-Nothing

Joseph Freiherr von Eichendorff

1

The splashing and clattering of my father's mill wheel was again in full swing, the snow on the roof was melting fast, and the twittering sparrows fluttered to and fro as I sat in the doorway and rubbed the sleep out of my eyes, reveling in the warm sunshine.

At that moment my father came out. Since the crack of dawn he had been stomping around irritably in the mill and now, his night-cap perched crookedly on his head, he shouted at me:

"You good-for-nothing! Here you are, basking in the sun again, stretching your limbs until they ache and leaving me to do all the work by myself. I don't see why I should keep you here any longer. Spring is just round the corner, so out you go into the world and earn your own living for a change!"

"So I'm a good-for-nothing, eh?" I retorted. "All right, then, I'll go off and seek my fortune."

The idea was indeed very much to my liking. In autumn and winter time the yellowhammer used to sing a lament outside our window: "Farmer, please hire me! Farmer, please hire me!" But a short time ago I had seen him sitting proudly on top of the tree, singing his merry springtime song: "Farmer, keep your work!"—and this had given me the idea of making for the open road.

So I went into the house and took down my fiddle—on which I was no mean performer, I may say. My father gave me a few coppers for the journey, and I set out down the long road that ran through the village. I smiled to myself as I saw all my old friends and companions leaving for work, going out to dig and plow as they had done yesterday, the day before yesterday and all the days before that, while I was free to roam the world.

With an air of pride and contentment I called out "Farewell!" to the poor folk around me, but none of them paid much heed. I felt as though every day would be like a Sunday. And when I finally got into the open country, I took out my beloved fiddle and played and sang as I walked along:

> The man who in God's favor stands,
> Has His command to wander free
> And seek the wonders of His hands,
> Revealed in wood and flower and tree.
>
> The listless man who sleeping lies
> Knows not the joy of morning's red;
> He only knows of children's cries,
> Of burdens, cares and daily bread.
>
> The streamlets from the mountains flow,
> The larks above make cheerful song;
> And in my joy of heart below
> I fain would join their happy throng.
>
> My guide in life is God alone,
> Who stream and lark and sea and land
> And earth and Heaven alike doth own:
> My life and fate lie in His hand.

At that moment I caught sight of an elegant carriage coming up behind me. It was traveling very slowly and must have been following me for some time, but so full was I of my song that I had not noticed it. Two aristocratic ladies were looking out and listening to me. One was younger than the other and particularly beautiful, but I found both of them very attractive. When I had finished singing, the older lady bade the coachman pull up.

"You seem to know some very charming songs, my good fellow," she said in a kindly tone.

"I could sing you far better ones, if you wished me to," I returned boldly.

"Where are you going so early in the morning?" she then asked.

I was ashamed that I did not even know myself, so I answered boldly:

"To Vienna."

The two ladies then began to talk to each other in a foreign tongue that I did not understand. The younger one shook her head a few times, but the other laughed and finally said to me:

"All right! Jump up behind! We are going to Vienna too!"

Who could have been happier than I! I bowed to the ladies and leaped up on to the box; the coachman cracked his whip and away we bowled along the shining road, the wind whistling round my ears.

The village with its gardens and church steeples receded into the distance, and new villages, palaces and mountains hove into view. Cornfields, hedgerows and meadows flew past in dazzling succession, while the larks soared in the clear blue sky above my head. It would have embarrassed me to shout out loud, but my heart was brimming over, and I jumped up and down on the footboard with such delight that I almost dropped my fiddle.

As the sun rose higher in the sky, heavy white clouds began to gather on the horizon, and an oppressive, empty silence settled over the broad expanse of gently waving grain. I thought of my village, of my father and his mill, of the cool shade by the side of our mill-pond—all that was now far, far behind me. I felt a strange urge to go back; then, tucking my fiddle inside my coat, I sat down pensively on the footboard and soon fell asleep.

When I opened my eyes, the coach was standing under a group of tall linden trees, behind which a broad flight of steps, flanked by columns, led up into a magnificent palace. Through the trees at the side could be seen the spires of Vienna.

The two ladies appeared to have left the coach long before, and the horses had been led away. I was frightened at finding myself left alone, and rushed into the palace, hearing the sound of laughter from an upper window as I did so.

I had some very strange experiences in this palace. First of all, as I stood looking around me in the cool spacious vestibule, someone tapped me on the shoulder with a stick. Turning round quickly, I found myself facing a tall man in uniform, a broad bandoleer of gold silk reaching down to his waist, a silver-knobbed swagger stick in his hand, and with a remarkably large, hooked, aristocratic nose. In the puffed-up manner of a pompous turkey-cock, he asked me my business there.

I was completely taken aback, and in my fear and trembling I could not utter a word. A number of servants came running from upstairs and downstairs, and looked me silently up and down. Then a chambermaid—as I later learned she was—came up to me and said that I was an attractive lad, and asked on behalf of her mistress whether I would like a job in the palace as a gardener's boy.

I felt in my pocket, but my few coppers had gone: they must have fallen out while I was dancing about on the coach. The only thing I had left was my fiddle, and the man with the swagger stick had already said that he would not have given me a farthing for it.

So, with great trepidation, I answered the chambermaid that I would, still looking out of the corner of my eye at the sinister figure moving to and fro in the vestibule like the great pendulum of a public clock, and just then looming up from the background majestic and frightening.

At last the gardener arrived, mumbling something about rascals and country bumpkins, and took me out into the park, giving me a lengthy lecture on the way. I was instructed to be sober and industrious, and not to wander about aimlessly or waste my time in unproductive activities: if I heeded this counsel, he said, I might in time achieve something. He gave me much other useful and well-phrased advice too, but I have since forgotten almost all of it. Indeed, I can barely recall how the whole situation came about, only that I said yes to everything. I felt like a bird that has been doused with water. But at least, praise God, I now had an occupation.

Life was pleasant in the park. I was given a generous meal every day and more than enough money to buy wine with, but there was unfortunately a good deal of work to do as well. I liked the little temples and arbors and attractive avenues, and would have gladly strolled along them at my leisure, and carried on enlightened conversation like the fine gentlemen and ladies who came there every day. Whenever the gardener went away, I used to take out my little pipe, sit down and think up fine, genteel phrases that I would have used if I had been a nobleman and able to saunter around with the lovely young lady who had brought me to the palace.

On quiet, sultry afternoons I would lie on my back and listen to the buzzing of the bees, watching the clouds sail past in the direction of my village, while the grass and the flowers swayed to and fro in the breeze. I would think then of my lovely lady, and in fact it often happened that she would walk through the distant garden with her guitar or with a book—tall, serene and gracious, like an angel—so that I scarcely knew whether I was awake or dreaming.

One day, as I was passing a summerhouse on the way to my work, I began to sing softly to myself:

> Where'er my footsteps wander,
> By mountain, field or spring,
> O'er hill or valley yonder,
> My love grows ever fonder,
> Fair lady, as I sing.

At that moment I caught sight of a lovely pair of bright, sparkling eyes peeping out from behind the half-drawn blinds and the flowers standing in front of the window. Startled, I did not finish my song but went on my way without looking back.

One Saturday evening I was standing, fiddle in hand, at the window of my cottage, thinking of the sparkling eyes I had seen and looking forward to the coming Sunday. Suddenly the little chambermaid came tripping along through the twilight.

"The fair lady sends you this," she said, "so that you can drink her health. Good night!"

With this she put a bottle of wine on the window-ledge, then turned round and disappeared again behind the flowers and bushes like a lizard.

I stood there for a long time looking at the remarkable bottle and wondering what to make of the incident. I had been playing my fiddle cheerfully enough before, but now my jubilation knew no bounds, and I sang the whole of the song about the beautiful lady, and all my other songs as well; by the time I had finished, the nightingales were awake, and the moon and the stars had long since risen above the park. It was indeed a good night—a wonderful night!

No one knows what Fate holds in store—every dog has his day—he who laughs last, laughs longest—the age of miracles is not past—Man proposes and God disposes: such were my rambling thoughts as I sat in the garden again the following day, smoking my pipe, and looking down at myself as I sat there I almost felt like a real wastrel.

Contrary to my former custom, I now rose very early every day, even before the gardener and the other laborers. The park was so beautiful at that time of day: the flowers, the fountains, the rose bushes—everything glittered like gold and jewels in the morning sunlight. In the avenues of tall beeches all was silent and cool and solemn, as in a church, and only the birds were fluttering back and forth, pecking at the sand.

Right in front of the palace, just below the windows of my lovely lady's room, stood a flowering shrub. Here I used to conceal myself each morning, looking up from between the branches, for I was afraid to show myself openly. And each day I watched her appear at the open window in her snow-white robe, still flushed and not yet fully awake. She would plait her dark brown tresses and look out across the park with tender, sparkling eyes, or tie up the flowers that grew in front of the window; at times she would even pick up a guitar, and cradling it in her white arms sing so touchingly that my heart still feels a twinge of melancholy whenever I remember her songs—yet how long ago it all was!

About a week went by in this way. But then one morning, as she was standing by the window in the stillness, a wretched fly began to buzz round my nose, making me sneeze again and again. Leaning out, she caught sight of me cowering behind the shrub. This made me feel so ashamed that for days I stayed away.

Finally I ventured there again, but the windows stayed shut, and although I hid in the bushes five or six mornings in succession, she did not appear. At last I grew impatient, and plucking up courage, I began every morning to walk boldly right past the palace and in front of all the windows. Yet there was still no sign of her. A few windows further on I used to see the other lady, whom I had not previously observed so closely—a fine, plump, rosy-cheeked person of proud and impressive aspect, like a tulip. I always bowed low to her, and, I must say, she always nodded appreciatively in return, glancing at me graciously as she did so. On one single occasion I thought I saw my lovely lady peeping out of her window from behind the curtain.

Days went by and still I did not see her. No more did she come into the park, no more did she come to the window. The gardener called me a lazy rascal; I grew irritable, and when I tried to gaze on the beauty of God's good earth I couldn't see past the tip of my own nose.

One Sunday afternoon I was lying in the park, watching the blue smoke rise from my pipe, annoyed with myself for not having chosen some other job, so that I could at least look forward sometimes to making Monday into an extra holiday. The other lads had put on their best clothes and gone off to the dancehalls in a nearby part of the town. There, out in the warm summer air, people in their Sunday best were surging backwards and forwards among the brightly lit houses and the roving barrel organs. But here was I, sitting in the park, like a bittern among the reeds at the edge of a lonely pool, rocking gently to and fro in the rowing boat that was tied up there, while the peal of the vesper bells rang out from the town and the swans drifted slowly back and forth alongside me. I was so depressed that I wished I were dead.

As I sat there, I heard the sound of cheerful voices and laughter in the distance. It came nearer and nearer; I caught a glimpse of red and white scarves, hats and plumes through the green branches, then suddenly a party of brightly dressed young gallants and their ladies ran across the field towards me from the palace, with my two ladies in their midst. Just as I was about to get up and run off, the elder of the two ladies noticed me.

"Well, well!" she cried, with a laugh. "Just the person we needed! We want you to row us across to the other side of the lake!"

One by one the ladies climbed carefully and somewhat apprehensively into the boat with the help of their escorts, who boasted confidently of their courage on the water. When the ladies had all taken their places on the wooden seat that ran around the side of the boat, I pushed off. One of the young gentlemen standing up at the bow began very gently to rock. The ladies were frightened and became uneasy; some even screamed. My lovely lady was sitting close to the side of the boat with a lily in her hand, and as she smiled at the ripples below her, touching them with her lily, her reflection shone in the water between the clouds and the trees, like an angel floating gently across the deep blue firmament.

As I was thus gazing at her, the second of my two ladies—the plump, cheerful one—had the idea of asking me to sing her a song during the trip. At this a young bespectacled dandy, who was sitting next to her, turned and kissed her hand.

"A brilliant suggestion!" he exclaimed. "Our collections of folk songs are like museums, but a popular song as really sung by the people in the woods and the open fields is like a wild Alpine rose actually growing on an Alpine slope—the very essence of our national spirit."

I replied, however, that I did not know anything worthy of such an exalted company. Thereupon the saucy little chambermaid, who, unbeknown to me, had been standing close by with a basket full of bottles and glasses, piped up:

"But you know a pretty little ditty about a lovely lady!"

"Then sing that!" cried the lady. "Come on, strike up!"

I went red all over. At that moment my lovely lady looked up, and her eyes lighted on mine, sending a tremor right through my body. I delayed no longer, and taking my courage in both hands, I sang boldly and cheerfully:

> Where'er my footsteps wander,
> By mountain, field or spring,
> O'er hill or valley yonder,
> My love grows ever fonder,
> Fair lady, as I sing.
>
> In Nature's peace reclining
> Mid flowers rich and rare,
> In pensiveness repining,
> And countless garlands twining,
> I see my loved one there.
>
> Yet my flowers shall ne'er come thither:
> She dwells so high above.

But though my garlands wither,
They shall yet take from hither
The memory of my love.

My mien conceals the very
Emotion I must save:
For though I seem so merry,
My fate is but to bury
Myself in mine own grave.

We reached the other side and the company got out of the boat. While I was singing, I had noticed that many of the young men made fun of me to the ladies, with sly glances and whispers. The man with the spectacles grasped me by the hand as he went away, and mumbled something or other, while the elder of my two ladies gave me a glance of appreciation. My lovely lady had cast her eyes down during the whole of my song, and now she left without saying a word. My eyes had filled with tears while I was singing, and the words of the song sent a feeling of shame and anguish through me, for I suddenly realized how beautiful *she* was and how poor and despised and forsaken I was myself. And when they had all disappeared behind the bushes, I could stand it no longer, and threw myself down on the grass and wept bitterly.

2

Close to the park, and separated from it only by a high wall, ran the highway. A neat little tollhouse with a red tile roof had been built here, and behind it was a small garden enclosed by a gaily colored fence and connected with the shadiest and most secluded part of the park by a gap in the wall. The tollkeeper who used to live there had just died.

Early one morning, while I was still sound asleep, the palace secretary arrived and summoned me to the bailiff. Dressing myself quickly, I sauntered along behind the cheerful secretary, who stopped every few moments to pick a flower and pin it to his lapel, or to make a few subtle passes with his cane at an imaginary opponent. From time to time he threw a remark at me over his shoulder but I did not understand a word he said, for I was still only half-awake.

As I entered the office, where it was not even properly light yet, the bailiff was sitting behind an enormous inkwell and piles of papers and books. Looking up from under his impressive wig, like an owl peering out of its nest, he said:

"What's your name? Where have you come from? Can you read and write figures?"

I said that I could, whereupon he continued:

"Well, in consideration of your good conduct and special qualifications, the lady of the house has assigned you the vacant post of tollkeeper."

I quickly thought over my conduct and qualifications, and came to the conclusion that, when all was said and done, the bailiff's compliments were well merited. So before I knew where I was, I found myself as tollkeeper.

I moved into my new quarters at once and was soon established. I also found a number of items which the late tollkeeper had bequeathed to his successor, among them a magnificent crimson dressing gown with yellow dots, a pair of green slippers, a nightcap and a few pipes with long stems. All these were things I had longed to have while I was still at home, where our village priest used to lead a leisurely life in this style. So, since I had no real duties to perform, I sat all day on the little seat in front of the house, wearing the dressing gown and the nightcap, smoking the longest pipe I could find among my predecessor's effects, and watching the people pass along the road in their carriages, on horseback or on foot. I only wished that some of those people in my own village who always said I would never get anywhere in life could see me now.

The dressing gown suited me very well, and I found the whole situation greatly to my liking. As I sat there, I reflected on questions such as how difficult it was to make a start in life, and how much more pleasant it was to live in luxury; and I made a secret vow to give up living like a vagrant and to save money like other people, so that in time I would make a real mark in the world. Yet for all these problems and worries and resolutions I did not forget my lovely lady for a single moment.

I pulled up all the potatoes and other vegetables that I found in my garden, and planted pretty flowers instead. When he saw this, the palace footman with the long, hooked nose, who often came to see me in my new residence and had become a firm friend, eyed me dubiously and seemed to think that my sudden good fortune had turned my head. But this did not deter me. For in the park close by I had heard the sound of soft voices, and although I could not see anybody because of the thick bushes, my lady's voice seemed to be among them. So every day I picked some of my finest flowers, waited until it was dark, then climbed over the wall and put them on a stone table that stood in an arbor. And every time I took a fresh posy, the old one had gone.

One evening the company were out hunting. The sun was just setting, covering the countryside with a carpet of glowing color, and the Danube, like a ribbon of fiery gold, meandered off into the distance, while from the vineyards on the hillsides beyond the plain came the singing and shouting of the vintners. Together with the footman I was sitting on the little bench in front of the tollhouse, enjoying the mild air and watching and listening as the happy day gradually darkened and grew silent.

Suddenly we heard the horns of the returning huntsmen in the distance, echoing each other's calls from both sides of the hills. This filled me with delight, and I jumped up in rapture and cried:

"How wonderful it must be to go hunting!"

The footman, however, calmly knocked out his pipe and rejoined:

"You may think so, but I know what it is like. You hardly earn enough money to replace the shoes you wear out, and you never get rid of the coughs and colds that come from permanently wet feet."

From some reason a senseless rage came over me at the sight of this detestable fellow with his conventional clothes, his permanently wet feet, his snuff taking and his long nose, and seizing him by the lapels, I cried:

"Get back to your own place, or I'll give you a good hiding here and now!"

This outburst only confirmed him in his opinion that I had gone out of my mind. He looked at me in fear and alarm, turned away without saying a word, and looking back suspiciously from time to time, hurried back with long strides to the palace, where he breathlessly announced that I had gone completely mad.

In the end I could not help laughing, though if the truth were known, I was very glad to be rid of the old wiseacre, for this was the time when I used to leave my posy. I jumped over the wall and was just creeping up to the little stone table when I heard the clip-clop of horses' hoofs close by. There was no time to escape, for at that moment my lovely lady, in green riding habit and with the plumes bobbing on her hat, rode slowly down the avenue, apparently deep in thought. As she emerged from beneath the tall trees in the fading light of evening, the sound of hunting horns coming closer and closer, the scene reminded me of the legend of the beautiful Magelone which I used to read in one of my father's old books at home, and I stood rooted to the spot.

When she caught sight of me, she gave a violent start and almost involuntarily pulled up. I was trembling like a leaf and my heart was thumping, yet I could not conceal my joy when I noticed that she was wearing in her lapel the posy that I had left the previous day. Unable to hold back any longer, I stammered:

"Most gracious lady, please accept this posy and all the other flowers in my garden and everything I own! I would go through fire and water for you!"

At first she had looked at me so gravely, almost angrily, that I had trembled like a leaf, but as I spoke, she cast her eyes down. Suddenly the sound of the huntsmen's voices came from the thicket, and snatching the posy from my hand, she rode away down the tree-lined avenue.

From this moment onwards I knew no peace. I was in the unshakable grip of that restless yet happy feeling which only used to come over me in springtime, an inexplicable feeling that some great stroke of fortune or other remarkable event was about to befall me. In particular I could not master the wretched bookkeeping at all, and when the rays of golden sunlight shone through the chestnut tree in front of the window and fell on the figures, lighting up now the balance, now the total, upwards and downwards, I became completely bewildered and could not even count up to two. The 8 came to look like my plump, tight-laced lady with a broad coiffure, while the wicked 7 was a signpost pointing backwards, or a gallows; the 9 caused me the greatest amusement, for whenever I turned my back, it stood on its head and became a 6; and the 2, shaped like a question mark, made a quizzical face as if to ask: "Where is all this going to get you, you puny zero? Without *her* your slender One and only you will never add up to anything!"

I even ceased to take any pleasure in sitting outside in front of my house. To make myself more comfortable, I now brought out a footstool as well; and the tollkeeper's old sunshade, which I had mended, I put up over my head like a Chinese pagoda. But all to no avail. As I sat and smoked and reflected, my legs seemed to be growing longer out of sheer boredom, and my nose to be getting bigger the longer I looked down it in idleness.

Occasionally a special post chaise came by before daybreak, and I would go out sleepily into the cool, fresh air: a pair of twinkling eyes would peep out from a pretty little face which looked down curiously from the coach and bade me a cheerful good morning; around me the crowing of the cocks echoed across the swaying cornfields, and a few early larks hovered high in the sky between the rays of the graying dawn; and then the coachman would blow his horn and drive on. I would stand and gaze after the coach for a long while, feeling that there was nothing left for me but to go myself on a long, long journey into the great, wide world.

I continued to lay my posies of flowers on the little stone table at sunset, but since that evening everything had changed. No one cared about them: every morning when I looked, the flowers were still lying there from the day before, looking at me mournfully with their drooping, wilting heads bathed in dewdrops, as though they were weeping.

This greatly vexed me, and I made no more posies. I let the weeds spread over the garden as they liked, while the flowers just stayed there until the wind blew the petals off. And the feelings in my own heart reflected this same disorder and wild abandon.

Once during this period of trial and tribulation, I was leaning in the window of my house, staring morosely up at the sky, when the palace chambermaid came hurrying across the road. She caught sight of me, and quickly turned in at my garden and came up to the window.

"The master came back from his travels yesterday," she said breathlessly.

"Did he?" I replied in surprise, for I had taken no interest in palace affairs for weeks, and did not even know that the master had been away. "Well, his charming daughter, my gracious young lady, will have been very pleased to see him."

The chambermaid looked me oddly up and down, so that I began to wonder whether I had said something foolish. Then, turning up her nose, she said:

"You don't know a thing, do you! Now listen. Tonight there is going to be a carnival in the palace in honor of the master. My mistress will be dressed as a flower girl—as a flower girl, do you hear?—and she has noticed that you have some beautiful flowers in your garden."

"How strange," I thought to myself; "there is now hardly a flower to be seen for weeds."

But she went on:

"My mistress needs flowers for her costume—nice, fresh ones. So she wants you to pick some and bring them this evening to the big pear-tree in the park, where she will come and collect them when it is dark."

This news filled me with delight, and in my happiness I left the window and ran outside.

"Shame on you, with that ugly old dressing gown!" she cried, as she saw how I was dressed.

This irritated me, but, anxious not to appear at a loss in matters of gallantry, I made a few graceful passes to try and catch her and kiss her. By some misfortune, however, the dressing gown, which was far too long for me, became entangled in my feet and I measured my length on the ground. By the time I picked myself up, she had vanished, and I heard her laughing merrily in the distance.

Now, at least, I had something with which to fill my thoughts and my dreams, for *she* still remembered me and my flowers. Going out into my garden, I tore all the weeds out of the flower-beds and flung them high into the air as though I were plucking out the very roots of all the world's evils and miseries. I saw the roses as *her* lips and the sky-blue convolvuluses as *her* eyes, while the snow-white lily with its sadly drooping head was like *her* alone.

I put my flowers carefully in a basket. It was a calm and beautiful evening without a cloud in the sky. A few stars were already out, the murmuring of the Danube could be heard across the fields, and from the tall trees in the nearby park came the cheerful singing of countless birds. Oh, how happy I was!

When darkness fell, I picked up my basket and made my way into the park. So bright and gay were my fragrant flowers, white, red and blue, that my heart rejoiced to see them. The moon had risen, and I walked lightheartedly along the neat, sand-covered paths, across the little white bridges beneath which the swans were sleeping, and on past the charming pavilions and arbors. I soon found the big pear-tree, for many were the times I had slept beneath it while I was still a gardener's boy.

All was dark and silent save for the silvery whisper of a tall aspen. From time to time the strains of dance music wafted across from the palace, and on occasions I even heard voices approaching, but then everything was still again. My heart was beating loudly and a strange feeling came over me, as though I were about to rob some-one.

For a long while I stood there motionless, leaning against the tree and listening, but still nobody came. I could not stand it any longer, and hanging my basket on my arm, I clambered up into the tree so as to be in the open air again, but up there the sound of music floated over to me even more clearly across the treetops.

I could see over the whole park and right into the illuminated windows of the palace: the chandeliers were turning slowly round and round like garlands of stars, while a host of elegant cavaliers and their ladies weaved, waltzed and whirled around in one dazzling body, as in a shadow play, and occasionally reclined at the open window to gaze down across the park. The lawn, the bushes and the trees shone like gold in the light that streamed from the ballroom, making the birds and flowers almost seem awake. Farther away from me, however, as well as behind me, everything remained dark and still.

"She is dancing in there," I thought to myself as I sat in the tree, "and has forgotten you and your flowers long ago. Everyone is happy, and nobody is worrying about you."

"Indeed, such has always been my fate," I mused on; "everyone else has his appointed place, has his own warm stove, his cup of coffee, his wife, his glass of wine in the evening, and is thoroughly content, even the long lanky footman. But I always seem to be a latecomer, arriving when nobody expects me any more—"

As I was meditating in this fashion I heard a rustling in the grass below me, and the gentle tones of two soft voices. Then the branches parted and the chambermaid, her inquisitive little eyes sparkling in the moonlight, peeped out and glanced round. I held my breath and stared downwards. A few minutes later the flower girl emerged from between the trees, just as the chambermaid had told me she would.

My heart was beating wildly. She was wearing a mask and seemed to be looking round her in surprise. Strangely enough, she did not seem to be at all slim and graceful now. Then at last she came close to the tree and removed her mask. It was the *other* lady!

How relieved I was, when I recovered from my first shock, that I had climbed up here to safety! How ever did *she* come to be here? And supposing my own lovely lady should arrive at this very moment to collect the flowers? A fine situation that would be! I felt like bursting into tears of fury over the whole affair.

"It is so stifling in the ballroom," I heard the flower girl say, "that I just had to come out into the open air to cool down a little."

She breathed heavily and fanned herself with her mask. In the bright moonlight I could plainly see that the veins in her neck were swollen with anger, and her face was flushed a deep red. Meanwhile the chambermaid was searching around in the bushes as though she had lost a pin.

"I simply must have some fresh flowers for my costume," the lady continued. "Wherever has he got to?"

The chambermaid went on searching, giggling to herself as she did so.

"Did you say something, Rosette?" snapped her mistress.

"I said what I shall always say," replied the chambermaid forthrightly, "and that is, that the tollkeeper is an absolute rogue, and always will be. He is probably asleep behind one of these bushes."

I was itching to jump down and redeem my reputation, but just then the music in the ballroom grew louder and the sound of drums was heard.

The lady could no longer control her impatience.

"They are already drinking to the master's return," she said irritably. "Come, or our absence will be noticed."

And putting her mask on again, she hurried back towards the palace in a rage, followed by the chambermaid. The trees and the bushes seemed to point their long noses and fingers at the retreating figure in some odd way, and the moonlight danced up and down her broad back as on a keyboard; indeed, her hasty departure, to the accompaniment of trumpets and drums, reminded me of the dramatic exit of the prima donna in an opera.

Sitting up in the tree, I did not really understand what was going on, and I kept my eyes fixed on the palace. A circle of tall lanterns at the foot of the steps cast a strange glow on to the shining windows and far out into the garden: it was a group of servants playing a serenade for their young master, and in the middle of them the footman, in a resplendent regalia like that of a minister of state, stood in front of his music stand, playing away for dear life on his bassoon.

As I sat back to listen to this serenade, the French windows leading to the upper balcony suddenly opened. A tall, handsome man in a fine uniform with many shining medals stepped out, leading by the hand my lovely lady all in white, looking like a lily in the darkness, or like the moon gliding across a cloudless sky.

I could not turn my gaze from the scene. I became oblivious to the park, the trees and the lawns, and had eyes only for the tall, slim figure as she stood there in the magical light of the torches, now exchanging a few charming words with the handsome officer at her side, now nodding graciously to the musicians below. The company assembled beneath the balcony were beside themselves with joy, and in the end I could no longer restrain myself and joined in the cries of "Hurrah!" at the top of my voice.

But when, after a while, she left the balcony, and one by one the torches went out, and the music stands were taken away, and the trees began to rustle again in the darkness, then the truth dawned on me, and I realized that it was only her aunt who had wanted me to bring the flowers, and that my lovely lady had long been married and had no thought of me, and that I was a stupid fool.

These thoughts made me ponder long and deeply, and I withdrew like a snail into the protective shell of my own brooding. The strains of the music in the palace became fainter and fainter, and the lonely clouds drifted away above the gloomy expanse of the park. And the whole night long I sat up there in the tree like an owl, contemplating the ruins of my happiness.

At last the cool air of morning woke me from my reveries, and as I looked about me, I was filled with astonishment. The music and dancing had long since ceased; the lawns, the pillars and the flights of steps, as well as the palace itself, presented a cool, silent, solemn aspect, and the only sound to be heard was the lonely splashing of the fountains. The birds were waking in the branches around me, spreading their wings and ruffling their gay feathers as they regarded their unexpected bedfellow in surprise. Cheerful rays of sunlight sparkled across the park and streamed into my eyes.

I sat up, and for the first time in a long while I looked out into the far distance, to where the boats were wending their way down the river past the vineyards, and where the country roads, still deserted, stretched out like bridges over the shimmering countryside, past distant mountains and valleys.

I know not how it happened, but suddenly I felt seized by my old wanderlust, my old feeling of mingled melancholy and joyous expectation. Yet at the same time my thoughts turned to the lovely lady slumbering peacefully between silken coverlets and surrounded by bright flowers up there in the palace, an angel sitting by her bedside in the stillness of the dawn.

"But no!" I cried aloud. "I must get away from here and travel onwards and onwards, as far as the sky is blue!"

And picking up my basket, I flung it high into the air, watching with delight as the flowers caught on the branches or fell on to the green grass below. Then I climbed quickly down and walked through the silent park towards the tollhouse, stopping from time to time at some spot where I had seen her or where I had lain in the shade, thinking of her.

Inside the house and around it everything looked just the same as when I had left it the day before. The garden lay waste and overgrown; inside the ledger was still open, and my fiddle, which I had almost forgotten, was hanging on the wall, covered with dust. At that moment a ray of sunlight from the window opposite lit up the strings, sounding a chord of joy in my heart.

"Come with me, faithful instrument!" I cried. "Our kingdom is not of this world!"

So, taking it down from the wall, and leaving the dressing gown, ledger, pipes and sunshade behind, I walked out of the little house and away down the shining highway, as poor as when I had arrived.

Many times I glanced back. My feelings were strangely mixed—on the one hand sadness, on the other unbridled happiness, like that of a bird that has escaped from its cage. So, after I had gone some distance along my way, I took my fiddle and sang for all to hear:

My guide in life is God alone,
Who stream and lark and sea and land
And earth and Heaven alike doth own:
My life and fate lie in His hand.

The palace, the garden and the spires of Vienna had vanished from sight in the haze behind me, and the larks soared jubilantly in the air above as I tramped over green hills and past merry towns and villages in the direction of Italy.

3

But now I was in trouble, for it had not occurred to me that I did not know the way, nor was there anyone around at that time of morning whom I could have asked. A short way ahead the highway divided into a number of different roads which led away into the distance and up over the highest mountains, as though to take the traveler right out of the world. It made me dizzy to look at them.

At last a farmer came into view, apparently on his way to church, for it was Sunday. He was wearing an old-fashioned coat with large silver buttons and carrying a long walking stick with a solid silver knob that glittered from afar in the sunshine.

"Can you tell me which road leads to Italy?" I asked him politely, when he came near.

He stopped, looked at me, reflected for a while, his lower lip protruding, then looked at me again.

"Italy," I repeated, "where the oranges grow."

"What do I care about oranges?" he snapped, and stalked on.

I would have given the man credit for better manners, for he had looked respectable enough.

But what was I to do now? Turn round and go back to my village? People would point their fingers at me, and the children would prance around and shout: "Welcome back from the big, wide world! What's the big, wide world like? Have you brought us back any gingerbread from the big, wide world?" The footman with the hooked nose, who was well-informed on matters of culture, used to say to me: "My dear tollkeeper, Italy is a beautiful country where

God Himself provides for all. You can lie on your back in the sun and the grapes will drop into your mouth. And if you are bitten by a tarantula, you will dance with remarkable agility, even though you may never really have learned to dance at all."

"Italy! Italy! Hurrah!" I cried in delight, and without considering the different routes, I ran on along the first road that I set eyes on.

After walking for some while, I spied a beautiful orchard on the right-hand side of the road. The morning sun was shining so attractively through the tree trunks and branches that the grass looked to be covered with a golden carpet. As I could not see anyone there, I climbed over the low hedge and lay down under an apple-tree to rest, for my limbs were still aching after the night I had spent up the tree.

There was a fine view of the surrounding landscape, and as it was Sunday the pealing of bells rang out across the silent fields from far and near, and country folk in their finery were making their way to church past the meadows and hedges. As the birds sang in the tree above me, I rejoiced and thought back on my mill and on my lovely lady's park, and how all that was now so far behind me—until at last I fell asleep.

In my dream I saw my lady, her long, white veils fluttering in the glow of dawn, emerge from the beautiful countryside and float gently towards me on the wings of the ringing chimes. In the next instant it seemed as though we were not in strange parts but in the shade of my father's mill at home: the people seemed to be in church, and only the sound of the organ could be heard through the trees, but everything was so silent and deserted that it made my heart ache. My lady, however, was kind to me and took me by the hand, and as we walked together through the lonely scene, she sang the words that she used to sing at the open window every morning to the strains of her guitar; and as she sang, I saw her reflection in the tranquil waters of the pond, but a thousand times lovelier, though also with such strange, staring eyes that I was almost frightened. Suddenly the mill wheel started to turn first slowly, then louder and faster. The pond clouded over, and ripples formed on its surface; my lady's features became pale and her veils grew longer and longer in the wind until finally they stretched out across the sky like sinister wisps of fog. The roar of the mill wheel grew even louder, and often I seemed to hear the footman playing his bassoon in the midst of it. At last, my heart thumping violently, I awoke.

A breeze had indeed risen and was rustling through the branches above me, but the deafening roar that I had heard came neither from the mill wheel nor from the footman, but from the farmer who had refused to show me the road to Italy a short while earlier. He had taken off his Sunday clothes and now stood before me in a white smock.

"Well, well," he said sarcastically, as I rubbed the sleep from my eyes, "are you reckoning on picking up a few oranges here, you laggard, trampling down my fine grass instead of going to church?"

I was annoyed that the ruffian had woken me up, and jumping indignantly to my feet, I retorted:

"What right have you to talk to me like that? I was a gardener before you ever knew me, and a tollkeeper too, and if you had come to the town, you would have had to doff your greasy nightcap to me. Besides that, I had my own house and my own crimson dressing gown with yellow dots."

But the villain took no notice of all this, and putting his hands on his hips, he said:

"What do you want here, eh?"

I saw that he was a short, stocky, bandy-legged fellow with protruding eyes and a red, slightly crooked nose. Saying "Eh? Eh?" all the time, he advanced slowly towards me, until at last I was filled with a strange sense of fear. Without hesitation, I leaped over the hedge and ran straight across the fields without looking back, my fiddle banging to and fro in the pocket of my cloak.

When I finally stopped to get my breath back, the orchard and the valley were lost to view, and I found myself standing in a lovely wood. But I paid little heed to the attractions of the scenery, for I was becoming more and more furious over the whole affair, in particular over the fellow's incivility, and I cursed him silently.

Hastening onwards, I got further and further away from the main road and closer and closer to the mountains. The track which I had been following now gave out, and all that remained was a narrow, little-used footpath. There was not a soul in sight and not a sound to be heard, yet it was pleasant to be walking there, for the trees were rustling and the birds were singing their merry ditties. So I commended myself to God's care, took out my violin and played all my favorite pieces, making the lonely wood echo to the sound.

But I did not play for long, for I kept on tripping over the confounded roots of trees; besides this, I was beginning to feel hungry, and there was no sign of the end of the wood. I wandered on the whole day, and the slanting rays of the sun were shining through the trees when at last I came out into a little grassy valley set around by mountains and full of red and blue flowers over which scores of butterflies were fluttering to and fro in the glow of evening.

So solitary was it here that the world seemed to be hundreds of miles away. The crickets chirped, and lying in the long grass on the other side of the valley, a shepherd played a mournful air on his pipe, filling the heart with melancholy. "How lucky to live a lazy life like him," I thought to myself, "while people like me have to wander about in unfamiliar parts and always keep their wits about them."

At the bottom of the valley flowed the beautiful clear water of a stream, and since I could not cross over to him, I shouted across and asked where the nearest village was. He did not trouble to get up but merely raised his head slightly from the ground and pointed with his pipe to the woods on the far side; then, completely unconcerned, he went on playing his tune.

I walked briskly onwards, for darkness was closing in. The birds, which had still been singing loudly as the last rays of evening sunshine gleamed through the wood, were suddenly quiet, and I almost began to feel frightened in the midst of the eerie rustling of the trees.

Then I heard the sound of dogs barking in the distance. I quickened my pace. The forest grew lighter, and through the last few trees I saw a lovely green open space where a group of children were playing noisily around a tall linden tree. There was also an inn there, in front of which a party of peasants were sitting round a table, playing cards and smoking; near the door on the other side a number of young lads and girls, the latter with their arms wrapped in their aprons, sat chatting to each other in the cool of the evening.

I immediately took out my fiddle and struck up a jolly country dance as I walked out of the wood towards them. The girls were surprised, while the old men broke into peals of laughter that echoed through the trees. However, as I strolled up to the linden tree and stood there leaning against it, still playing my fiddle, the young folk began to murmur and whisper to each other; then, putting down their pipes, the lads got up, each took his girl by the hand, and before I knew where I was, they were all dancing merrily round me, with the dogs barking, smocks flying and the children staring at me in curiosity as my agile fingers moved over the strings.

When the first dance was over, it was plain for all to see how deeply a piece of good music can affect people. For a few moments ago these lads had been lolling on the benches, their legs outstretched and their pipes in their mouths, whereas now they were suddenly transformed, letting their brightly colored kerchiefs hang down from their buttonholes and dancing so charmingly round the girls that it was a real delight to watch.

One of them, who obviously had a high opinion of himself, then fumbled in his waistcoat pocket for a long while, so as to be sure that the others would notice it, and finally produced a silver coin which he tried to press into my hand. This offended me, even though I did not have a penny to my name, and I told him to keep his charity for himself, since I was only playing out of happiness at being among people again.

A little later a pretty girl came up to me with a large goblet of wine.

"Musicians are thirsty folk!" she said with a smile, revealing a row of pearly white teeth behind her ruby lips, which made me want to kiss her. Flashing me a glance with her sparkling eyes, she lifted the goblet to her dainty lips, then passed it to me. I drained it, then struck up again, and they all began to whirl happily around.

The old men had finished their game, and gradually the young folk became weary and drifted off home. Finally all was still and deserted in front of the inn. Even the girl who had brought me the wine was about to leave but she walked away very slowly and looked back from time to time as though she had forgotten something. Then she stopped and appeared to examine the ground, but I could see that, as she bent down, she glanced back towards me from under her arm. The polite manners that I had learned at the palace now stood me in good stead, and I ran over to her and asked:

"Have you lost something, fair maid?"

"No, no!" she replied, blushing. "It was only a rose. Would you like it?"

I thanked her and put it in my buttonhole. Then giving me an affectionate glance, she added:

"You play very nicely."

"It is a gift from God," I answered.

"There are not many musicians in these parts," she went on, hesitating and casting her eyes down. "You could make a good living here. Besides, my father plays the violin a little too, and likes hearing about the world outside—and he is very rich."

Then she burst out laughing and cried:

"If only you wouldn't wag your head about when you play!"

"Dearest maiden," I replied, "do not address me so disrespectfully. And as concerns my head movements, that is something all we virtuosos do."

"Oh, I see," she said, and was about to go on, when a terrible noise came from inside the inn. The door burst open with a crash, and a lanky fellow flew out like a ramrod from a gun barrel; then the door was slammed shut again.

The girl had fled like a scared rabbit the moment she heard the first sound, and had vanished into the darkness. The figure on the ground sprang to his feet and began to hurl a remarkable barrage of insults at the door.

"What? Drunk?" he cried. "Not paid the debts chalked up on the grimy door? Wipe them out! Did I not shave you over the spoon* yesterday and cut your nose in the process, so that you bit the spoon in half? Shaving accounts for one debt, the spoon for two, a piece of plaster to stick on your nose for three—how many miserable debts do you expect me to pay? All right, then, all right—I'll leave the whole village and the whole world unshorn. You can all go around with long beards for all I care, and when the Day of Judgment comes, even God Himself won't be able to tell whether you're Jews or Christians! Go and hang yourselves by your own beards, you shaggy bears!"

At this point he suddenly burst into tears, and his voice became a pitiable falsetto:

"Do you expect me to drink water, like a wretched fish? Is that

---

* The German expression *über den Löffel barbieren* connotes in its literal meaning the village barber's primitive way of putting a wooden spoon inside his customer's cheek in order to stretch the skin and smooth out the wrinkles. From this it came to mean "to treat someone like a peasant," i.e. summarily and none too gently, and eventually "to pull the wool over someone's eyes," which is the only meaning it has today. Eichendorff uses it here as a deliberate pun. [*Trans.*]

what you call brotherly love? Am I not a human being and an experienced surgeon? How furious it all makes me—me, a man of compassion and human kindness!"

But no one stirred in the house, and step by step he moved away. When he caught sight of me, he advanced towards me with open arms, and for a moment I thought the madcap was going to embrace me, but I sprang to one side and he stumbled past. For a long while afterwards I still heard him talking to himself in the darkness, now in a harsh voice, now gently.

My thoughts were in confusion. The girl who had given me the rose was young, attractive and rich—that way I could make my fortune in the twinkling of an eye: there would be lamb and pork, turkey and fatted goose stuffed with apples, and I could even see the footman coming up to me and saying: "Go to it, tollkeeper, go to it! Youthful wed eats happy bread, and the lucky man gets the bride! Stay at home and feather your nest!"

Turning over such thoughts in my mind, I sat down on a stone in the now deserted forecourt of the inn, for since I had no money, I did not venture to knock at the door. The moon was shining brightly, the wooded mountainsides rustled in the stillness of the night, and sometimes the barking of a dog came from the village that lay hidden in the valley beyond the trees. I watched the wisps of cloud drift slowly across the face of the moon, and sometimes caught sight of a falling star in the distance.

"That same moon," I thought to myself, "is shining at this moment on my father's mill and on the white palace; my lady is asleep, all is quiet, and the fountains and trees in the park are rustling as they always did, and nobody cares whether I am there or not—or even whether I am alive or dead."

The world suddenly seemed so vast, and I felt so utterly alone in its midst that I could have cried my heart out.

I was still sitting there, when suddenly I heard the sound of horses' hoofs in the distance. I held my breath and listened. It came closer and closer, and soon I could hear the horses snorting. Then two riders appeared from beneath the trees. They stopped at the edge of the forest and began an animated conversation with each other in low tones: this I could see from the two shadows that stretched out across the moonlit clearing and gesticulated with their long dark arms, now in this direction, now in the other.

Before she died, my mother had often told me stories about wild forests and fierce bandits, and I had always wished I could have an adventure like that. Now I was to pay the penalty for my rash and stupid ideas!

Getting softly to my feet, I reached up stealthily, and grasping the lowest branch of the tree quickly pulled myself up. But half my body was still dangling from the branch, and as I was just about to swing up my legs, one of the horsemen trotted out into the open. I shut my eyes tight and lay there motionless on the branch.

"Who's there?" came a voice from behind me.

"No one!" I shouted at the top of my voice, afraid that he had already caught me. At the same time I could not help smiling at the thought of how disconcerted the two fellows were going to look when they turned out my empty pockets.

"Is that so?" said the bandit. "Then whose are these two legs hanging down?"

There was no way out now.

"They only belong to a poor musician who has lost his way," I answered, and with this I lowered myself to the ground, for I felt foolish sprawling over the branch like a broken fork.

The horse shied as I dropped from the tree, but patting its neck, the bandit said with a laugh:

"Well, well! We've lost our way too, so that makes us friends! I thought you might help us find the road to B. You won't regret it!"

It was useless for me to insist that I had no idea where B. was, and that it would be better for me to ask first at the inn or show them the way down to the village. He paid no heed but calmly produced a pistol from his belt and let the cold moonlight glint upon it. Then polishing the barrel and inspecting it critically with one eye, he turned to me and said in a quiet, friendly tone:

"Perhaps, my dear fellow, you will be so kind as to lead the way to B."

Now the fat was properly in the fire. If I happened to take the right road, I should certainly end up in the robbers' lair and get a beating when they discovered that I had no money; and if I did not take the right road, I would also get a beating. So without further ado I took the first road I saw, which led past the inn and away from the village. The horseman galloped back to his companion, and then they rode along together behind me.

So in this aimless and rather foolish manner we moved on through the moonlit night. The road led through the forest and along the mountainside. From time to time, across the tops of the dark, swaying pines that stretched up from the slopes below, I caught a view of deep, silent valleys; here and there a nightingale sang, and dogs barked in the distant villages. The sound of a running stream came from the bottom of the valley and its waters glistened in the moonlight.

On and on we went. The monotonous clip-clopping of the horses' hoofs was always behind me, and the two riders chattered away to each other the whole time in some foreign tongue; the long shadows of the trees fell across the two figures in turn, making them look now light, now dark, now small, now gigantic. My thoughts were in turmoil, and I felt as though I were dreaming and could not wake up. I stepped out boldly, however, for in the end, I thought, the darkness will have to give way to daylight and we shall reach the end of the wood.

At last a few long rays of pale, red light spread across the sky, quite faintly, as when one breathes on a mirror, and the sound of the first lark came from high above the silent valley. At this welcome from the dawn a weight was lifted from my heart, and my fear left me.

The two riders stretched their limbs and looked round on all sides, apparently realizing now that we could hardly be on the right road. They jabbered away to each other again, and I could not fail to notice that they were talking about me; one of them even seemed to be rather apprehensive of me, perhaps taking me for a highwayman in disguise who was out to lead them along a false path. This thought greatly amused me, for the lighter it became, the bolder I grew, especially as we were just then coming out into a clearing in the wood. So glancing fiercely to left and right, I whistled a few times between my fingers as robbers do when they want to signal to each other.

"Stop!" shouted one of the two, in a voice that made me tremble. I looked round and saw that they had both dismounted and tied their horses to a tree. One of them came quickly towards me, looked me straight in the eye and then began to roar with laughter in a ridiculous manner that I found very irritating. Then he said:

"Well, I do declare! It's the palace gardener—or tollkeeper, I should say!"

I stared at him wide-eyed but could not recall him; indeed, I should have been hard put to remember all the young men who used to ride in and out of the palace.

"Splendid! Splendid!" he went on, still laughing. "I see you are on holiday. We are in need of a servant, so if you stay with us, you can be on holiday the whole time."

I was taken aback by this, and stammered that I was on a trip to Italy.

"Italy!" he cried. "That's where we are going too!"

"Well, in that case . . . !" I exclaimed. And taking out my fiddle, I played a happy tune that roused the birds in the forest, whereupon he seized his companion and waltzed round on the grass with him like one possessed.

Suddenly they both stopped.

"Heaven be praised!" cried one. "I can see the steeple of the church at B. We'll soon be there now!"

He took out his watch, caused it to strike the hour, looked at it, then shook his head and let it strike again.

"No, that won't do," he said, "we shall get there too soon, and that could have unpleasant results."

So they fetched cake, roast meat and bottles of wine from their saddlebags, spread out a gaily colored cloth on the grass, and stretching themselves out beside it, began to eat a hearty meal. They gave very generous portions of everything to me as well, which was just what I needed, since I had not eaten properly for days.

"For your information," began one of them, ". . . but you recognize us, do you not?"

I shook my head.

"Well, then, for your information, I am Leonhard, a painter, and the gentleman over there is Guido, also a painter."

I now looked at the two painters more closely in the light of dawn. The one called Leonhard was tall, slim and suntanned, with vivacious, flashing eyes; the other was much younger, shorter and more delicate, dressed in the old German style, as the footman used to call it, open-necked and with a white ruff around which hung dark brown curls, which he often had to shake out of his handsome features.

When this younger person had finished his meal, he picked up my violin, which I had laid on the ground beside me, sat down on a branch of a nearby tree that had just been felled, and plucked the strings a few times. Then, in clear, birdlike tones that moved me deeply, he sang:

> When the glow of morning pales
> Over woods and over dales,
> Warmth and light to all things bringing,
> Birds in joy are upwards winging.
> And all who see them, man or boy,
> Are filled with happiness and joy,
> And swear, the bird-song round them ringing,
> That they shall share the joy of singing.

As he sang, the morning sun cast a cheerful glow over his rather pale cheeks and his dark, amorous eyes. But I was so tired that I could no longer follow the words or the tune that he was singing, and I soon fell asleep.

When I began to wake, I heard the two painters, as in a dream, still talking away beside me and the birds still singing above my head. The brightness of the day shone through my closed eyes and produced a kind of bright darkness, as when the sun shines through red silk curtains.

"Come è bello!" I heard someone exclaim. Opening my eyes, I found the young painter bending over me in the sparkling light of morning, so closely that all I could see of his face was his dark eyes set between his dangling curls.

I jumped up quickly, for it was now broad daylight. Leonhard seemed somewhat peevish and frowned as he bade us get ready to continue the journey. The other painter, shaking the curls out of his face, hummed a tune to himself as he bridled his horse, and in the end Leonhard burst out laughing, seized a bottle that was still standing on the ground and cried, pouring the remainder of its contents into the glasses:

"Here's to a successful journey!"

They clinked their glasses, and the sound was pleasant to hear. Then Leonhard took the bottle and hurled it high into the air so that it glittered in the sunlight.

At last they mounted their horses, and I set off, walking cheerfully at their side. Before us stretched an endless valley, and we made our way down to it. Everywhere there was the stirring of nature and a flashing of lights and an air of celebration. I felt so cool and so happy that I could have taken wing and sailed from the mountain-side right out into the glorious landscape below.

4

Farewell, O mill and palace and footman! Here I was, perched high on the box and bouncing sometimes a yard into the air, the two painters in the coach behind me, and a team of four horses with a splendid postilion in front of me. The wind whistled round my ears; villages, towns and vineyards flashed by on both sides at such a speed that it set my head in a whirl.

But I must tell how all this happened. When we arrived at B., a tall, gaunt, morose-looking man in a thick green coat came out to meet us, bowed several times to the painters and conducted us into the village. Beneath the tall lime trees in front of the posting house there stood a fine coach-and-four. Leonhard had remarked a number of times, as we rode along, that I had grown out of my clothes, and he fetched out of his portmanteau a new waistcoat and tailcoat, which he made me don. These made me look very elegant but were too long and too wide, and hung down limply on all sides. I was also given a new hat which shone in the sun as though it had just been greased.

The morose-looking man then took the two horses by the bridle, the painters jumped into the coach, while I took my place on the box, and off we went, just as the postmaster, still wearing his nightcap, poked his head out of the window. The postilion sounded his horn, and we set off merrily for Italy.

I had a wonderful time up there, living like a bird yet without having to fly. All I had to do was to sit on the box day and night, and occasionally fetch food and drink from the inns at which we stopped. The painters never left the coach, and during the daytime they drew the curtains across the windows as if they were afraid of sunstroke. Now and again, however, Guido did put his handsome head out and carry on a friendly conversation with me, and he laughed at Leonhard when the latter took offense at our long dia-logues.

On a few occasions, indeed, I was in danger of falling out with my masters—once, for example, when I began to play my fiddle one beautiful starlit night as I sat on the box, and another time because of my propensity for sleeping.

This latter was a remarkable affair. I wanted to see everything in Italy that there was to see, and every few moments my eyes goggled at the things we passed. But after a while the sight of the sixteen galloping hoofs in front of me became a jumbled pattern of crisscross threads which so bewildered me that my eyes began to water, until at last I could keep them open no longer and fell helplessly into a deep sleep from which I could not be roused. Whether it was day or night, rain or shine, I hung down over the box, now to one side, now to the other, and sometimes even backwards; on occasion my head drooped so far down that my hat flew off, and Guido, sitting in the coach below, cried out in alarm.

In this manner—though I can now scarcely remember it—we traveled most of the way through what they call Lombardy. Then one fine evening we stopped at a country inn. The post-horses were not due to be ready in the nearby village for a few hours, so the painters left the coach and asked to be shown to a private room where they could rest a little and write a few letters. I was very glad at this and went immediately into the tavern, hoping to be able to eat and drink at my leisure for the first time in a long while.

It was a disorderly place. The serving girls were walking about with unkempt hair, and their loose neckerchiefs were draped untidily over their yellow skins. The menservants, wearing blue smocks, were sitting at a round table eating supper, and from time to time they glanced at me out of the corners of their eyes. They all wore short, thick pigtails, and had the elegant appearance of young aristocrats.

"Well," I said to myself, continuing to eat heartily, "here I am in that country from which those odd folk used to bring our village priest mousetraps, barometers and paintings. What things one can learn if only one ventures out into the world."

As I was meditating thus over my meal, a little man who had been sitting in a dark corner of the room drinking a glass of wine suddenly darted out towards me like a spider. He was short and humpbacked and had a large, terrifying head with a long Roman nose and thin red side-whiskers, and the hairs of his powdered wig stood on end as though he had been in a gale. He wore a discolored, old-fashioned tailcoat, short plush knee britches and faded silk stockings. He had been to Germany once, he said, and he prided himself on understanding the language perfectly.

Sitting down beside me, he asked all manner of questions, taking pinches of snuff the whole time: was I the *servitore,* he inquired, and when did we *arrivare,* and were we going to Rome? I did not know the answers myself, and besides that I could not understand his gibberish. So at last I asked in desperation:

"*Parlez-vous français?*"

He shook his head—to my great relief, since I did not speak French either. But it was no use. The fellow now had the bit between his teeth and went on asking question after question. The more we talked, the less the one understood of what the other was saying, and eventually we both became so heated that I thought the *signore* was going to peck at me with his long beak. By this time the maids, who had been following our babel of tongues, were having a good laugh at our expense.

So, quickly putting down my knife and fork, I went outside. I felt in this foreign land as though I had sunk a thousand fathoms down into the sea, where all kinds of strange, writhing creatures were crawling about, glaring and snapping at me in the murky depths.

The warm night air outside was perfect for a stroll. A snatch of song came floating across from the distant vineyards, occasional flashes of lightning could be seen in the distance, and the whole scene was bathed in shimmering moonlight. Sometimes I imagined that I saw a tall, dark figure creeping past the hazel bushes in front of the house and peeping out at me through the branches, but the next moment all was quiet again.

Just then Guido came out on to the balcony of the inn. He did not notice me, and playing skillfully on a zither that he must have found in the inn, he sang as sweetly as a nightingale:

Man's delights are laid to rest—
Such is the message of the breeze
That rustles through the leafy trees,
Stirring memories, long repressed,
Of olden times, of poignant sorrow;

Soft forebodings of the morrow
Flash like lightning through the breast.

Whether he sang any more than this one verse, I do not know, for so gentle was the mild night air that I lay down on the bench in front of the door and, weary as I was, fell sound asleep.

Some few hours later I was awakened from my dreams by the cheerful sound of the post horn. It took me a while to collect my senses, then I jumped up and saw that the dawn was glowing on the mountaintops. The fresh morning air made me shiver. Then I remembered that we had intended to be well on our way by this time. "Aha!" I thought, "this time it's my turn to do the waking and laughing. What a shock the sleepy-headed Guido will get when he hears me outside!"

I went into the little garden, crept up to the window of my masters' room, drew myself up and sang in a cheerful voice:

When the hoopoe's on the wing,
Dawn is closely following;
And when the sun reveals his treasure,
Sleeping is a double pleasure!

The window was open, yet everything was quiet but for the breeze blowing through the tendrils of the vine that trailed along the wall and into the window itself.

"What has happened?" I cried in surprise, then ran into the house and down the passage that led to the room. When I opened the door, a sudden stab of pain went through my heart: the room was empty—no coat, no hat, no boots. The only thing left was the zither that Guido had been playing the previous evening.

On the table in the middle of the room lay a fine, full moneybag with a note on it. I took the note to the window and saw to my amazement that it had written on it "For the Tollkeeper."

But what use was this if I did not find my cheerful masters again? I dropped the moneybag into the deep pocket of my cloak, and it sank like a stone in a well, weighing me down heavily. Then I rushed out and raised the alarm, rousing all the menservants and maidservants in the place. They had no idea what I was trying to say, and thought I had gone mad, but when they found the empty room, they were as astonished as I.

No one knew anything about the painters. The only information came from a maid who appeared to have noticed—as far as I could understand from her signs and gestures—that when Guido was singing on the balcony the previous evening, he had suddenly given a loud cry and rushed back into the room; later in the night, she said, she had been woken up by the sound of galloping horses, and when she looked out of her window, she saw the humpbacked *signore* who had been talking so animatedly to me gallop away on a white horse across the moonlit fields, sometimes bouncing up a yard into the air above the saddle; he had looked like a ghost on a three-legged horse, and she had crossed herself in fear.

I stood there, not knowing what to do. Meanwhile the horses had been harnessed and the coach was waiting in front of the inn. The postilion was blowing his horn fit to burst, impatient to get off, for he had to be at the next station by the appointed time, and everything had been planned to the minute. I ran round the house one last time, calling the painters, but there was no reply. The people in the inn gathered outside and stared at me, the postilion began to curse at the delay and the horses snorted and pawed the ground. At a loss what to do, I finally jumped into the coach; the hostler slammed the door behind me, the postilion cracked his whip and off I went again into the great, wide world.

5

I journeyed onwards day and night without rest. I had no time to collect my thoughts, for wherever we stopped, fresh horses were waiting ready harnessed; moreover I could not speak to the people, and my protestations therefore served little purpose. Sometimes, when I was in the middle of an excellent meal at an inn, the postilion would blow his horn and I had to drop my knife and fork and jump back into the coach, without having the slightest notion where I was supposed to be going at such breakneck speed, or why.

In other respects this mode of life was not at all unpleasant. I stretched myself out in the coach as though I were lying on a sofa, facing first one way, then the other, and came to know new lands and new peoples. Whenever we passed through a town, I rested both my arms on the window and looked out, acknowledging the salutations of the inhabitants who doffed their hats to me, or waving like an old friend to the girls sitting at their windows, making them gaze after the coach for a long time in surprise and curiosity.

Eventually, however, I began to feel worried. I had never counted how much there was in the moneybag, and I had to pay the postmasters and innkeepers a great deal wherever I went, so before I knew it, the bag was empty. My first thought was to jump out of the coach while we were riding through a lonely wood, and thus escape. But in the next moment I felt sad at the thought of leaving the coach to travel on alone, for together we might have journeyed right to the ends of the earth.

As I sat there deep in thought, not knowing what course to follow, the coach suddenly swerved off the main highway.

"Where are you going?" I shouted to the postilion.

But shout as I might, the only thing he would say was:

"Si, si, signore!"

And he drove on furiously, so that I was tossed from one side of the coach to the other.

I could not understand what he was about, for the highway at this point ran through splendid country, and beyond it the sun was sinking as though into a flashing sea of fire. In the direction in which we were now traveling, however, there rose up a barren mountain range with deep, sinister ravines which had long been shrouded in darkness.

The farther we went, the wilder and more desolate the country became, and when all of a sudden the moon shone out from behind the crags and trees, the scene presented a grim and gruesome aspect. The narrow, rocky passes forced us to go slowly, and the monotonous rattle of the wheels echoed loudly against the stony slopes as though we were driving into a huge tomb. From invisible waterfalls in the depths of the forest came a continuous roar, and owls cried in the distance: "Follow, follow!"

I now noticed that the coachman had no uniform and was in fact not a postilion at all. He appeared to be glancing uneasily from side to side, and began to urge the horses on even faster. As I leaned out of the window, a horseman suddenly rode out from behind the bushes, galloped across our path and vanished into the forest on the other side. This caused me great alarm, for in the moonlight I thought I recognized the horseman as that hunchback on the white horse who had pecked at me with his beaky nose in the inn. Shaking his head, the coachman burst out laughing at such reckless riding, and turning round, chattered away to me with great animation—though I did not understand a word—and drove on all the faster.

A short while later I was relieved to see a light in the distance. Gradually more and more lights came into view, growing steadily larger and brighter until at last we approached a group of smoke-blackened cottages which clung to the rocks like swallows' nests. It was a warm night and the doors were open, and in the brightly lit rooms I could see all kinds of rough-looking folk squatting round the hearth like murky shadows.

The coach rattled past the houses and on to a stony track that led up a steep mountainside; at some moments tall trees and overhanging creepers completely hemmed us in, at others the whole of the heavens lay open, and below us the immense, silent pattern of mountains, valleys and woodlands was spread out to my gaze. On the summit of the mountain stood a large, ancient castle, its numerous turrets glistening in the moonlight.

"The Lord be praised!" I cried, wondering eagerly where they were going to take me.

It must have been at least half an hour before we reached the castle. The entrance led through a large round tower, the top of which had completely crumbled away. The coachman cracked his whip three times; the sound echoed round the old building and scared a crowd of jackdaws out of their nooks and crannies, making them fly noisily to and fro. Then the coach rolled through a long, dark passage. The horses' hoofs sent up sparks from the cobblestones, a large dog barked, and the coach rumbled on past the curved stone walls, while the jackdaws still cawed overhead. And so, with a clatter and a commotion, we finally emerged into a narrow, paved courtyard.

"What a strange place," I said to myself, as the coach came to a halt. Suddenly the door was opened from outside and a tall old man carrying a small lantern looked at me suspiciously from beneath his bushy eyebrows. Taking me by the arm, he helped me out of the coach as though I were a gentleman of rank.

In front of the door stood an ugly old woman in a black smock and skirt, a white apron and a black cap with a long ribbon that hung down at the side of her nose. A big bunch of keys dangled from her waist on one side, while in her hand she carried an antiquated candelabra with two candles burning in it. As soon as she caught sight of me, she began to curtsy very low and chatter incessantly to me. I could not understand a word she said but just went on bowing to her, and the whole affair, I may say, made me feel very uneasy.

Meanwhile the old man had been shining his lantern on the coach from all sides and was now shaking his head and muttering to himself because he had found no cases or baggage. The coachman, without asking me for a tip, then drove the coach into an old shed at the side of the courtyard.

Having respectfully invited me, with all kinds of strange signs and gestures, to follow her, the old woman with the candles led me down a long, narrow passageway and up a short flight of stone steps. As we passed the kitchen, some young maidservants poked their heads through the half-open door, staring at me in curiosity and motioning surreptitiously to each other as though they had never seen a man before.

At the top of the steps the woman opened a door, and to my astonishment I found myself in a magnificent chamber, the ceiling of which was decorated in gold, and the walls hung with superb tapestries of flowers and various human figures. In the middle stood a table ready laid, with enough roast meat, cake, salad, fruit, wine and sweetmeats to make one jump for joy. Between the two windows there hung an immense mirror that reached from the floor to the ceiling.

I must confess that the sight of all this gave me tremendous pleasure. Stretching my limbs a few times, I paced up and down the room like an aristocrat. Then I could not resist looking at myself in the long mirror. To be sure, the new clothes from Leonhard were most becoming, and the sojourn in Italy had given my eye a certain fiery look, but for the rest I was as much a stripling as I had been at home, and only on my upper lip were the first few downy hairs showing themselves.

The old woman kept masticating away with her toothless mouth, looking as though she were chewing the tip of her own nose. Then she made me sit down, stroked my chin with her skinny fingers and called me *poverino*. At the same time she looked at me so mischievously with her bloodshot eyes that one corner of her mouth was drawn halfway up her cheek. At last, making a low curtsy, she went out.

I sat down at the table, and a pretty servant-girl came in to wait on me. I tried to engage her in all kinds of gallantries, but she did not understand me and looked at me oddly out of the corner of her eye. The food was delicious, and I enjoyed every morsel.

When I was full, I got up, and the maid, taking a candle from the table, led me into another room, in which there was a sofa, a small mirror and a magnificent bed with green silk curtains. I made signs to her to ask whether I was meant to lie down on it. She nodded, but it was impossible for me to do so, for she still stayed in the room, as though rooted to the spot. Finally I fetched myself a large glass of wine from the dining room, and raising it to her, cried:

"Felicissima notte!"

For I had learned at least this much Italian. As I drained the glass, she giggled and flushed crimson, then went into the dining room and closed the door behind her.

"What is there to laugh at," I wondered; "everybody in Italy seems to be mad."

My only fear now was that the postilion would sound his horn at any moment. I went to the window and listened, but all was quiet. "Let him blow his horn if he wants to!" I thought to myself, and taking off my clothes, I got into the wonderful bed. I felt as though I were floating on a sea of milk and honey. Down in the yard the old lime tree in front of my window was rustling in the wind, an occasional jackdaw flew up from the roof—and at last, in a mood of complete serenity, I fell asleep.

6

When I awoke, the first rays of dawn were shining on the green curtains above my head. I could not remember where I was; it felt as if I were still riding in the coach and had dreamed about a moonlit castle and an old witch and her pale-faced daughter.

Jumping out of bed, I dressed and looked around me. My eyes

lighted on a small door which I had not noticed before. It was ajar, so I pushed it open and found myself in a neat, attractive little room into which the sun was shining brightly. Women's clothes were strewn untidily over a chair, and on a divan close by lay the girl who had waited on me at table the previous evening. She was sleeping peacefully, her head cradled in her bare, white arm, over which hung her black, curly hair. "Supposing she knew that the door was open!" I thought. And I returned to my own bedroom, closing and bolting the door behind me lest she should feel embarrassed when she woke up.

Outside there was not a sound to be heard save the early song of a little forest-bird that was sitting on a bush in front of my window.

"I shall not allow you to put me to shame," I said, "by being the only one to sing the praise of the Lord so early in the morning!"

And picking up my fiddle, which I had left on the table the night before, I went outside. There was a deathly silence everywhere in the castle, and it took me a long while to find my way through the dark corridors and out into the open.

Leaving the castle, I came upon a large garden arranged in a series of broad terraces, one below the other, which stretched halfway down the mountainside. But everything was in a disgraceful condition. The paths were overgrown with grass, and the figures carved out of the box trees had not been trimmed, so that their long noses and pointed caps stretched high up into the air, making them look like ghosts waiting to frighten a passerby. Someone had even hung some washing on the broken statues that overlooked the dried-up fountain. Cabbages were growing here and there, then came a few common flowers—everything in utter disorder and overgrown with tall weeds through which brightly colored lizards slithered and darted. Through the tall trees lay a vast expanse of desolate landscape, one mountain peak after another as far as the eye could see.

After I had been walking about in this barren waste for a time, I noticed on the terrace below me a tall, slim, pale young man in a long, brown hooded cloak, pacing up and down with folded arms. Apparently he had not seen me, for after a while he sat down on a stone bench, took a book out of his pocket and began to read aloud as though he were delivering a sermon; now and again he raised his eyes to the sky, then lowered his head sadly and rested it on his right hand.

For a long while I stood watching him. Then, curious to know why he was behaving so strangely, I went quickly down to him. He had just uttered a deep sigh, and when I approached, he sprang up in alarm. We were both confused and at a loss for words, and kept bowing to each other, until he finally turned on his heel and strode off through the bushes.

The sun had now risen, and jumping on to the bench in joy, I sent the strains of my violin echoing far out into the silent valleys below.

The old woman with the keys, who had been anxiously looking for me in the castle in order to bring me my breakfast, came out on to the terrace above me, amazed that I was such a skillful violinist. Soon she was joined by the sullen old man, who shared her amazement, and in the end even the servant-girls came out. There they all stood, full of astonishment, while I played away, inventing ever more rapid and complicated cadenzas and variations, until I became quite tired.

There was something very strange about the castle. No one, for example, thought of leaving it. Moreover it was not a lodging house at all, but, as I learned from one of the maids, belonged to a wealthy count. Once or twice I asked the old woman what his name was and where he lived, but she just leered at me, as on the evening when I had first arrived, screwing up her face and squinting at me so slyly that I thought she was out of her mind. If I drank a whole bottle of wine on a hot day, the maids would giggle when they were asked to bring me another; and once, when I felt like smoking a pipe, and explained to them in signs what I wanted, they all burst into senseless laughter.

The most remarkable thing of all, however, was that in the evenings, and especially on very dark nights, the sound of music could often be heard beneath my window, as of soft chords being struck at intervals on a guitar. Once I thought I heard a voice calling softly from below, and I jumped out of bed, put my head out of the window and shouted:

"Hey there! Who's that?"

But there was no reply, and all I could hear was a stirring in the bushes. The big dog in the courtyard barked at me a few times, then all was quiet again, and I did not hear the music again.

For the rest, my life was all that a man could wish for. That good old footman had known what he was talking about when he said that in Italy the grapes just dropped into one's mouth. I was living in the lonely castle like an enchanted prince, and wherever I went, the people showed me great respect, although they all knew that I had not a penny to bless myself with. I only had to utter the magic formula "Abracadabra!" and wonderful foods—rice, wine, melons and Parmesan cheese—appeared on the table.

I enjoyed it all to the full: I slept in the grand four-poster bed, went for strolls in the garden, played my violin and sometimes lent a helping hand with work in the garden. I would lie for hours in the long grass, while the thin young man in the long cloak—a student, and a relative of the old couple in the castle, who was here on holiday—walked round me in wide circles, mumbling things out of his book like a magician and finally sending me to sleep.

So one day after another went by, until at last I began to grow very unhealthy as a result of all this good living. My limbs grew stiff from continuous inactivity, and I felt as if I would collapse from sheer indolence.

One sultry afternoon I was sitting high up on a tree that grew on the mountain slope, rocking gently to and fro on the branches which stretched out over the deep, silent valley. But for the buzzing of the bees around me, all was still; there was not a soul in sight, and in the meadows far below me the cows were lying on the rich grass.

Then from across the tops of the trees came the distant sound of a post horn; at times it grew clearer and louder, at others it became almost inaudible. An old song came to my mind that I had learned from a wandering journeyman at my father's mill, and I began to sing:

> Whoe'er desires to wander,
> Must take his loved one too;
> For he who's alone out yonder,
> Is an exile to all but a few.

> O dark and verdant grasses,
> What know ye of times gone by,
> Of human joy that passes,
> And of hopes beyond the sky?

> The stars shone down so brightly

On my happiness of yore,
And the nightingale trilled so lightly,
When I went to my loved one's door.

With joy I greet the dawning
That shines on sea and sand;
And in the glow of morning
I praise my German land!

The distant post horn seemed to accompany my song, coming closer and closer as I sang, and finally emerging from the woods and echoing in the courtyard. As I jumped down from the tree, the old woman came out of the castle carrying a packet.

"There is something here for you as well," she said, taking a dainty envelope from the packet and handing it to me.

It had no name or address on it, and I broke the seal. When I opened it, my face went as red as a peony, and my heart beat so loudly that I was sure the old woman must have heard it. For the letter was from my lovely lady, whose writing I had often seen on notes she had sent to the bailiff's office! With trembling hand I read:

Everything is settled. I took advantage of this opportunity so as to be the first to tell you the happy news. Hurry back. Life is so dreary here, and I have scarcely been able to go on living since you left.

Aurelie

Tears of mingled fear and rapture filled my eyes, making me feel ashamed in the presence of the old woman, who was leering at me again in her repulsive way, and I fled to the remotest corner of the garden. I threw myself into the grass by the hazel bushes and read the letter once more, recited every word by heart, then read it again and again. The sun's rays glinted through the branches and on to the words, making the letters intertwine before my eyes like gold and green and red blossoms. Perhaps she is not married at all, I thought, and the handsome officer was her brother, or perhaps he has died, or perhaps I have taken leave of my senses, or . . .

"What does it matter?" I cried, jumping up. "Now it's all clear. She loves me! She loves me!"

As I crept out of the bushes, the sun was beginning to set. The sky was red, the birds were singing merrily in the trees, and the valleys were full of shimmering light, but in my heart everything was a thousand times brighter and happier!

I called to them in the castle to bring my supper out into the garden, and made the old woman, the sullen old man and the maids all come out and sit down with me at the table under the tree. While I was thus enjoying my meal, I drew out my violin and began to play. This made everybody cheerful: the old man relaxed his stern expression as he drained one glass after another, the old woman prattled away on everything under the sun, and the girls began to dance with each other on the lawn.

Even the pale student, curious as to what was going on, put in an appearance. He glanced disdainfully at the scene and was about to move haughtily on when, losing no time, I jumped up, caught hold of him by his long coat and, before he knew what had happened, was waltzing madly around with him. He made an effort to dance very daintily and in the most modern style, making such subtle and intricate steps that the perspiration soon poured down his face, and his long coattails flew round like the spokes of a wheel. Sometimes he rolled his eyes and looked at me so queerly that I almost began to be afraid of him, and quickly let him go again.

The old woman, of course, would have given anything to know what the letter contained, and why I was suddenly so merry, but it would have been far too long a story to explain to her. All I did was to point to a group of cranes that were flying overhead at that moment, and say that I, too, would soon have to leave and fly far, far away.

At this she opened her puckered eyes wide and looked spitefully now at me, now at the old man. Then I noticed that, whenever I turned away, the two of them put their heads together and talked excitedly, eyeing me suspiciously from time to time. That surprised me. I wondered what plans they were hatching, but at the same time I became more relaxed, and as the sun had long since set, I bade the company good night and went thoughtfully up to my bedroom.

So happy and excited was I that I walked up and down in my room for a long while. Outside the wind drove heavy black clouds across the sky above the castle tower, and the darkness almost blotted out the nearby mountain peaks.

Suddenly I thought I heard voices in the garden below, and putting out the light, I stood close by the window. The voices seemed to be coming nearer but were still very soft. Then a gleam of light shone from a small lantern which one of the figures was carrying under his cloak, and I recognized the surly old caretaker and the housekeeper. The light lit up the old woman's face, which looked uglier than ever, and flashed on to a long knife that she was holding in her hand. They were both looking up at my window. Then the caretaker wrapped his cloak more tightly round himself, and everything was dark and still again.

"What are they doing down there at this time of night?" I wondered, and I shuddered as I thought of all the murder-stories I had heard, and the tales of witches and robbers who cut up human beings and devoured their hearts.

As I was standing there, I heard soft footsteps coming up the stairs and along the passage to my door, and voices seemed to be whispering secretly to each other. I ran quickly to the other end of the room and hid behind a table which I prepared to hold in front of me, rushing at the door full tilt the moment it opened. But in the darkness I overturned a chair and made a terrible noise. Everything was quiet outside. I listened intently from behind the table, my eyes fairly popping out of my head and fixed unwaveringly on the door, as though I were trying to bore a hole in it.

I stayed like this for a while, keeping so still that I could have heard the flies crawling up the wall. Then came the sound of a key being slipped into the lock. I prepared for my assault with the table. But after the key had turned slowly three times, it was cautiously withdrawn, and the footsteps retreated along the passage and down the stairs.

I drew a deep breath. "Ah," I said to myself, "they have locked me in so as to make it easy for themselves once I am fast asleep." I tried the door. Sure enough, it was locked tight; so also, for the first time since I had been there, was the door that led to the maid's room.

So here I was, a captive in a foreign land. My lovely lady was probably standing by her window and looking out across the silent park towards the road, waiting for me to come strolling past the tollhouse with my violin. The clouds were racing across the sky, time was slipping away from me—and here I sat, imprisoned in my room. I did not know which way to turn in my desperation. And whenever the leaves rustled outside, or a rat scurried across the floor, I imagined that the old woman had crept through a concealed door in the wall and was prowling softly round the room with the long knife in her hand.

As I sat there miserably on my bed, I suddenly heard the strains of music beneath my window again, and the sound of the guitar sent a ray of hope through my heart. I opened the window and called out softly.

"Sh! Sh!" came a voice from below.

Without further hesitation I put the letter in my pocket and picked up my fiddle. Climbing out of the window, I clambered down the broken old wall, holding on to the creepers that grew in the cracks. Then a few stones gave way; I began to slip, and slid down faster and faster until I landed on the ground with a thump that made my brain shake.

Before I could collect my senses, somebody embraced me so violently that I gave a cry. My savior placed his finger on my lips, took me by the hand and led me out of the bushes on to the lawn.

Then I saw with astonishment that it was the lanky student, with his guitar hanging from his neck by a broad silk ribbon. Hastily I made him understand that I wanted to get out of the garden. He seemed to know this already, and took me along all kinds of hidden, roundabout paths to the bottom gate in the high garden wall. The gate was shut, but the student had anticipated this, and producing a big key, he opened it cautiously.

We entered the forest, and I was on the point of asking him the way to the nearest town, when he suddenly fell on his knees in front of me, raised one hand high in the air and began to curse and swear in the most terrible manner. I had no idea what he meant by this behavior, and all I could hear was *idio* and *cuore* and *amore* and *furore*. Then he started to shuffle closer and closer towards me on his knees. I realized to my horror that he was mad, and without looking where I was going, I ran off into the densest part of the forest.

I heard him shouting after me like a lunatic, then came another, rougher voice from the direction of the castle, and I thought they must be searching for me. I did not know which way to turn, and the night was dark, so I could easily have fallen into their clutches. So I decided to climb into one of the tall fir trees to wait until the situation became quieter.

From this vantage point I could hear one voice after another coming from the castle, and a number of torches cast their fiery gleam on to the ancient walls and far out into the darkness. I breathed a prayer as the tumult grew louder and louder and came closer and closer.

Then the student, carrying a torch, rushed past my tree, his coattails flying in the wind, but from this moment on they all seemed to turn their attention to the other side of the mountain. The voices became fainter and the wind murmured again through the silent forest. At last I climbed down and ran breathlessly on through the night into the valley below.

7

Day and night I hurried on, my ears still ringing with the shouts of my pursuers, as though they were still coming after me with their torches and their long knives. Then I learned from a passerby that I was only a few miles from Rome. This news, happy though it made me, also gave me a shock, for back in my childhood days I had heard many glorious tales about the splendors of that city, and as I lay on the grass in front of the mill in the stillness of a Sunday afternoon, I had imagined that it looked like the clouds above me, with wonderful hills, and ravines that plunged down to the deep-blue sea, and golden gates, and tall, shining towers on which angels in golden raiment stood and sang.

Darkness had long since fallen, and the moon was shining brightly as I came out of the woods. Then mounting a hilltop, I saw the city before me. The sea sparkled in the far distance, the heavens were studded with a myriad of twinkling stars, and beneath it lay the Holy City, of which only a long, misty strip was visible, like a lion sleeping on the silent ground, while the mountains round about stood like sinister giants watching over him.

I walked on and came first upon a great expanse of lonely moorland, where everything was as silent as the grave. Here and there stood a crumbling old wall or a withered, grotesquely twisted bush; night birds whirred overhead, and my long, dark shadow stretched out beside me. People say that Venus is buried here in the ruins of a sunken city, and that the old pagans sometimes rise from their graves at dead of night and make travelers lose their way across the moor. I walked firmly on, however, and did not allow anything to deflect me from my purpose.

The city now rose clearly before me in all its glory. The high fortresses, the gates and the golden domes shone in the bright moonshine as though angels in golden robes really were standing on the towers and singing out across the plain.

I passed a number of small cottages, then entered the famous city through a magnificent gate. The moon shone down between the palaces all around, making everything look as bright as day, but the streets were empty save for an occasional ragged beggar lying in a marble doorway like a corpse, sleeping in the warm night air. The fountains were playing in the silent squares, while the gardens along the street rustled and filled the air with refreshing scents.

As I walked along in a daze at the moonlight, the beautiful scents and the glories all around me, I heard the sound of a guitar in one of the gardens. "My goodness!" I said to myself. "The mad student must have secretly followed me here!"

Then came the sweet tones of a woman's voice singing to the guitar. I stood there transfixed, for it was the voice of my lovely lady, and she was singing the same Italian song as she used to sing at her window in the palace!

At this the memory of that happy time returned to me with such poignancy that I felt like weeping—the palace garden in the stillness of early morning, and those joyful occasions when I used to hide behind the bushes, until that wretched fly had buzzed round my nose.

I could restrain myself no longer, and climbing over the golden gate with its rich ornamentation, I jumped down into the garden from which the song was coming. Then in the distance I caught sight of a slim, white figure standing behind a poplar tree. The figure looked towards me in astonishment, then turned and ran so swiftly towards the house that I could hardly follow her movements in the moonlight.

"It was her!" I cried, and my heart throbbed with joy. But to my chagrin I found that I had twisted my ankle when I jumped from the gate, and I had to shake my leg a few times before I could follow her to the house. By the time I got there, the doors and windows were all shut. I knocked gently, listened, then knocked again. I thought I heard soft whispers and giggles coming from inside, and once I even imagined that a pair of twinkling eyes peeped out from behind the shutters, then all was quiet again.

"She does not know who it is," I said to myself, and taking out my fiddle, which I always carried with me, I walked up and down the path in front of the house, singing the lovely lady's song and playing merrily all the songs that I used to play on beautiful summer evenings in the park, or on my seat in front of the tollhouse, sending the melodies ringing out towards the palace. But it was of no avail. Not a soul stirred. So in the end I put my violin away sadly and lay down on the stone step in front of the door, for the long walk had made me very weary.

It was a warm night. The flowers that grew in front of the house sent forth their sweetness, and from a distance came the splashing of a fountain. I dreamed of sky-blue flowers, of lonely, beautiful, dark green valleys with bubbling springs and rippling brooks, and the melodious songs of gaily colored birds overhead—until at last I fell asleep.

When I awoke, the cool morning air was caressing my limbs, and the birds were twittering in the trees as though trying to make a fool of me. Jumping to my feet, I looked around. I could still hear the fountain in the garden but not a sound came from the house. I peeped through the green shutters of one of the rooms, and saw a sofa and a large round table covered with a gray cloth; the chairs stood neatly around the sides of the room, but all the blinds were drawn, as though the house had not been lived in for years.

Suddenly I began to feel afraid of the eerie house and its garden, and of the white-clad figure I had seen the evening before, and without waiting any longer, I ran along the paths and through the shrubberies, and quickly climbed the gate again. The sight of the glorious city before me took my breath away; the morning sun was flashing and sparkling across the rooftops and flooding the long, silent streets with light. Shouting for joy, I jumped down on to the roadway below.

But where was I to go in this great strange city? The mysterious events of the previous night were still buzzing through my head, and the lovely lady's song still echoed in my ears. I sat down by a fountain in a deserted square, washed the sleep from my eyes in the cold water and sang:

> If I were a little bird,
> I know what I'd be singing;
> And if I had two tiny wings,
> I know where I'd be winging.

"Hey there, my merry fellow!" called a young man who had approached the fountain while I was singing. "You sing like a lark at the first ray of dawn!"

The unexpected sound of someone talking my native tongue made it seem as though the bell of my village church were tolling out on a quiet Sunday morning.

"A hearty welcome to you, countryman!" I cried, jumping down in delight.

The young man smiled and looked me up and down. Then he asked:

"What are you doing in Rome?"

For the moment I did not know what to say, for I certainly did not feel like telling him that I was engaged in following my lovely lady. Finally I replied:

"I am just wandering around, seeing something of the world."

"Well, well!" said the young man with a laugh. "Then we share the same profession. For I, too, want to see something of the world, and then paint what I have seen."

"So you're a painter!" I exclaimed joyfully, thinking of Leonhard and Guido. But he cut me short.

"You had better come with me," he said, "and we will have breakfast together. Afterwards I'll paint a likeness of you that will be a delight to behold."

This suited me admirably, and I accompanied him through the deserted streets. A few shops were beginning to open their shutters, and here and there a pair of white arms or a sleepy little head would appear at the window.

He led me through a maze of dark, narrow alleys until we eventually slipped into an old, smoke-blackened house and ascended first one flight of stairs, then another, as though we were climbing up to Heaven. At last we stopped in front of the attic door, and the painter began to search feverishly through his pockets. It transpired, however, that he had forgotten to lock the door and had left the key in the room: he had gone out before dawn, he told me, in order to see the sun rise over the surrounding countryside. So he merely shook his head and kicked the door open with his foot.

It was a room of immense size, big enough to dance in, if only the floor had not been strewn with all manner of things—boots, papers, clothes, upturned paintpots, in complete disorder. In the middle stood a number of large easels, looking like the scaffolds used for picking pears, and some large paintings were leaning against the walls. On a long wooden table there was a dish with bread and butter on it, and next to it a large paint stain. By the dish stood a bottle of wine.

"First let's eat and drink, my friend!" said the painter.

I wanted to make myself a few slices of bread and butter, but there was no knife, and we had to rummage about among the papers on the table for a long while before we finally found it under a large parcel. The painter than pushed the window open, and the fresh morning air streamed into the room. There was a wonderful view across the city and far up into the mountains, where the sun shone upon the vineyards and lit up the cheerful white houses.

"Here's to our fertile native land beyond the hills!" he cried, taking a draft from the bottle and then passing it to me. I drank his health in return, praising over and over in my heart the beauties of my distant homeland.

The painter now went over to a wooden easel on which a large sheet of paper was resting, and moved it closer to the window. On the paper was a picture of an old cottage, skillfully drawn with bold, black strokes. Inside the cottage sat the figure of the Virgin Mary, a blissful yet profoundly somber expression on her beautiful countenance. The Christ-child sat on a little bed of straw at her feet, looking up with affectionate but grave eyes. At the entrance to the cottage two shepherd-boys were kneeling, each carrying his crook and his bag.

"Look," said the painter, "I want to set your head on one of these shepherd-boys. Your features will become famous, and if God wills, the world will take pleasure in the sight years after the two of us are dead and buried, and when we ourselves come to kneel in peace and joy before the Virgin and her Son, like these two happy boys."

He picked up an old chair, but the arm came off in his hand as he lifted it. Putting it together again quickly, he pushed it across to the easel and made me sit on it and turn my face half towards him.

For a few minutes I sat in this position without moving, but after a while I began to itch, now in one place, now in another, and could not stand it any longer. Besides this, on the wall opposite me hung half a cracked mirror, and while he was painting me, I could not resist looking into it and making all kinds of grimaces, out of sheer boredom. He noticed this and laughed, eventually motioning me to get up. My features had now been transferred to the shepherd with such faithfulness that I felt very proud of myself.

He worked on busily in the cool morning air, singing as he did so and sometimes stopping to look out of the window at the superb view. I cut myself another piece of bread and butter and strolled up and down the room, looking at the paintings that were leaning against the wall. Two of them took my particular fancy.

"Did you paint these too?" I asked him.

"Indeed, no!" he answered. "They are the work of the great masters Leonardo da Vinci and Guido Reni. But you don't understand anything about such things!"

This last remark offended me, and I retorted:

"On the contrary. I know these two masters as well as I know myself."

He looked at me wide-eyed.

"How is that?" he asked quickly.

"Well," I began, "I traveled with them day and night on horseback, on foot and by coach, and the wind whistled round my ears, and I lost them in the inn and traveled on at breakneck pace in their coach, speeding over the terrible cobblestones on two wheels, and—"

"Wait!" the painter broke in, staring at me as though I had taken leave of my senses. Then he burst out laughing. "Aha!" he cried. "Now I understand! You mean you traveled with two painters called Leonhard and Guido?"

I nodded. Then, jumping up, he studied me again closely from tip to toe.

"Well, it could be," he began, "and then . . . do you play the violin?"

I patted the pocket of my cloak, and the strings of my instrument gave out a twanging sound.

"Upon my word!" he exclaimed. "It is! Do you know that a young German countess was here, inquiring in every corner of Rome after the two painters and a young musician with a fiddle?"

"A young German countess!" I cried in delight. "Is the footman with her?"

"I don't know about that," he replied, "I only saw her a few times, at the house of a friend of hers some distance from the city. Do you know her?"

At this he went over to a corner of the room and pulled aside a cloth from a large picture. It was as though someone had opened the shutters in a dark room and let the dazzling sun flood in. For—it was the lovely lady! Wearing a black velvet dress, she was standing in the garden, raising her veil with her hand and looking out with a kind and gentle expression across a fine, wide landscape. The longer I looked, the more it came to resemble the park around the palace, with the flowers and the branches swaying gracefully in the breeze, my little tollhouse down below, the road stretching out across the green countryside, and the Danube and the hazy blue mountains in the distance.

"It's her! It's her!" I cried. And snatching up my hat, I ran out of the room and down the endless flights of stairs, as the astonished painter shouted after me that if I came back that evening, we might be able to find out more.

8

I hurried through the city towards the house where I had heard my lady singing the previous evening. The streets were now full of life. Gentlemen and their ladies strolled in the sunshine, bowing to each other and exchanging cheerful greetings, splendid coaches rattled past, and from the church towers the bells pealed out for mass, resounding through the clear air above the bustling scene.

I was overwhelmed with happiness at the clamor around me. I ran on and on, and when I finally stopped, I had no idea where I was. Everything seemed bewitched, as though the garden, the house and the fountain in the silent square had been a dream, and as though the bright light of day had driven it all from the face of the earth. Nor could I ask anybody, for I did not know what the square was called.

It now began to grow oppressively hot. The sun's rays burned down on the cobbled streets like flaming arrows, and people crept wearily into the confines of their own houses and let down the blinds. Everywhere there was a deathly hush.

In despair I threw myself on the ground in front of a fine, large house whose balcony, resting on wide columns, cast a broad shadow across the street. I gazed first at the silent city, to which the suddenly deserted streets had now given a sinister aspect, then at the blue, cloudless sky, until finally I fell asleep with weariness.

I dreamed that I was lying in a lonely green meadow near my village: the warm, gentle rain of summer sparkled in the sun as it set behind the mountains, and as the raindrops fell, they were transformed into bright flowers, completely covering me as I lay there.

How great, therefore, was my astonishment when I awoke to find myself really surrounded with flowers! I jumped to my feet but could see nothing unusual except for an open window on the top floor of the house above me, where there was a mass of sweetly scented plants and flowers, behind which a parrot chattered and squawked without pause. Picking up the flowers, I made them into a nosegay which I put in my buttonhole.

Then I tried to start up a conversation with the parrot, for it gave me great pleasure to watch him clamber up and down in his gilt cage and perform all manner of contortions, in the course of which he always contrived to trip over his big toe.

Suddenly he shouted *"Furfante!"* at me, and even though he was only a stupid animal, this annoyed me. So I called him an insulting name in return, and we both got angry; the more I insulted him in German, the more he shrieked away at me in Italian.

At that moment I heard someone laughing behind me, and turned round quickly. It was the painter I had met that morning.

"What ridiculous pranks are you up to now?" he said. "I have been waiting for you for half an hour. The air is cooler now, so let us go to a park outside the city where we shall find a number of our compatriots. Maybe they can tell you more about the German countess."

I was overjoyed at this, and we started out at once, while the parrot went on hurling insults at me for a long while afterwards.

After walking along narrow, stony paths that led uphill past farmhouses and vineyards, we came to a small park high on the hillside, where a group of young men and girls were sitting round a table in the open. As we approached, they motioned to us to keep still and pointed to a large, leafy grove on the other side of the lawn where two comely ladies were sitting. One of them was singing, the other accompanying her on a guitar. Between them stood a pleasant-looking man who beat time now and again with a little baton.

The evening sun glittered through the foliage, lighting up the fruit and the bottles of wine on the table, and shining on the shapely, pearl-white shoulders of the lady with the guitar. Her companion was in raptures, and the veins in her neck stood out as she sang a group of Italian songs with great artistry.

She was in the middle of a cadenza, her eyes raised heavenwards, and the man at her side was waiting with raised baton for the moment when she would pick up the time again. Nobody dared to breathe.

Suddenly the gate burst open and in rushed a girl, her face crimson, pursued by a young man with pale, delicate features. The two were quarreling violently.

The startled conductor stood there with upraised baton like a petrified magician, but the lady broke off her final trill and got up in fury. The others all hissed angrily at the young man.

"Philistine!" shouted one of the men sitting at the table. "You've interrupted the fascinating tableau based on the description by the late E. T. A. Hoffman on page 347 of the *Ladies' Almanach for 1816*—the story about Hummel's best picture at the Berlin exhibition in the autumn of 1814!"*

But this outburst had no effect.

"What do I care about your precious tableaus!" cried the young

* A reference to Hoffmann's tale *Die Fermate (The Pause)*, which was published in Fouqué's *Frauentaschenbuch auf 1816*, and has as its starting point a painting by J. E. Hummel depicting, like this episode in Eichendorff's story, a soprano singing the final trill of her cadenza, watched anxiously by the conductor with upraised arm. Eichendorff's description follows, word for word in parts, that of Hoffmann. [*Trans.*]

man. "My self-portrait for the others, and my girl for me—that's the way I want it!"

Then turning to the poor girl, he went on:

"You faithless, wanton creature! You carping critic, with an eye only for the glint of silver in a painting, and the golden thread in a piece of literature, and with many sweethearts but no true love! May you come to have as a husband, not a poor, honest painter but an old duke with a whole mine of diamonds on his nose, a silver sheen on his bald pate and gilt edges on his few remaining hairs! Come on, out with that wretched note you hid from me a moment ago! What are you up to now? Who is the note from, and who is it meant for?"

The girl, however, stubbornly refused to give way, and the more pressing the others became, trying noisily to console and pacify the angry young fellow, the more heated and agitated he became. The girl, moreover, would not hold her tongue and finally burst out of the crowd and quite unexpectedly threw herself into my arms for protection, weeping bitterly. I at once assumed an appropriate attitude of concern, but then, when she noticed that the others in the noisy gathering were no longer paying any attention to us, she suddenly looked up at me and whispered breathlessly, without betraying any emotion:

"You miserable tollkeeper! It's all your fault that I have to put up with this! Take this slip of paper quickly; our address is on it. And when you come through the gateway, keep to the deserted road that leads to the right."

I was speechless with amazement, for as I looked at her I recognized her as the saucy little chambermaid from the palace who had brought me the bottle of wine that Sunday evening. As she clung to me excitedly, her curly black hair falling over my arm, she had never looked so pretty.

"But, fair madam," I began, "how did you——"

"Keep quiet, for heaven's sake!" she interrupted, and before I could collect my thoughts, she had run off to the other side of the park.

Meanwhile the others had almost completely forgotten what they had originally been doing, and were arguing heatedly away, trying to prove to the young man that he was drunk and that this sort of behavior was unbecoming to a decent-living painter. The stout, lively man—who, as I later found out, was a great friend of the arts and interested in all branches of knowledge—had thrown his baton aside and was moving around excitedly in the center of the throng, his chubby face positively gleaming with friendliness. He sought tirelessly to mediate and to console, expressing at the same time his disappointment over the interruption of the cadenza and of the attractive *scena* that he had been at such pains to prepare.

My heart was now happy again, as on that blissful Saturday when I had stood by the open window and the wine bottle and played my fiddle until far into the night. So, since the uproar seemed as though it would never end, I took out my instrument and struck up an Italian ditty which they used to dance to in the mountains and which I had heard while at the lonely castle in the forest.

At this they all pricked up their ears.

"Bravo! Bravo! A fine idea!" cried the friend of the arts, and ran from one person to another to arrange what he called a "rustic entertainment." He set things going himself by offering his hand to the lady who had been playing the guitar, and then began to dance with remarkable skill, designing letters on the grass with his steps and sometimes even pirouetting and making quite tolerable *saltos* in the air. He soon grew tired of this, however, for he was somewhat portly, and as his leaps became lower and clumsier, he finally removed himself from the circle, coughing violently and mopping the perspiration from his brow with a snowy white handkerchief.

The young man had in the meanwhile regained his composure and fetched some castanets from the inn, and before I knew where I was, they were all dancing merrily together. The sinking sun cast its last red rays through the dark shadows and on to the old walls and the decaying, ivy-covered columns in the background; and beyond the vineyards on the other side lay the city of Rome, bathed in the glow of evening.

The whole company was dancing gaily in the cool, calm air, and my heart rejoiced to see the slender young girls, the chambermaid among them, skip among the bushes with arms outstretched, like nymphs of the wood, clacking their castanets merrily in the air at each bound. In the end I could hold back no longer, and leaping into their midst, I danced some very pretty steps, playing my fiddle without pause at the same time.

On and on I danced, oblivious to the fact that the others had begun to tire and were drifting away one by one. Then I felt a hard tug at my coattails. It was the chambermaid.

"Don't be so foolish!" she whispered. "You're jumping about like a billy goat! Look properly at the note I gave you and follow me a little while later. The young countess is waiting!"

With this she slipped through the gate and vanished into the darkness that was settling over the vineyards.

My heart was thumping wildly, and I felt like running after her, but fortunately the servant arrived at that moment and lit the large lantern which hung over the gateway. Moving over to the light, I quickly took the note out of my pocket. On it was a hasty pencil sketch of the gate and road, as the chambermaid had told me, and underneath it the words: "Eleven o'clock by the small door."

Eleven o'clock was still a few long hours away, but I intended to set out at once, for I had no peace of mind. At that moment, however, the painter who had brought me here came up.

"Did you speak to that girl?" he asked. "I cannot see her here any more, but she was the countess's chambermaid."

"Quiet! Quiet!" I replied. "The countess is still in Rome."

"So much the better," he said. "Come and join us and drink to her health!"

And in spite of my protests he drew me back into the garden.

Everything was now dark and deserted. The merry couples were strolling back to the city; as they wended their way through the vineyards, their conversation and laughter echoed through the still night air, becoming fainter and fainter until finally the sound of their voices merged with the rustle of the trees and the murmur of the brook in the valley below. The painter and I, together with Eckbrecht, the young man who had started the quarrel, were the only ones left. The moon shone through the tall trees, and a lone candle flickered in the breeze, lighting up the pools of wine that had been spilled on the table in front of us.

The painter made me sit down and tell them about my home, my journey and my aim in life. Eckbrecht ordered the pretty little waitress to bring us some bottles, then took her upon his knee, put his guitar in her hands and taught her how to strum a tune on it. Her little fingers soon moved daintily over the strings, and the two of them then sang an Italian folk song together, first the painter a verse, then the girl, making a delightful scene in the evening stillness.

The girl was soon called elsewhere. Eckbrecht leaned back on the bench, stretched out his legs on a chair in front of him, and to the accompaniment of his guitar, sang a whole collection of fine German and Italian songs, without paying the slightest heed to the painter or myself. The stars were shining out of a clear sky, and everything was bathed in silver moonlight. My thoughts wandered to the lovely lady and to my distant homeland, and I quite forgot the painter at my side.

Now and again Eckbrecht had to stop to tune his instrument, and this made him very angry. On one occasion he twisted and tugged at it so violently that a string broke. Throwing the guitar on the ground, he jumped up, and only then did he observe that the painter had in the meantime stretched out his arm across the table and fallen fast asleep.

Taking his white cloak, which was hanging from a branch near the table, he threw it over his shoulders. Then he hesitated, looked sharply first at the painter, then at me, and eventually sat down on the table right in front of me. Clearing his throat, he pulled at his neckerchief and embarked on a long speech:

"My dear friend and countryman," he began, "since the bottles are almost empty, and since morality is unquestionably the citizen's first duty when virtue is at a discount, I feel compelled by a sense of national loyalty to make you aware of certain moral values.

"It might be thought that you are a mere stripling—though your coat has certainly seen better days; one might also concede that a few moments ago you were leaping about in a remarkable fashion like a satyr; while yet others might maintain that you are a mere bird of passage, since not only are you passing through but you also sing like a bird. For my part, however, I care nothing for such superficial judgments. In my view you are a genius on holiday."

His exaggerated mode of speech irritated me, and I was about to interrupt him, but he went on heedlessly:

"You see? These few words of praise have already gone to your head. Reflect, and consider this dangerous vocation! We geniuses—I am one myself—care as little about the world as the world cares about us. In our seven-league boots—which we shall soon be equipped with at birth—we stride resolutely on towards eternity. Yet what an unhappy and uncomfortable position we are in: one leg is in the future, with the prospect of a new dawn, a new life; the other is still in the Piazza del Popolo in Rome, where the masses of today sense a good opportunity to tag along with us, and hang on to our boots so tightly that they almost pull our legs off! And this shivering and starving and wine bibbing is all for the sake of immortality!

"Look at my companion on the seat over there. He is a genius too. But if he finds time too long, what will he do with eternity? You and I and the sun, comrade, all rose at the same time this morning; all day we have been busy thinking and painting, and everything was splendid. Now suddenly sleep-ridden night has drawn her fur-clad arm across the scene and wiped out all the colors."

On and on he chattered, and with his disheveled hair, and all his drinking and dancing, his face took on a deathly pallor in the moonlight. His wild talk was beginning to make me afraid, and as he turned round towards the sleeping painter, I seized the opportunity to creep round the table and out of the garden without attracting his attention, and made my way past the vine trellises down into the moonlit valley, happy to be alone once more.

In the city the clocks were striking ten. The distant sounds of a guitar floated across to me on the still air, together with the voices of the two painters, as they, too, wandered homewards, and I ran on as fast as I could, lest they should start to ask me more questions.

At the gate I took the road to the right and hurried with beating heart past the silent houses and gardens. To my surprise, however, I came out into the square with the fountain in the center, which I had been unable to find earlier in the day. There, in the glorious moonlight, stood the lonely summerhouse and in the garden I heard the lovely lady singing the very same Italian song as yesterday.

Joyfully I ran to the small door, then to the main door, then tugged with all my might at the big garden gate, but they were all locked. Then I remembered that eleven had not yet struck. The time was passing with agonizing slowness, but I did not feel it would be proper for me to climb over the gate again, so having walked up and down in the square for a while, I sat down by the fountain and meditated.

The stars were twinkling in the sky and the square was deserted. I sat there happily and listened as my lady's song was wafted towards me from the garden, mingling with the murmur of the fountain.

Suddenly I caught sight of a white figure approaching from the other side of the square and making for the small door. Straining my eyes in the moonlight, I saw that it was the mad painter in the white cloak. He took out a key, opened the door, and before I knew it, had slipped into the garden.

From the very beginning I had taken a special dislike to this fellow because of his absurd ideas, and now was beside myself with rage. "The mad genius is probably drunk again," I said to myself. "He must have got the key from the chambermaid, and now intends to creep up on my lady and assault her."

I rushed through the little gateway, which he had left open, and into the garden. At first everything seemed quiet. The double door of the summerhouse was ajar, and a soft beam of light lit up the grass and the flowers in front of the house. Keeping my distance, I looked inside. In a luxurious green room, dimly lit by a single lamp, lay the lovely lady, reclining on a silken couch and holding her guitar, blissfully unaware of the threatening danger.

I could not look for long, however, for at that moment I saw the figure in white slink past the bushes and approach the house from the other side. The lady was singing a song of lamentation that pierced me to the quick. Without hesitating, I broke off a thick branch, and brandishing it above my head, charged towards the figure shouting: "Murder! Murder!" with all my might, making the whole garden tremble.

When he saw me coming, the painter gave a terrible scream and ran off. I screamed even louder and chased him towards the house. I had almost caught up with him when I tripped over some wretched flowerpots and fell full-length in front of the door.

"So it's you, you young fool!" came a voice from above me. "You frightened the life out of me!"

Stumbling to my feet, I wiped the sand and the earth out of my eyes. There stood the chambermaid, whose white cloak had fallen from her shoulders with her last jump.

"But I thought the painter was here," I stammered in confusion.

"Of course he was," she replied cheekily. "At least, his cloak was, which he put round my shoulders when I came in the gate, because I was cold."

While we were talking, the lady had got up from the sofa and come to the door. My heart was thumping as though it would burst. Then, as I looked more closely, I saw that it was not my lovely lady at all but a completely different person! She was a tall, stout, impressive lady with a hooked nose and arched black eyebrows, and of intimidating beauty. She looked at me imperiously with her large, flashing eyes, and I was so awestruck that I did not know what to do. I bowed to her time after time in my confusion, and finally made to kiss her hand, but she pulled it away and said something in Italian to the chambermaid which I did not understand.

In the meantime the whole neighborhood had been awakened by the noise. Dogs were barking and children screaming, and the sound of men's voices came closer and closer. The lady looked at me as if she would like to pierce me through, then turned quickly away and went back into the room, slamming the door in my face with a haughty but somewhat forced laugh.

The chambermaid grabbed me unceremoniously by the coattails and pulled me towards the gate.

"So now you've made a fool of yourself again," she said to me angrily.

At this I saw red.

"What do you mean?" I retorted in fury. "Was it not you who told me to come here?"

"That's just it!" she cried. "My countess has been so kind to you, throwing posies to you from her window and singing arias, and this is the reward she gets! You are a hopeless fellow, trampling your good fortune underfoot like this!"

"But I meant the German countess, my own lovely lady," I protested.

"Oh, she returned to Germany ages ago," she replied, "and took your mad passion with her, so you had better go back there yourself. She is languishing for you, so the two of you will be able to play the violin and gaze together at the moon—but take care not to let *me* set eyes on you again!"

Suddenly there was a great clamor behind us. Men armed with clubs were climbing over the fence from the adjoining garden, others were uttering oaths and searching up and down the paths, and frightened faces wearing nightcaps peeped over the moonlit hedges. It was as though the Devil himself were suddenly giving birth to a whole unruly rabble in the bushes and hedgerows.

The chambermaid did not waste a moment.

"Thief! Thief! Over there!" she cried, waving towards the other side of the garden. Then she pushed me quickly through the gate and slammed it shut behind me.

So there I was, back in the deserted square and without a friend in the world, just as when I had arrived the day before. The fountain that had been flittering so cheerfully in the moonlight, as though little angels were climbing up and down the column of gushing water, was still playing, but all my joy and happiness had been washed away. I resolved to turn my back for ever on this deceitful land of Italy with its mad painters, its oranges and its chambermaids, and within an hour I had left the gate of the city behind me.

9

Like sentinels the mountains stand;
Each peak looks outwards like a tower
To see who, in this morning hour,
Approaches from a foreign land.
Their luster bright shall never cloy,
And at their sight I jump for joy
And shout aloud to greet the day:
Austria for ever!

Everybody knows me there,
Every tree and every brook
And every bird above. And look—
The Danube's waters, blue and fair!
St. Stephen's spire, now drawing near,
Looks o'er the hill to greet me here—
Or will do soon, one happy day.
Austria for ever!

I stood on a mountain peak and looked down on the Austrian countryside below, waving my hat in delight. As I was singing the last verse, I heard a splendid group of wind instruments join in the tune, and I turned round to see three young journeymen in long blue coats standing behind me. The first was playing an oboe, the second a clarinet, and the third, who was wearing an old cocked hat on his head, a French horn, and the sound of their musical accompaniment rang out through the forest. By no means loath to join them, I produced my fiddle and played and sang cheerfully along with them.

After a while they began to exchange suspicious glances; first the horn player stopped puffing out his cheeks and laid down his instrument, and eventually they all stopped playing and stared at me. I, too, stopped in surprise and stared back. At last the horn-player said:

"We thought that because of your long tailcoat you must be an Englishman who was enjoying the beauties of nature on foot, and we hoped we might pick up a few coppers. But it seems that you are a musician yourself."

"Actually I am a toll-collector," I replied. "I have come straight from Rome, but it is some time since there were any tolls to collect, and I have been living on the proceeds of my playing."

"That doesn't bring in much these days," said the horn-player, who had walked back to the edge of the wood and was using his hat to fan a little fire that they had kindled there. "Wind instruments are better. Whenever we find a nobleman lunching quietly, we creep unnoticed into the covered porch and start to blow away as hard as we can—and a servant soon comes out with money or food to make us stop our noise. But will you not have a bite with us?"

The fire was glowing merrily, and we all sat round it in the fresh morning air. Two of the musicians took a jug of coffee and milk off the fire, fetched some bread out of their pockets and took it in turns to dip the bread in the coffee and drink from the jug. It was a joy to watch them. The horn-player, however, said:

"I cannot stand that horrible black stuff."

He handed me half of a large slice of bread and butter, and then produced a bottle of wine.

"Would you not like a drop?" he asked.

I took a deep draft but put the bottle down again quickly with a grimace, for it tasted like vinegar.

"A local growth," he explained. "But your stay in Italy has ruined your German taste."

Thereupon he rummaged in his pocket and pulled out all manner of oddments, among them a tattered old map with the portrait of the Emperor on it in full regalia, the scepter in his right hand, the orb in his left. He spread it out carefully on the ground, and the others gathered round to discuss what route to take.

"The holidays will soon be over," said one. "We must turn off to the left immediately after we leave Linz—that will bring us in good time to Prague."

"What!" cried the horn-player. "Who can you play to there? There's nothing along that road but woods and charcoal-burners— no true appreciation of art and no decent free lodgings."

"Rubbish!" retorted the other. "I like those charcoal-burners best. They know where the shoe pinches, and are not so particular if you happen to play a wrong note."

"That means you have no *point d'honneur*," said the horn-player. "*Odi profanum vulgus et arceo,** as the Roman poet said."

"But we pass some churches on the way," remarked the third man, "so we can always stay with the priest."

"You won't find me there!" answered the horn-player. "Priests give short rations and long sermons, always preaching at us for leading useless lives and urging us to apply ourselves to the pursuit of knowledge. They are particularly prone to do this if they suspect that you might become a brother yourself some day. No, no— *clericus clericum non decimat*. But what is all the trouble about, in any case? The professors are still in Karlsbad and won't be back exactly to the day."

"*Distinguendum est inter et inter*," replied the other; "*quod licet Jovi, non licet bovi!*"

I now realized that they were students from Prague, and began to feel a deep respect for them, particularly as the Latin simply poured from their mouths.

"Are you also a man of learning, sir?" the horn-player asked me. I replied humbly that I had always felt a desire to learn but had never had the money.

"That doesn't matter," he cried. "We have no money either, nor rich friends. But a man with any sense must learn to help himself. *Aurora musis amica*—in plain language, don't dillydally over your breakfast. And when the bell tolls out at noon across the town from spire to spire and from mountain to mountain, and the noisy schoolchildren burst out of their gloomy old buildings and wend their happy way through the sunlit streets, then we betake ourselves

---

* The Latin quotations mean, in order, "I hate the common crowd and keep it at a distance" (Horace); clergy doesn't attack (decimate) clergy; one must make distinctions; what is proper for Jupiter is not proper for an ox; dawn is the friend of the Muses.

to the brother in charge of the Capuchins' kitchen, and find the table ready laid for us; and even if it is not laid, there is a full bowl waiting for each of us, so we do not ask any questions but sit down and eat, and perfect our knowledge of Latin at the same time. In this way, sir, we keep up our studies from day to day. And when vacation time arrives, and the others go off home to their parents by coach or on horseback, we tuck our instruments under our coats and wander out of the town, and the whole world is at our feet."

For some reason it made me sad to think, as he was talking, that such learned men could be so lonely, and as I came to realize that my own fate was really no different from theirs, the tears came to my eyes.

The horn-player stared at me in surprise.

"It makes no difference," he eventually went on; "I would not wish to go where clean beds and nightcaps and bootjacks and horses and coffee had all been ordered in advance. The real attraction when we go out early in the morning, with the birds of passage flying high above our heads, is that we do not know over what fire our meal is going to be cooked that evening, nor what special fortune may befall us before the day is done."

"And wherever we go," the second man joined in, "and take out our instruments, there is jollity. When we go into some country villa at midday and play in the hall, the maids dance in the garden outside and the gentry open the door of the dining room so that they can hear the music better; the clatter of plates and the smell of roast meat mingle with our cheerful music making, and the young ladies at the dinner table crane their necks to catch a glimpse of us through the half-open door."

"That's right," cried the horn-player, his eyes shining. "Let the others learn their textbooks by heart—*we* are going to learn from the great picture book which the good Lord has opened for us in the world outside. Believe me, sir, we are the kind of people who really have something to talk to the peasants about, and who smite the pulpits with our fists, uplifting the hearts of the congregation and making them tremble with contrition."

As they were talking, I felt so happy that I would have gladly joined them in their studies. I could have listened endlessly to their conversation, for I enjoy being in the company of educated people from whom one can learn.

However, there was little chance that an intellectual discussion would develop, for the first student was worried that the end of the vacation was so near. He put his clarinet together, laid a sheet of music across his knees, and began to practice a difficult passage from a mass in which he was supposed to play when they got back to Prague. He puffed and twiddled away, often playing so many wrong notes that it was agony to listen to him and made it impossible for one to hear one's own words.

Suddenly the horn-player exclaimed in his deep bass voice:

"I've got it!"

And he brought his fist down triumphantly on the mat at his side.

The zealous clarinetist paused for a moment and looked at him in surprise.

"Listen," the horn-player continued, "Not far from Vienna there is a palace, and in that palace is a footman, and that footman is a cousin of mine. That is the place for us, my fellow students! We can pay our respects to my cousin, and he will help us along our way."

At this I pricked up my ears.

"Does he play the bassoon?" I asked excitedly. "And is he tall and upright in build, with a long hooked nose?"

The horn-player nodded. I threw my arms round his neck in delight, dislodging his cocked hat in the process, and we all resolved to take the ferryboat down the Danube to the countess's palace.

When we arrived at the riverbank, all was set for departure. The portly innkeeper by whose tavern the boat had been anchored overnight was standing there cheerfully with his legs wide apart, completely blocking the entrance to the house and making hearty quips and jests to the departing passengers. Girls were looking out of every window, exchanging greetings with the sailors who were carrying the last of the parcels on board.

An elderly gentleman wearing a gray overcoat and a black neckerchief, who was also traveling on the boat, stood on the bank talking earnestly to a slim young man in long leather breeches and a short scarlet jacket who was mounted on a fine English steed, and I had the strange impression that they occasionally glanced in my direction and were talking about me. Finally the old gentleman gave a laugh, and cracking his whip, the young man galloped off at a furious pace through the clear morning air and out into the sun-drenched countryside, as though trying to race the larks in the sky above him.

Meanwhile the students and I had decided to pool our resources, and the captain of the vessel chuckled and shook his head as the horn-player counted out our fare all in copper coins which we had raked together out of our pockets.

I jumped for joy at being by my beloved Danube once more. We hurried on board, the captain gave the signal, and away we sailed between meadows and mountains in the bright glow of morning. The birds were singing in the woods, and from distant villages came the sound of the bells tolling for matins, while overhead the occasional twittering of larks could be heard. There was also a canary on board the boat, and its cheerful trilling was a delight to hear.

This bird belonged to a pretty girl who was traveling with us. She kept the cage close by her and was carrying a small bundle of clothing under one arm; she sat quietly by herself, looking with an air of contentment, now at her new traveling shoes which peeped out from under her skirt, now at the water below her, and the sun shone on her pale brow and her carefully parted hair. I could see that the students would have liked to engage her in conversation, for they kept walking past her, and the horn-player would clear his throat and adjust first his cravat, then his cocked hat. But they could not pluck up enough courage to do so, and every time they approached, the girl lowered her eyes.

They also felt embarrassed by the presence of the elderly man in the gray overcoat, who was sitting on the other side of the boat and whom they took for a priest. He was reading a breviary, and as he looked up from time to time to gaze at the scenery, the gilt edges of the book and the brightly colored devotional pictures lying between its pages shone in the sunshine. At the same time he kept a keen eye on what went on in the boat, and quickly recognized the passengers for what they were: thus he addressed one of the students in Latin, whereupon all three of them approached, doffed their hats and answered him also in Latin.

Seating myself in the bow of the boat, I let my legs dangle over the side, and as we sailed on over the foaming waves, I gazed happily into the hazy distance, where spires and palaces appeared one by one above the riverbank, grew larger and larger, then receded again into the background.

"If only I had wings!" I thought to myself. And in my restlessness I took out my beloved violin and played all the oldest pieces that I had learned at home and in my lovely lady's palace.

Suddenly someone tapped me on the shoulder. It was the reverend gentleman, who had laid aside his book and been listening to my playing.

"Well, well, good *ludi magister,*"* he said to me with a smile, "you are forgetting to eat."

And telling me to put my fiddle away, he invited me to share his repast, taking me over to a pretty little awning which the sailors had built out of young birches and firs in the center of the boat; he had asked for a table to be put there, and all of us—I, the students and the young girl as well—were made to sit round it on crates and barrels.

The reverend gentleman now unpacked some slices of bread and butter and a large joint of meat, which had been carefully wrapped in paper. He drew out of a box a number of bottles of wine and a silver cup inlaid with gold, poured out some wine, tasted it, sniffed it and tasted it again, then handed it round to each of us.

The students all sat bolt upright on their barrels and ate and drank very little, out of respect for their host. The girl, too, only sipped her wine, glancing now at me, now at the students, but gradually becoming bolder each time she did so. Finally she confided to the priest that she was leaving home for the first time and going into service, and was now on her way to the palace where her new mistress lived.

At this I began to blush deeply, for the palace she named was that of my lovely lady.

"She must be my future chambermaid," I thought, and as I looked at her wide-eyed, I began to feel dizzy.

"There is going to be a big wedding at the palace soon," said the priest.

"I know," replied the girl, who would have liked to learn more about the matter. "People say it is a secret childhood love which the old countess refused to allow."

To this the priest merely said, "Mm, hm!" filling his hunting-cup with wine and sipping it thoughtfully. Then he noticed that I was leaning across the table with both arms and listening attentively to the conversation, and he went on:

"It so happens that the two countesses sent me to try and find out

---

* "Master of the games" or "schoolmaster."

whether the bridegroom-to-be had already arrived in these parts, for a lady wrote from Rome that he had left there a long time ago."

When he mentioned the lady in Rome, I began to turn red again.

"Do you know the future bridegroom, reverend sir?" I asked in confusion.

"No," he replied, "but he is said to be a gay bird."

"Indeed he is," I said hastily, "a bird who escapes from every cage the moment he can, and sings merrily whenever he finds his freedom again."

"And wanders about in foreign parts," continued the priest calmly, "and sings serenades by night and sleeps in front of people's houses by day."

This remark annoyed me.

"Reverend sir," I cried heatedly, "you have been misinformed. The bridegroom is a slim, virtuous, confident young man who lived in fine style in an old Italian castle and associated only with countesses, famous painters and chambermaids, and husbands his funds very wisely—when he has any, that is—and who——"

"Well now," he interrupted, laughing so heartily that the tears rolled down his cheeks and he turned almost blue in the face, "I had no idea that you knew him so well."

"But I heard that he was a tall man, and fabulously rich," the girl interposed.

"Confusion, confusion and nothing but confusion!" cried the reverend gentleman, and went on laughing uproariously, until he finally broke into a violent fit of coughing. When he had recovered somewhat, he raised his cup aloft and cried:

"Here's to the happy couple!"

I did not know what to make of the man and his strange talk, but my adventures in Rome made me too embarrassed to tell him in front of all the others that I myself was the happy bridegroom he had been sent to look for.

The cup was again being passed round, and the priest conversed amicably with the members of the company. They all came to like him, and in the end everyone was talking away gaily at the same time. The students became more and more communicative, telling of their travels in the mountains and eventually even taking out their instruments and starting to play. The cool air was wafted through the branches of the little awning, and the evening sun cast its golden hue over the woods and valleys which slipped quickly by, while the riverbank echoed to the sound of the horn.

The longer they played, the more cheerful the priest became and he began to tell a number of amusing anecdotes about his youth— how he, too, used to wander over hill and dale during his holidays, often hungry and thirsty but always merry, and how a student's life was in reality one long holiday, stretching from the dullness and dreariness of school life to the seriousness of earning one's living. The students drank another round and struck up a new song, making it ring out into the mountains:

> The birds are southwards winging,
> Rejoicing as they go,
> With travelers blithely swinging
> Their hats in the morning glow.
> Behold the students going
> To roam o'er hill and dell!
> Their instruments they're blowing,
> To sound their last farewell.
> We leave thee, Prague, with heavy hearts
> And travel on to distant parts:
> *Et habeat bonam pacem,*
> *Qui sedet post fornacem!**
>
> At night, the windows shining,
> We wander through the town,
> And watch the couples dining
> In elegant cloak and gown.
> Whether earlier or later,
> We play to every class,
> And our thirst grows ever greater—
> Mine host, another glass!
> And then, with gestures willing,
> Our earnest wish fulfilling,
> *Venit ex sua domo*
> *Beatus ille homo!*

* The Latin refrains mean "may he live in peace who sits behind the stove"; "out of his house he comes, the happy man"; "happy the man who sits at home, sits behind the stove, and lives in peace."

Boreas sends its icy blast
O'er wood and stream and field;
Our brief security is past,
To rain and snow we yield.
Our coats are worn and shoddy,
Our shoes are patched and old;
Yet we play for everybody
And sing in accents bold:
Beatus ille homo,
Qui sedet in sua domo,
Et sedet post fornacem
Et habet bonam pacem!

Although we understood no Latin, the sailors, the girl and I all joined in the refrain with gusto. I sang the most lustily of all, however, for in the rays of the evening sun I had just caught sight of my old tollhouse above the trees on the distant horizon, and next to it the palace itself.

10

The boat landed and we jumped ashore, scattering in all directions like birds suddenly released from their cage. The priest bade us a hurried farewell and strode off towards the palace, while the students hastened towards a secluded thicket to brush their coats, wash in the nearby stream and shave each other. The new chambermaid, carrying her canary and her bundle of clothes under her arm, made her way at my suggestion to the inn at the bottom of the hill: there the landlord's wife would help her change her dress before she presented herself to her new mistress in the palace. The beauty of the evening filled my heart with joy, and when all the others had disappeared from view, I ran straight up to the palace garden.

My tollhouse, which I had to pass, looked the same as before, and the tall trees still rustled above it; even the yellowhammer, that used to perch every evening on the chestnut tree in front of the window and sing its serenade as the sun went down, was still there, as though nothing in the world had changed since those days.

The window was open, so I ran up to it excitedly and looked in. No one was there, but the clock on the wall was still ticking quietly away, the desk still stood close by the window, and the long pipe was in the corner as it used to be. Unable to restrain myself, I jumped through the window and sat down at the desk in front of the big ledger. As I sat there, the sun's golden rays cast a greenish light on the figures before me, and the bees buzzed outside the window, while the yellowhammer went on singing his merry tune.

Suddenly the door opened and in came a tall, elderly tollkeeper, wearing my old dressing gown with the dots on it. When he caught sight of me, he stopped in his tracks, took off his spectacles and glared. I was startled, jumped up without a word and rushed out into the garden, where I narrowly missed tripping over the potato plants which the footman had instructed this old tollkeeper to plant in place of my flowers. I heard him blunder through the door, cursing me as he did so, but by this time I was sitting on top of the high wall and looking down into the garden with a beating heart.

The sweet scent of flowers rose through the quivering air, and all the birds were rejoicing. The groves and paths were deserted but the golden trees inclined their heads towards me in the evening breeze, as though bidding me welcome, and through their branches came an occasional glint of the Danube in the deep valley below.

At that moment I heard a voice singing in the garden some distance away:

> Man's delights are laid to rest—
> Such is the message of the breeze
> That rustles through the leafy trees,
> Stirring memories, long repressed,
> Of olden times, of poignant sorrow;
> Soft forebodings of the morrow
> Flash like lightning through the breast.

The voice and the song both sounded strangely familiar, as though I had heard them some time in a dream. Then everything came back to me.

"It's Guido!" I cried in delight, climbing down into the garden as fast as I could—for it was the very song he had been singing on the balcony of the Italian inn that summer evening when I had last seen him.

He went on singing, and I jumped across hedgerows and flower beds in the direction of his voice. Then, as I burst through the last of the rosebushes, I stood there spellbound. For on the grass near the lake, in the glow of the evening sun, my lovely lady was sitting on a bench, wearing a wonderful gown and with a garland of red and white roses in her black hair. Her eyes were cast down, and she was playing with her riding crop on the grass in front of her, just as she had done in the boat when I had sung the song about the lovely lady. Opposite her, and with her back to me, sat another young lady, over whose smooth, white neck fell a mass of brown curls, and as the swans glided slowly past on the still waters of the lake, she was singing to her guitar.

Suddenly the lovely lady raised her eyes, and as she caught sight of me, she gave a scream. The other lady turned round so quickly that her curls flew into her face, but when she saw me, she burst into uncontrollable laughter, jumped up from her seat and clapped her hands three times. To my surprise a group of little girls emerged from behind the rosebushes, dressed in short, snow white frocks with green and red bows on them. They were holding a long flower chain in their hands, and quickly forming a circle round me, they began to dance and sing:

> A chain of purest flowers,
> And silk of violet hue,
> A wedding's happy hours
> And thoughts of pleasures new.
> A chain of purest flowers,
> With silk of violet hue.

The song was from Weber's *Freischütz,* and I recognized a few of the singers as girls from the village. I pinched their cheeks in fun and would have liked to escape from them, but the saucy little creatures would not let me go. I had no idea what it was all about and simply stood there in a daze.

At that moment an elegant young man in riding habit stepped out from the bushes. I could hardly believe my eyes—for it was the cheerful Leonhard! The girls broke their circle, and balancing miraculously on one leg, with the other stretched upwards, they lifted the flower chain high above their heads. My lady stood there motionless, glancing in my direction from time to time. Then, taking her by the hand, Leonhard led her over to me and said:

"Love—as all learned men agree—is one of the strongest forces in the human heart. With a single fiery glance it breaks down the fortresses of rank and class; the world is too cramped for it, and eternity too short. Indeed, it is like a poet's mantle, which every romantic spirit dons in the world of cold reality when he wishes to escape to Arcadia. The farther apart two lovers move, the broader becomes the sweep of this shining mantle in the wind behind them, and the bolder and more original become its configurations; its train grows longer and longer, and in the end not even a dispassionate observer can avoid stepping on one or other of its folds.

"My beloved tollkeeper and bridegroom! Although you wandered in this mantle as far as the banks of the Tiber, your betrothed still held on to the end of its train with her tiny hand, drawing you back into the quiet spell of her beautiful eyes, however much you might resist and play your fiddle and make a fuss. But now that we have finally reached this point, my two poor, dear, foolish people, wrap yourselves in this blissful mantle and forget the world outside. Love each other like turtledoves, and be happy!"

Scarcely had he finished his speech when the lady who had just been singing came up to me, placed a fresh myrtle wreath on my head and teasingly sang the following verse, her little face close to me as she set the wreath more firmly on my hair:

> In memory of heartfelt pleasure
> This wreath I place upon thy brow;
> Thy music I shall ever treasure:
> Its poignant beauty fills me now.

She stepped back a few paces.

"Do you remember those bandits who found you hiding up the tree?" she asked, curtsying to me with a charming smile that made my heart leap. Without waiting for my answer, she walked round me, looking at me from all sides.

"He really is! Just as he was, without a trace of anything Italian!" she exclaimed to the lovely lady. "And just look at his bulging pockets—violin, clothes, razor, traveling case, all mixed up together!"

She turned me around and about, and could not stop laughing.

The lovely lady had kept silent all this time, and for shame and embarrassment did not dare to raise her eyes; she even appeared to me to be secretly angry at all the banter and jesting. Then suddenly her eyes filled with tears; she hid her face on the breast of her companion, who looked at her in astonishment at first, then embraced her affectionately.

I stood there in utter confusion. For as I looked more closely at this lady, I recognized her as none other than Guido, the painter!

I did not know what to say, and was on the point of asking what it was all about, when Leonhard came over and whispered something to her.

"Doesn't he know!" I heard him ask.

She shook her head. Then, after a moment's reflection, he said:

"No, no. We must tell him everything at once, or there will only be more gossip and confusion."

Then, turning to me, he began:

"My dear tollkeeper, we have not got a great deal of time, but please be so good as to dispose of all your astonishment here and now, so that you do not go about stirring up old tales by your ignorant questions and your mystification, or inventing new stories and explanations."

He drew me further into the bushes, while the young lady took the riding crop that my own lovely lady had laid aside and flourished it in the air, making her brown curls fall over her face but not concealing the deep flush that spread over it.

"Now," he went on, "although Flora is behaving as though she knew nothing of the whole affair, she once gave her heart away on the impulse of a moment. Meanwhile along comes another man, and with trumpets and drums and many fine words offers her *his* heart, seeking hers in return. But her heart belongs to someone else, and his heart belongs to her; and as he does not want *his* heart back, so neither does he wish to return *hers*. A great rumpus follows—but have you never read a romance?"

I admitted I had not.

"Then at least you have taken part in one," he continued. "Anyway, there was such confusion over these hearts that in the end that someone—in other words, I myself—had to take a hand in the matter.

"One warm night I jumped on my horse, made the lady mount the other, dressed as a painter called Guido, and rode off with her to Italy, where she could hide in one of my lonely castles until the hue and cry over hearts had passed. But we had been followed, and Flora caught sight of our pursuers from the balcony of the inn at which you showed your prowess as a sleeping sentry."

"So the hunchback——"

"—was a spy. We crept into the woods and let you drive off alone in the coach, which had its fixed route to follow. This put not only our pursuers off the scent, but also my servants at the castle, who were expecting the disguised Flora at any moment and then, with more enthusiasm than discernment, took you for her. Even down here at the palace people believed that she was in the fortress; they inquired, and then wrote—did you never get the letter?"

"This one?" I stammered, taking the note shamefacedly from my pocket.

"It was meant for me!" cried Flora, who had not seemed to be taking any interest in the conversation. She seized it, read it hastily and put it in her bosom.

"Now we must go up to the palace," said Leonhard; "everybody is waiting for us. As you see, we have come to the right and proper conclusion of the story, and everything has turned out as it ought to in a respectable romance—revelation, then sadness, but finally consolation. We are all happily united again, and the wedding takes place the day after tomorrow."

As he spoke, a deafening noise of trumpets and drums, horns and trombones came from behind the bushes, together with cries of "Hurrah!" and the sound of salvos being fired from the cannons; the little girls had started to dance again, and all around heads popped out of the bushes like plants sprouting from the ground. In the melee and confusion I leaped from one side to the other and recognized one by one the familiar faces in the darkness: the old gardener was beating the drums, the students from Prague in their long coats were playing away in the middle, and next to them was the footman, twiddling with his fingers up and down his bassoon like one possessed. So surprised was I to see him there that I rushed over and embraced him affectionately, which made him completely forget what he was playing.

"Well, bless my soul!" he cried to the students. "Even if he travels to the farthest corners of the earth, he will still be a clown when he gets back!"

And picking up his instrument, he resumed his furious playing.

In the meantime the lovely lady had quietly slipped away from all this confusion and was running across the grass and out into the garden like a frightened deer. I saw her just in time and flew after her. The musicians were too busy to notice; when they did discover that we were no longer there, they thought that we had gone up to the palace, and they all marched off in that direction, still playing away as hard as they could.

I had almost caught up with her, when we reached a summerhouse standing at the very edge of the garden, its open windows overlooking the wide valley. The sun had almost set behind the mountains, leaving only a shimmering red glow in the warm air as the sounds of evening died away, and the quieter it became, the clearer grew the murmur of the Danube below.

The lovely countess stood before me, flushed with her exertions, and I could almost hear her heart beat. I could not take my eyes away from her, but such was my trepidation at finding myself alone with her, that the words I wanted to utter stuck in my throat. At last, summoning all my courage, I took her hand in mine. Quickly she drew me to her and threw her arms round my neck, and I held her tightly in my embrace. Then she suddenly tore herself away and went across to the window, where she stood for a while to cool her burning cheeks in the evening air and regain her composure.

"Oh, my heart is almost bursting!" I cried. "And I still do not understand what has been happening. It all seems like a dream!"

"It does to me as well," she replied. Then after a pause she went on:

"When I returned from Rome with the countess last summer, after we had found Flora and brought her back with us, but had heard nothing of you either here or there, I never thought that everything would work out like this. For it was only at noon today that the messenger, speedy and reliable lad that he is, came galloping up to the palace with the news that you were arriving on the mailboat."

She smiled to herself. Then she resumed:

"Do you remember the last time you saw me, on the balcony? It was a quiet evening just like this, and there was music in the garden?"

"Then who has died?" I asked breathlessly.

"What do you mean?" she asked, looking at me in amazement.

"Is it your ladyship's husband—the man who stood by your side on the balcony?"

She flushed a deep red.

"What strange notions you have!" she exclaimed. "That was the countess's son, who had just returned from his travels. That day was also my birthday, and he took me out on the balcony with him for them to give me a cheer as well. So that's the reason why you ran away!"

"Why, of course it was!" I cried, striking my forehead with my hand, while she shook her dainty head and laughed merrily.

As we thus stood there talking happily, I was so enchanted that I could have listened to her till morning. Delving into my pocket, I fetched out a handful of almonds which I had brought with me from Italy. She took one or two, and together we cracked them, looking out in joy over the peaceful countryside. After a little while she said:

"Do you see that little white villa over there in the moonlight? The count has given it to us to live in, together with the garden and the vineyards. He has known for a long while that we were in love with each other; besides, he is very well-disposed towards you, for had you not been with him that time when he escaped with Flora from the inn, they would both have been caught before they could make their peace with the old countess, and things would have turned out very different."

"Oh my dearest, most noble countess!" I cried. "I am so confused by all these surprises that I do not know whether I am standing on my head or my heels! You mean that Leonhard——"

"That's what he called himself in Italy," she broke in. "He owns those estates over there, and he is now going to marry Flora, our countess's beautiful daughter. But why do you keep calling *me* countess?"

I stared at her.

"I am not a countess at all," she went on: "I was brought here as a poor orphan child by my uncle, the footman, and the countess has allowed me to grow up in the palace."

I felt as though a weight had been lifted from my heart.

"God bless the footman for being your uncle and mine!" I cried in jubilation. "I always held him in high esteem."

"He thinks a great deal of you, too," she said. " 'If only he would behave with a little more decorum!' he always says of you. You really must wear more respectable clothes now!"

"English frock coat, straw hat, knee breeches and spurs! And right after the wedding we'll go to Italy—to Rome, where the wonderful fountains are—and we'll take the students with us and the footman as well!"

She smiled happily and looked affectionately at me. The sound of music still echoed from afar, and flares lit up the night sky as they shot across the garden from the palace. The waters of the Danube rippled past beneath us—and all of it, all of it was so good.

Translated by Ronald Taylor

ACKNOWLEDGMENTS

Every reasonable effort has been made to locate the owners of rights to previously published translations printed here. We gratefully acknowledge permission to reprint the following material:

"An Unexpected Reunion" by Johann Peter Hebel from *Deutsche Erzahlungen. German Stories,* Harry Steinhauer, ed. © 1984 The Regents of the University of California. Used by permission of the University of California Press.

"Kannitverstan" by Johann Peter Hebel, translated by Paul Pratt, from *German Stories and Tales,* edited by Robert Pick. Copyright 1954 by Alfred A. Knopf, Inc. Reprinted by permission of the publisher.

"Undine" by Friedrich de la Motte Fouqué, translated by P. Turner, is reproduced by kind permission of John Calder (Publishers) Ltd., London, and Riverrun Press, Inc., New York.

"Peter Schlemihl" by Adelbert von Chamisso in *Twelve German Novellas,* Harry Steinhauer, ed., pp. 181–226. © 1977 The Regents of the University of California. Used by permission of the University of California Press.

"The Madman of Fort Ratonneau" by Achim von Arnim from E. J. Engel, *German Narrative Prose,* London: Oswald Wolff, Ltd., 1965. Reprinted by permission of Berg Publishers Limited.

"Memoirs of a Good-for-Nothing" by Joseph Freiherr von Eichendorff, translated by Ronald Taylor, is reproduced by kind permission of John Calder (Publishers) Ltd., London, and Riverrun Press, Inc., New York.

THE GERMAN LIBRARY
in 100 Volumes

Gottfried von Strassburg
Tristan and Isolde
Edited and Revised by Francis G. Gentry
Foreword by C. Stephen Jaeger

German Medieval Tales
Edited by Francis G. Gentry
Foreword by Thomas Berger

German Humanism and Reformation
Edited by Reinhard P. Becker
Foreword by Roland Bainton

Immanuel Kant
Philosophical Writings
Edited by Ernst Behler
Foreword by René Wellek

Friedrich Schiller
Plays: Intrigue and Love and Don Carlos
Edited by Walter Hinderer
Foreword by Gordon Craig

German Romantic Criticism
Edited by A. Leslie Willson
Foreword by Ernst Behler

Heinrich von Kleist
Plays
Edited by Walter Hinderer
Foreword by E. L. Doctorow

E.T.A. Hoffman
Tales
Edited by Victor Lange

German Literary Fairy Tales
Edited by Frank G. Ryder and Robert M. Browning
Introduction by Gordon Birrell
Foreword by John Gardiner

Heinrich Heine
Poetry and Prose
Edited by Jost Hermand and Robert C. Holub
Foreword by Alfred Kazin

Heinrich von Kleist and Jean Paul
German Romantic Novellas
Edited by Frank G. Ryder and Robert M. Browning
Foreword by John Simon

German Poetry from 1750 to 1900
Edited by Robert M. Browning
Foreword by Michael Hamburger

Gottfried Keller
Stories
Edited by Frank G. Ryder
Foreword by Max Frisch

Wilhelm Raabe
Novels
Edited by Volkmar Sander
Foreword by Joel Agee

Theodor Fontane
Short Novels and Other Writings
Edited by Peter Demetz
Foreword by Peter Gay

Wilhelm Busch and Others
German Satirical Writings
Edited by Deiter P. Lotze and Volkmar Sander
Foreword by John Simon

Writings of German Composers
Edited by Jost Hermand and James Steakley

Arthur Schnitzler
Plays and Stories
Edited by Egon Schwarz
Foreword by Stanley Elkin

Rainer Maria Rilke
Prose and Poetry
Edited by Egon Schwarz
Foreword by Howard Nemerov

Essays on German Theater
Edited by Margaret Herzfeld-Sander
Foreword by Martin Esslin

Friedrich Dürrenmatt
Plays and Essays
Edited by Volkmar Sander
Foreword by Martin Esslin

Hans Magnus Enzensberger
Critical Essays
Edited by Reinhold Grimm and Bruce Armstrong
Foreword by John Simon

Georg Büchner
Complete Works and Letters
Edited by Walter Hinderer and Henry J. Schmidt

Gottfried Benn
Prose, Essays, Poems
Edited by Volkmar Sander
Foreword by E. B. Ashton
Introduction by Reinhard Paul Becker

German Essays on Art History
Edited by Gert Schiff